HER MAJESTY

BRIAN HOEY

HER MAJESTY

Fifty Regal Years

HarperCollins*Publishers*

HarperCollins*Publishers*
77–85 Fulham Palace Road,
Hammersmith, London W6 8JB

www.**fire**and**water**.com

Published by HarperCollins*Publishers* 2001
1 3 5 7 9 8 6 4 2

A catalogue record for this book is
available from the British Library

ISBN 0 00 257079 3

Set in Galliard by
Rowland Phototypesetting Ltd,
Bury St Edmunds, Suffolk

Printed and bound in Great Britain by
Omnia Books Limited, Glasgow

For my wife
Diana

Contents

Illustrations

Queen Elizabeth with the Queen Mother and Princess Margaret at Royal Ascot, June 1956. © Topham Picturepoint

Queen Elizabeth and Princess Anne at Liverpool Street Station. © Fox Photos/Hulton Archive

Queen Elizabeth filming the Crossing the Line ceremony on board the *Gothic* in 1953. © Fox Photos/Hulton Archive

The Royal Family and corgis on holiday at Balmoral. © PA News

Queen Elizabeth and Earl Mountbatten of Burma. © Topham Picturepoint

King George VI and Douglas Fairbanks Jnr in Scotland during the Second World War. Reproduced courtesy of Mrs Vera Fairbanks

Queen Elizabeth and Prince Philip with President John F. Kennedy and his wife Jackie. © PA News

Queen Elizabeth with Richard Nixon and his wife Pat at Chequers. © Keystone/Hulton Archive

Queen Elizabeth with Nelson D. Rockefeller and President Gerald Ford at the White House. © Colin Davy/Camera Press

Queen Elizabeth dancing with President Ford. © Colin Davy/Camera Press

Queen Elizabeth and President George Bush. © Doug Mills/Associated Press

Dr Henry Kissinger with the royal party in their open carriage at Royal Ascot. © Stewart Mark/Camera Press

The Clintons meet the Queen. © Camera Press

Queen Elizabeth joins five prime ministers at 10 Downing Street in December 1985. © PA News

Queen Elizabeth and Prince Philip with Neil Kinnock at Cardiff University in June 2000. © Cardiff University

Queen Elizabeth and Margaret Thatcher. © PA News

Queen Elizabeth and Nelson Mandela. © PA News

Queen Elizabeth and Tony Blair. © PA News

Queen Elizabeth with the Archbishop of Canterbury, Dr Robert Runcie, and Sir Shridath Ramphal, the Commonwealth Secretary General. © Reuters/Popperfoto

Queen Elizabeth and Prince Philip at the Vatican with Pope John Paul II in 1980. © Topham Picturepoint

Queen Elizabeth and Prince Philip at the Vatican with Pope John Paul II in 2000. © Stewart Mark/Camera Press

Queen Elizabeth and Prince Philip visit Aberfan, South Wales in October 1966. © Popperfoto

Prince Charles and Princess Diana at the State Opening of Parliament in 1984. © Popperfoto

Queen Elizabeth and Prince Philip, in their Garter robes, escorted by Her Majesty's Silver Stick in Waiting, Colonel Andrew Parker Bowles. Private Collection

Queen Elizabeth and Prince Philip with Chief Superintendent Jim Beaton GC, in Australia in 1992. © Rex Features

The Earl of Carnarvon greets Princess Anne at Ascot.
© S Djukanovic/Camera Press

Sir Robert Fellowes and Sir Robin Janvrin. © Photographers International

Queen Elizabeth and William Farish. © Mark Elias/Associated Press

St George's Hall, Windsor Castle. © Stewart Mark/Camera Press

Balmoral Castle. © Earl Beesley/Camera Press

Queen Elizabeth and Princess Margaret with Princes William and Harry on the steps of St Paul's Cathedral. © PA News

Queen Elizabeth and members of the Royal Family on the last summer cruise on board the Royal Yacht *Britannia*. © PA News

The wedding of Prince Edward and Sophie Rhys-Jones. © Camera Press

Queen Elizabeth with the Queen Mother and Princess Margaret at the ballet. © Fiona Hanson/Topham Picturepoint

Princess Anne celebrating her fiftieth birthday at Windsor Castle.
© PA News

Queen Elizabeth and Prince Philip. © PA News

Acknowledgements

I am indebted to a great many people for their contributions and other assistance during the preparation of this book. Past and present members of the royal household have been generous with their time and expertise; some I am able to name, others have asked me to respect their confidentiality. Friends of the Queen and Prince Philip spoke openly and also provided me with some unique photographs.

Among those to whom I am particularly grateful are the following: Ronald Allison, Harry Arnold, Jocelyn Barrow, James Beaton GC, Countess Mountbatten of Burma, ex-President George Bush and Mrs Barbara Bush, Lady Myra Butter, the Earl of Carnarvon, Lord Carrington, Marge Champion, Geoffrey Crawford, Michael Dannenhauer, Lady de Bellaigue, Lord Deedes, Oliver Everett, Paul Flynn MP, Bryan Forbes, ex-President Gerald Ford, Princess George of Hanover, Geordie Greig, Lorna Hogg, Sir Bernard Ingham, Lady Georgina 'Gina' Kennard, Neil Kinnock, Dr Henry Kissinger, Lee Kwan Yew, Austin Mitchell MP, Christina Neuman, Lord [David] Owen, Andrew Parker Bowles, Colin Parker, David Rankin-Hunt, Maureen Rose, James Whitaker, Alan Williams MP, and George Wiltshire.

I was also fortunate enough to be allowed to speak to the

late Lord Runcie just a few weeks before he died. Although in considerable pain, he gave no indication of his discomfort. I am glad to record my appreciation of his unfailing courtesy and good humour.

Similarly, the late Douglas Fairbanks Jnr and his wife Vera were equally kind in corresponding with me in spite of his illness.

My thanks must also go to Richard Johnson at Harper-Collins for his encouragement and constructive criticism right from the beginning of this project, and to Juliet Davis for her picture research; to my agent Michael Shaw at Curtis Brown for his unfailing efforts on my behalf; to Eric Bailey and Peter Dobbie at the *Mail on Sunday*, and to Janice Robertson, to whom I owe a massive debt for her extraordinary energy and perception when editing the manuscript.

This book has not been 'vetted' by Buckingham Palace, or anyone else; therefore any opinions which are not attributed are mine and mine alone – as are any errors.

Prologue

I have had the opportunity to observe the royal family at fairly close quarters for thirty years and have met all of them, including the Queen, on a number of occasions. As the Princess Royal's biographer, I was given unprecedented access, both at Buckingham Palace and during her travels at home and abroad, and never once did she insist on – or even ask for – any power of veto. The present family is changed dramatically from that of fifty years ago, not only in size, but in its own and the public's perception of its role. Gone is the near-worship the country once felt for royalty, to be replaced by a demand that they now have to earn the respect they took for granted as their God-given right.

If there has been a decline in public support for the monarchy in recent years, this lack of confidence appears to be partly the result of media exposure of the private lives of some of the younger members of the royal family. But this could not have taken place if the behaviour of the culprits had not caused the stories to be investigated. The result has been a growing disenchantment and increasing scepticism about the ability of the monarchy to survive once the present sovereign has gone. Elizabeth II is admired and respected as much today as when she first came to the throne in 1952;

her heirs are the ones who do not inspire the same level of confidence.

In 1999, Australia voted narrowly to keep the monarchy – and the Queen as its Head of State – in spite of an energetic and well-organized republican campaign to remove her. Yet in her opening address in Sydney in March 2000, at the start of her State Visit, she gave no hint of her own feelings about the result of the referendum. It was an important speech, arguably the most significant since the famous 'Annus Horribilis' address at the Guildhall in 1992. But Her Majesty has the ability to say something meaningful without causing offence. This is due as much to the way in which she delivers her speeches as to their content. The lack of emotion with which she speaks is an enormous advantage when it comes to mentioning uncomfortable topics. No one can even hazard a guess as to her own thoughts and opinions, even when the subject is so obviously one which involves her personally.

The enthusiastic reception she received on that visit, when even committed republican sections of the population joined in the welcome, must have given Her Majesty a moment of quiet satisfaction – to know that in spite of the thousands of miles that separate them, and that she is still wanted as Queen of Australia. It may also have been seen as a warning to those politicians in Britain who have held thinly disguised similar ambitions for the United Kingdom. Perhaps they now realize that they threaten the Queen and the monarchy at their peril.

In 1991 President Ronald Reagan summed up the feeling towards Elizabeth II when he said, 'Throughout the world, with respect to all other female monarchs, whenever we speak about "The Queen" we all know which one we are referring to.' For half a century the Queen has shown that she is able to embrace change without showing any sign that she feels discomfort. Her demeanour has been impeccable throughout her reign and continues to be so. She is the perfect example of the modern constitutional monarch.

She is unique, a working sovereign and clearly a woman who has fulfilled her destiny. Elizabeth II is simply The Queen.

CHAPTER ONE

A Typical Day

*'Glenys and the Queen spent half an hour
discussing the problems of incontinent dogs.'*
NEIL KINNOCK

It is 7.30 in the morning and Buckingham Palace is starting to stir. The police sergeant sitting outside the Queen's bed-room is coming to the end of his overnight shift. He used to go off duty at 6.30, but after an intruder entered the bedroom at about 7 a.m. on the morning of 9 July 1982, when no one was on guard, the extra hour was added. Her Majesty's personal maid walks towards him carrying the 'morning tray' for her royal mistress. On it are pots of Earl Grey tea and hot water, both in solid silver, cold milk but no sugar, and a few Marie biscuits (appropriately named after the Grand Duchess Marie of Russia, the wife of Prince Alfred, Queen Victoria's fourth son, and a former Duchess of Edinburgh). The cup and saucer are of bone china and there is also a fine linen napkin draped across the tray which bears the royal cypher EIIR.

The maid gives a light tap on the door, which bears the legend 'The Queen' on a white card in a plain brass holder.

Without waiting to be called she enters the room and walks quietly across to the bedside table with its family photographs and telephone, complete with 'panic button' – the one which was so spectacularly ignored on the morning when Michael Fagan became the only man – apart from her husband – to see the Queen asleep in bed. The large double bed has white linen sheets, measuring 80 × 112 inches and bearing the monogram HM The Queen, exactly 3½ inches high, and featherdown pillows complete with lace border and the same monogram, but this time a more modest 1½ inches high. The colour scheme of the room is pale green, the Queen's favourite shade.

Putting the tray down, the maid draws back the curtains and reveals the early morning traffic, already building up on Constitution Hill, and the joggers in Green Park. She switches on the radio which is tuned to BBC Radio 4 as the Queen likes to wake up to the sound of John Humphrys or James Naughtie giving the day's early news and grilling unfortunate politicians on the *Today* programme.

Quite often the Queen is already awake; she is an early riser, and she will bid her maid 'Good morning' and ask what the weather outside looks like. Then, while Her Majesty is enjoying her first cup of tea, her maid will go into the adjoining bathroom to draw the bath, which has to be exactly the right temperature: 62 degrees, tested with a thermometer, and no more than seven inches of water. The Queen prefers to bathe in a deep, old-fashioned Victorian cast-iron bath with massive brass taps whose flow is fierce enough to allow the bath to be filled in minutes, while Prince Philip, in his suite a few yards away, hates to waste time and has a shower, after drinking the first of many cups of coffee.

Prince Philip's set of rooms are workmanlike and functional, with an office, complete with state-of-the-art computer, a library, bedroom, bathroom and massive dressing room where his valet stores just some of HRH's collection of suits, sports coats and uniforms. The bulk of both his wardrobe and the

Queen's, all numbered and catalogued, is housed on the second floor in an entirely separate apartment. Prince Philip also has a fully equipped barbershop for his exclusive use.

Soon a footman returns from the gardens where he has been walking the royal corgis and trying to get them to 'do their business'. He doesn't enter the royal bedroom. It is a rule in the royal household that no male servant is permitted to go into a lady's bedroom when she is there. So he hands the dogs over to the maid who is waiting outside. The corgis, all female, sleep in their own room, next door to the Page's Pantry, each with her own basket and silver feeding bowl.

The staff at Buckingham Palace do not share the Queen's love for her dogs as they are apt to 'spend pennies' on the carpets and furniture, causing extra, and very unpleasant work for the domestic staff. Two of the most useful and used items in the royal household are a plentiful supply of blotting paper and soda water, both excellent for removing stains. A common, though unspoken, complaint is that the royal family do not regard house-training as of paramount importance for their dogs. However, when Glenys Kinnock, wife of the former Labour leader, joined her husband and the Queen for tea one afternoon, they spent almost their entire time discussing the problems of incontinent dogs.

While the Queen is in her bath, one of her three dressers lays out the first outfit of the day in the adjacent dressing room with its floor-to-ceiling mirrors and walk-in wardrobes. She knows exactly what is needed as she was given the Queen's daily programme the evening before. Depending on the engagements for the day, the Queen may have to change as many as five times, but she rarely makes her own choice; that is what she pays her dressers to do, she says. The dresser removes the clothes the Queen has worn the night before and each article is examined and brushed before being returned to its place in one of the giant wardrobes on the floor above.

Once the Queen has dressed, her hairdresser brushes and

arranges her hair in the style that hasn't changed in decades. Breakfast is served promptly at 8.30 in the Queen's own private dining room, where she is joined by Prince Philip. Another footman has brought the food to a hot-plate – a silver 'muffin dish' with the food on top and hot water underneath – and once he has served the couple he leaves the room so they can eat in peace. It might be the last time that day they will get the opportunity to be alone together.

As with everything the Queen uses, the breakfast utensils are of the best, the cutlery solid silver, the crockery Sèvres bone china and even the butter imprinted with the royal cypher. The milk will have been delivered early that morning from the royal dairy at Windsor, in bottles again bearing the royal cypher. The Queen is said to have once remarked that the first time she really realized she was Queen was when she saw those milk bottles with EIIR on them.

The Queen has a healthy appetite, but these days she does not care for a 'full English' at breakfast time, occasionally enjoying a plate of scrambled eggs but more often preferring toast, marmalade and tea. Prince Philip eats as he does everything – in a rush, with coffee, served black, his favourite drink. He rarely drinks tea – Earl Grey or any other brand.

A selection of the morning's newspapers will have been placed on a side table and the Queen and Prince Philip glance through them all as they eat. The Queen prefers the *Daily Telegraph* while Philip scans all the papers making loud comments on items that irritate him. Otherwise early morning conversation is kept to a minimum, but they like to talk over the plans each has for the remainder of the day. Meanwhile a lone piper from one of the Scottish regiments prepares to march up and down on the terrace below. The Queen loves the music of the bagpipes and every morning she listens to some of her favourite tunes.

By 9.30 the Queen will be seated at her desk in her sitting room cum office, accompanied by a couple of her corgis, ready for two solid hours of paperwork. The room is comfortable rather than luxurious with armchairs and sofas upholstered in country-house style chintz. The Chinese carpet is another shade of green. The room is very much as it was in the King's day and, like his daughter, George VI preferred this colour to any other. Much earlier that morning the palace florist arrived to arrange fresh flowers which are in profusion around the room. The desk is Chippendale and the Queen brought it with her when she moved from her earlier home at Clarence House in 1952. It is cluttered with personal treasures and family photographs, including one of the Queen Mother taken during the Second World War and another of 'Grannie' – old Queen Mary. There is also a favourite small leather-framed folding album showing a young, smiling Princess Elizabeth and Prince Philip. A heavy crystal double inkwell contains the black ink which the Queen uses to sign official documents and the special green colour she likes for personal letters. She rarely uses a ballpoint pen, insisting on her favourite old fountain pen with a heavy gold nib. There's also a pristine sheet of blotting paper (destroyed every day), black in colour so that one cannot see what she has written by holding it up to a mirror. A leather folder, again with the royal crest, contains Her Majesty's stationery; there is a sponge for dampening envelopes and memo pads for writing notes to her staff.

This is very much a working desk. As a former Page says, 'It may appear cluttered and untidy to the average eye, but the Queen knows where everything is and hates it if anything is moved without her permission.' The Queen's chair is made of solid mahogany with an upright back and wide arms.

Her press secretary will have already clipped any items of interest from all the morning newspapers and prepared a digest of the day's news from the early morning radio and television bulletins. Once she has read this and any other papers she might have needed to see, she presses a button on the console in front of her which connects her directly with several members of her household. Usually the first person she calls is her private secretary, Sir Robin Janvrin. He is waiting in his office on the ground floor and when he hears the words, 'Robin, would you like to come up?' he knows it's time to start the day's work. Carrying a small wicker basket containing the documents the Queen has to read and initial, he enters the room, gives a brief neck bow and says, 'Your Majesty.' Thereafter, he addresses her as 'Ma'am' to rhyme with ham not smarm. Sir Robin and his colleagues have already read all the letters and telegrams that arrived overnight and filtered out those they are able to handle themselves. Even so, the Queen's mailbox normally runs to scores of items every day, so it's fortunate that she has mastered the knack of 'scanning' or speed-reading. Now, sitting in a chair alongside the desk he goes through the day's programme and offers a briefing on any visitors expected. These written briefs are short, concise and sometimes quite irreverent. A heavyweight diplomat was described as 'Rather like an overweight bear, so don't invite him to sit in one of the armchairs; he'll never get up again.'

If guests are expected at the Palace, the housekeeper, Heather Colebrook, is summoned so that the domestic arrangements for their comfort can be discussed. Miss Colebrook who, although single, is given the courtesy title of 'Mrs', lives in what must be the finest position of any apartment in London. Her flat is on the ground floor of Buckingham Palace looking out on the front quadrangle from where she can see and hear the changing of the guard every morning. But although Mrs Colebrook is in charge of all the housemaids and cleaners in the royal household, the Queen always checks the rooms of her guests herself before they arrive. And while her housekeeper will let the Queen know, through the Master of the Household, if an item of furniture needs repair or a carpet or some bedlinen should be replaced, Her Majesty herself has to give approval for the money to be spent if it's a major piece of expenditure.

Later in the morning the duty lady-in-waiting is called into the sitting room. The Queen shows her some of the letters she has received which require a personal reply. Those from children and the elderly get special attention and the lady-in-waiting writes the letters and signs them on behalf of the Queen. Personal friends who write to Her Majesty put their initials in the lower left-hand corner of the envelope and when the staff see these they know they are not to open them, for the Queen likes to open her personal mail herself.

Official guests, such as incoming or outgoing foreign emissaries coming to present their credentials or take their leave, have an audience at noon. This takes place in the Audience Room, also part of the Queen's suite, and lasts for around ten minutes. The Queen might also be seeing commanding officers of the regiments of which she is Colonel-in-Chief as they assume or relinquish their posts. Certain senior naval and Royal Air Force officers also have the right to be received by the sovereign, and when this happens, the Queen pays them the compliment of wearing the brooch or emblem of their particular service unit.

Twenty-two times a year an investiture is held in the palace ballroom, when 150 men and women receive their honours from the Queen, or occasionally, from the Prince of Wales. This ceremony starts promptly at mid-day and lasts exactly one hour. The Queen has performed this particular royal duty nearly seven hundred times, yet she still manages to make it appear as if it is the first time for her also, and that she is enjoying the occasion as much as the recipients.

Lunch is usually eaten alone. The Queen is occasionally joined by a lady-in-waiting, but rarely by another member of the royal family, even if they happen to be in the Palace. Formality exists between mother and children, so there's no question of just popping a head around the door or dropping in for a bite to eat. If the Queen wants one of them to join her, her Page of the Backstairs is despatched to deliver the invitation.

Her Majesty prefers light meals. Poultry and fish are preferred to the heavier red meat dishes, and eaten with fresh vegetables and salad and very few potatoes. A great favourite is lamb cutlets with artichokes. But although the dishes may be simple they are superbly presented, every sprout, carrot or potato exactly matching its neighbour in shape and size. The Queen does not have a starter and neither does she care for stolid desserts. She is not a great lover of cheese either, so fresh fruit is more often her choice. And during the day she doesn't drink alcohol, sticking instead to her favourite still Malvern water, of which she is said to drink 'gallons every day'. If the Duke of Edinburgh is at home, he joins her and perhaps drinks a glass of beer with his meal.

In the early days of the Queen's reign, the royal chef would arrive in her quarters at the start of the week with a complete list of suggestions – including three alternatives – for every meal over the coming seven days. The Queen would tick those she preferred, occasionally making choices of her own. These days, the system is basically the same, except that the chef does not come upstairs in person. Instead he sends the list to Her Majesty's Page, who returns it when she has indicated what she wants. Even so, she still knows on Monday what she is having for dinner on Thursday, and all menus continue to be written in French.

Immediately after lunch, the Queen likes to walk in the gardens with several of her dogs. Household staff know they should keep well out of the way at this time. She doesn't welcome company or want to see anyone else in the gardens. Only the gardeners may remain, and they only speak if first addressed by the Queen. Sometimes she might ask why a particular plant or bush is being moved, but more often than not she prefers solitude. Then she relaxes for half an hour with the *Sporting Life* and *Racing Post*, the 'bibles' of the racing fraternity; and several times a week she also speaks on the telephone to her racing manager, the Earl of Carnarvon.

He is one of the few people who is always put through to her.

Sometimes there are engagements in the afternoon. They will be in the London area, and when the Queen is ready to leave, her Page telephones her personal police officer, in his office on the ground floor, to warn him to be waiting at the Garden Door with the car door open. The Queen's chauffeur, whose name is Joe Last, never leaves his place behind the wheel. As Her Majesty walks downstairs – she rarely uses the ancient lift – a small knot of people materializes and wait to see her off. These are her private secretary and several of the household. They will also be there when she returns.

All afternoon engagements are scheduled to finish before 4.30 so that the Queen can be back at the Palace in time for tea at five. It's an immovable feast and the meal she enjoys the most: tiny sandwiches, cut to precise size, without crusts, warm scones with cream and strawberry jam and, always, her favourite Dundee fruit cake. The ritual never changes and neither does the fare. However, Her Majesty doesn't eat the scones herself; they are ordered solely for the corgis.

There may be liveried footmen at her beck and call twenty-four hours a day, but, as with breakfast, the Queen likes to serve herself at teatime. She insists on pouring her own cup of tea, which she replenishes from a kettle mounted on a swivel stand, and which was designed for her by Prince Philip, so she wouldn't have to lift a heavy kettle full of boiling water.

After tea, Her Majesty returns to her office for another hour. Most of the clerical staff at Buckingham Palace finish at 5.30 but the senior members of the household: her private secretary, the Crown Equerry, the Keeper of the Privy Purse, the Master of the Household and the press secretary, are often at their desks until seven.

If there is no evening engagement, the Queen retires to her own rooms just after six to rest before changing for dinner. The exception is Tuesday evening, when the Prime Minister arrives for his weekly audience at 6.30. It used to be an hour earlier, but when Prince Charles and Princess Anne were small, the Queen liked to spend that time with them so she changed the appointment to half past six – and it has remained so ever since. The meeting is official, so it takes place in the Audience Room, on the north-west corner between the Royal Closet and the Queen's dining room, and lasts for no more than half an hour.

Unlike the Queen Mother and Princess Margaret, who still insist on dressing for dinner every evening, even when they are alone, the Queen and Prince Philip simply change into something more comfortable. For her it's a short dress and for him a lounge suit or smoking jacket. It's all a far cry from the days of King George V, who not only donned a frock coat for dinner every evening, but also wore the Garter Star, with Queen Mary in full-length gown and diamond tiara.

Dinner for the Queen and Prince Philip is the most relaxed meal of the day when they both enjoy a couple of glasses of their favourite German wine. The meal consists of three courses, again with no red meat. Roast beef and Yorkshire puddings have been off the royal menus for some years. Prince Philip often has a separate engagement in the evening, but the Queen rarely accompanies him. She likes to remain in her private quarters, reading or watching television in the sitting room next door to her office. She also enjoys solving jigsaw puzzles and in each of her houses there is usually a giant, complicated one waiting to be finished. Frequently she spends part of the evening working on her 'boxes' – the official despatch cases which contain correspondence from government departments in the United Kingdom and the Commonwealth. Every evening a report on the day's proceedings in Parliament is delivered to her, written by the Vice-Chamberlain of the Household, a senior MP. At one time it was handwritten and took hours to write and deliver. These days a word processor is used and the report is electronically transferred to Buckingham Palace, where it is invariably read by the Queen before she retires.

Her Majesty is not a late night person. She is usually in bed by eleven, but she likes to read in bed. So, often, the last lights seen shining out of the north side of the Palace are those in her rooms. They are easy to identify; they are the only ones with bow windows, overlooking Constitution Hill.

CHAPTER TWO

Queen Regnant

'I believe it's a tribute to the Queen's
professionalism that she has developed the
monarchy to what it is today – a steady fixture
in our lives.'
NEIL KINNOCK, LABOUR LEADER 1983–1992

'By the sudden death of my dear father I am called upon to assume the duties and responsibilities of sovereignty.' With this simple yet totally moving accession speech, made in London on 8 February 1952, the former Princess Elizabeth became Her Majesty Queen Elizabeth II, forty-second sovereign of England since William the Conqueror, yet only its sixth reigning queen.

Some thirty-six hours earlier she had been a contented twenty-five-year-old wife and mother, enjoying the pleasures – and climate – of a Kenyan summer, when she learned that her beloved father, King George VI, had died in his sleep at the age of fifty-six. She was immediately flown back to an icy Britain to be greeted at London airport by seventy-seven-year-old Winston Churchill, her father's, and now her, Prime Minister. Waiting at Buckingham Palace, determined to be the first member of the royal family to pay homage to the new monarch, was her eighty-five-year-old grandmother. Queen Mary, widow of King George V, gave a deep curtsy as she kissed her granddaughter's hand. It was an emotional and moving experience for those who witnessed the brief ceremony, particularly as she was the only queen to see her granddaughter become sovereign. Queen Mary would live for only another year, missing the coronation by two months, but insisting in her final weeks that the ceremony should go ahead in spite of the traditional period of court mourning.

Elizabeth II is now the longest-reigning British sovereign since her great-great-grandmother, Queen Victoria, the last Queen Regnant, who had occupied the throne for more than sixty-three years when she died in 1901, and whose empire controlled one-fifth of the earth's land surface and a quarter of the world's population. Their joint ancestor, the first Elizabeth, reigned for forty-five years (1558–1603).

Born on 21 April 1926 in a private house in London when her parents were then the Duke and Duchess of York, the Queen is also the first female sovereign to bear the family name of Windsor. It was adopted by her grandfather, King George V, who issued a proclamation on 17 July 1917, during the First World War. Intended to counteract any anti-German feeling, it changed the family's official name from Saxe-Coburg and Gotha to Windsor.

Crowned in Westminster Abbey on 2 June 1953, Her Majesty's full titles are: Elizabeth the Second, by the Grace of God, of the United Kingdom of Great Britain and Northern Ireland, and of her other Realms and Territories Queen, Head of the Commonwealth, Defender of the Faith. She is not, and never has been, Empress. By the time she came to the throne, India had won its independence. The title, which related only to India, had been created for, and at the insistence of, Queen Victoria in April 1876 and adopted by every sovereign since.

But it disappeared for ever in 1947, when King George VI was forced to relinquish it.

There is a little-known story about the Queen's wedding that exemplifies the human side of this very public figure. She and Prince Philip were eager to hear the radio commentary when they were travelling in the procession from Westminster Abbey. This was long before transistors made it possible for tiny sets to be hidden in a pocket, so the Crown Equerry, Sir Dermot McMorrough Kavanagh, who had held the post since 1941, arranged for what passed for a 'portable' wireless set to be installed inside the Irish State Coach. The trouble was that even 'portable' radios needed huge – and very heavy – batteries, so these were fitted underneath the seats on both sides of the coach. The reception wasn't terribly clear but at least the Queen and Prince Philip were able to hear the scene being described by the BBC commentator as they waved to the crowds. The radio set was a secret known to only a few inside the Palace, but the Queen later said it added to her enjoyment of the day tremendously and also helped to fend off any nervous feelings.

Elizabeth II is recognized as monarch or Head of the Commonwealth by fifty-one countries throughout the world, mainly in what was once the British Empire. These range from the sub-continent of India with its 900 million people, to tiny island dependencies in the South Pacific whose populations are smaller than those of many London boroughs. The monarchy is Britain's oldest secular institution, pre-dating Parliament by 400 years and the Law Courts by 300. The Queen can trace her descent in direct line back to King Egbert, the first Monarch of All England in 829. She is the latest in a line that stretches for over a thousand years with a continuity that has been interrupted only once; when Oliver Cromwell's Commonwealth ruled from 1649 to 1660.

One of Her Majesty's titles: Defender of the Faith, first granted to Henry VIII by the Pope – when the faith he was supposed to defend was Roman Catholicism – seems strangely archaic in a land where fewer than one in twenty now professes to be a practising Christian and where there are more Hindus and Moslems attending their places of worship than belong to the Anglican Church of England, of which she is Supreme Governor.

She is by far the most experienced monarch in British history and during her reign she has been served by seven private secretaries, and seen ten Prime Ministers arrive and depart (eleven if you count Harold Wilson's two terms of office). The first was an ageing Winston Churchill, the latest, the youthful Tony Blair, had not been born when she ascended the throne.

She is said to have no political power yet when Harold Wilson's Labour Party won the 1974 election by a very small majority she still sent for the defeated Ted Heath, as the sitting Prime Minister, and gave him the opportunity to form a Conservative–Liberal coalition. It wasn't until he failed in this that she invited Wilson to form a government. She had been reluctant to summon Heath at first, although he had requested the opportunity, as she realized the choice would be seen in some quarters as the monarch over-ruling the wishes of the democratic electorate; and indeed it was mistakenly believed that she had shown her own political leanings. Yet there is little evidence that she prefers Conservative politicians to Labour. James Callaghan is believed to have been one of her favourite Prime Ministers, while Margaret Thatcher has never been considered the most popular.

Even here there is a contradiction. A well-publicized difference of opinion between the Queen and Margaret Thatcher in the eighties was officially denied by the Palace, even though the source had been one of Her Majesty's senior courtiers. And both the Queen and Prince Philip attended Lady Thatcher's 70th birthday party in 1995; hardly the action of someone who disliked her former Prime Minister.

Sir Bernard Ingham, who was Margaret Thatcher's press secretary throughout her time at Number 10, had this to say about his former boss's relationship with the Queen. 'They got on very well. Mrs Thatcher [as she then was] held royalty in almost God-like awe. She had a traditional feeling of reverence for the royal family and willingly paid obeisance to the Queen. As far as I am aware there was only one area where there were disagreements and that was over the Commonwealth. Mrs Thatcher never held the Commonwealth in quite the same degree of affection or importance as the Queen. Mrs Thatcher felt it to be an expensive luxury with few benefits for Britain, while the Queen obviously regards her position as Head of the Commonwealth as of prime importance. But on a personal level, the Queen showed her appreciation of Mrs Thatcher quite soon after she left office, giving her the Order of Merit and making her a Lady of the Garter. I feel this was to put paid to the rumours – mostly started by courtiers at the Palace – that the Queen did not relish the thought of having to deal with a woman prime minister.'

Another myth relating to the Queen's relationships with her Prime Ministers is that she preferred Winston Churchill to all the others. In the very early days of her reign, the Queen was said to be occasionally irritated by what was described as 'Winston's patronizing attitude'. However, it did not take Churchill, ever a pragmatist, many months to assume his well-documented sycophantic 'adoption' of his young sovereign.

When Elizabeth came to the throne Harry Truman was President of the United States. Since then she has seen another ten occupants of the White House, as well as five Popes in the Vatican, and she must have lost count of the other heads of state who have come and gone. But Buckingham Palace has a record of every single one, including when and where they met the Queen, what they spoke about and the gifts they exchanged. Such is the attention paid by the Palace to the minutest detail, they probably also know what Her Majesty was wearing at the time and what she had for breakfast that day.

The former United States President George Bush recalls a visit to Buckingham Palace in 1989 when he noticed an unusual three-legged silver dish which intrigued him. 'What is that, I asked Her Majesty. She replied, "I don't know. You gave it to me."

Another former US President, Gerald Ford, formed a warm friendship when he welcomed Her Majesty to Washington. After the official banquet they opened the dancing (to the tune of Getting to Know You), and he recalled, 'I was dancing with the Queen of England. It sure was a long way from my origins in Omaha, Nebraska.' This was in 1976 when the Queen and Prince Philip paid their first State Visit to the United States for nearly twenty years. Their previous visit had been in 1957 when President Eisenhower was tenant of the White House. Dr Henry Kissinger recalls some of the highlights of the 1976 occasion. 'There were a number of celebratory events to mark the bicentenary of America and the Queen and Prince Philip came to several; first in New York, another at the White House and there was one splendid evening when she returned President Ford's hospitality and invited us to dinner on board the Royal Yacht. *Britannia* was anchored off Newport, Rhode Island and it made a magnificent spectacle, dressed overall and with the Royal Marines Band playing. She appeared to enjoy it and we certainly did. I was lucky enough to be seated next to the Queen twice which made it even more enjoyable.'

It was during the 1976 visit that Dr Kissinger made his memorable remark about the Queen 'being a very interesting lady with a lot of savvy'. 'The reason I made this assessment of her was that I had sat next to her shortly after she had returned from one of the Commonwealth Conferences. She painted vivid word pictures of various leaders which showed how completely in tune she was with what was happening in these countries. We also discussed other aspects of foreign policy when she displayed a keen knowledge. She is a serious woman who is world class in her understanding of international affairs, and she is able to make shrewd judgements of people. And, far from being the mere figurehead she sometimes appears to be, she also knows a great deal about the electoral system in Britain. She knows all about the arithmetic needed by the different parties and how much of a majority is required to form a working government.'

A former Secretary of State and Presidential Adviser on National Security, Henry Kissinger has known the Queen and Prince Philip since just after Richard Nixon was first elected President in 1968. 'This was when I first met the Queen. Nixon was making a visit to England which was not a State occasion. I accompanied him and the Queen asked us to a lunch at Buckingham Palace. I thought from her public image that Her Majesty would be a very formal lady; very aloof and stern. But from the moment I met her – and this was confirmed on subsequent occasions – I was struck by how lively and animated she was and also her great sense of humour, without sacrificing any of her dignity.'

Henry Kissinger was once on the board of 20th Century-Fox, and Ronald Reagan, a former movie star turned politician, used his connections to arrange a function at the Hollywood studios at which both the Queen and Henry Kissinger were guests. 'It was the idea of Nancy Reagan and on this occasion I was nowhere near the Queen or Prince Philip. Someone, in their wisdom, had decided, with appalling bad taste, that the only people who would sit near the Queen would be those who were the major fund-raisers for Reagan. Anyway, we were all lined up in two rows, along which the Queen and Prince Philip walked, acknowledging the applause and stopping to have a word with some of the stars they recognized. Prince Philip paused to chat to me for a few moments. Immediately, a rather officious executive plucked at his sleeve urging him to continue the procession. He was having none of it, retorting, "Surely I can stop for a second to talk to an old friend without someone trying to pull me back into line?"'

One of the nicest occasions when Henry Kissinger met the Queen was when she knighted him. (Dr Kissinger was made a Knight Commander of The Most Distinguished Order of St Michael and St George on 25 June 1995, for his services to international diplomacy, though, as a United States citizen, he does not use the title Sir.) As he recalled, 'The Queen was most gracious and gave me lunch at Windsor. It was during the meal that Prince Philip saved me from making what could have been a *faux pas*. Towards the end of lunch the Queen's corgis came in and sat at her feet. Now I am very fond of dogs – in fact I regard myself as a "dog-nut", and for the moment I forgot where I was, calling across the table to my wife Nancy, who was sitting next to Prince Philip, 'Look what's sitting under the table.' There was complete silence and everybody – there were around forty of us present – stopped what they were doing. Prince Philip jumped to my rescue, making a remark about them being the bane of his life and everyone laughed. He had said it in a joking fashion that defused the situation straight away and I was very grateful.

'On the same occasion, during Royal Ascot Week, I was invited to ride with the Queen and Prince Philip in an open carriage as they processed down the racecourse in front of the grandstands and waved to the crowds. Even though I have never thought of myself as a man who is easily intimidated, I have to confess I was slightly overawed. What happened was that we left the Castle in a fleet of cars and drove down the Long Walk to the entrance to the racecourse, then changed over to the horse-drawn carriages for the final mile. It was fascinating because as we were being driven, the Queen was making comments about little mistakes she had spotted – but which nobody else would have noticed. She didn't do it in a nasty way; more humorous and witty. For example, she noticed that the band had started a couple of beats too soon, little things like that. She made the whole thing very enjoyable.'

Dr Kissinger also observed the attention to detail that accompanies all things royal. 'When we arrived at the Royal Box everything was meticulously arranged. There was no scrabbling around looking for seats, everyone had an appointed place and the Queen knew exactly where everyone and everything should be. To the outsider it all looks so spontaneous, but the planning is brilliant and all done with excellent taste. She is a wonderful hostess.'

Henry Kissinger also has a great respect for Prince Philip and, despite Philip's reputation for being aggressive and overbearing on occasion, enjoys his company: 'I've never found him to be difficult. He's always the same to me. I like his honesty and the way he says what he believes.'

Britain has long liked to think it enjoys a special relationship with the United States. Henry Kissinger believes the character and personal qualities of the Queen make a significant contribution. 'Whenever I see her with American Presidents, I cannot believe she can behave the same way with every other country. She has made a unique and enormous contribution to Anglo/US relations. There is no doubt in my mind that she is admired and respected here more than any other head of state.'

During the half-century Elizabeth II has sat on the throne she has never put a foot wrong in her public life, and her personal life has also been exemplary. However, the life of her family has not always been so unblemished. With three of her four children married and divorced and one of them, the Prince of Wales, involved in one of the nation's most publicized, and criticized, love affairs, her success as a parent has been questioned. With Elizabeth, duty has always come first, even at the expense of her own family's happiness. At the same time her devotion to her public responsibilities has provided the protective wall against any private emotional grief other parents might have felt when faced with the troubles the royal family has encountered in recent years.

The Queen has a political acumen that has often been underrated. Her influence on affairs of state is recognized by those in authority but rarely fully appreciated by the man or woman in the street. Why should it be, when to many people she is associated only with the pomp and ceremony connected with the ritual of royalty? As Lord Callaghan once said, 'The Queen has astute political judgement which sometimes seems at odds with the general public perception of her.'

She has also refined into an art form the business of dealing with political leaders whose beliefs may be far removed from her own. One of her oldest and most cherished friends is the former Prime Minister of Singapore, Lee Kwan Yew, a man of singularly independent views. He remembers the first time they met in 1966. 'She was amazingly good at putting her guests at ease without seeming to do so. It was a social skill perfected by training and years of experience.'

Her sense of humour has also been witnessed by a wide-ranging if comparatively select audience. The journalist Geordie Greig tells an amusing story involving the Nobel Prize-winning West Indian poet, Derek Walcott. When he was about to receive the Queen's Gold Medal for Poetry in 1989, Walcott was briefed beforehand by the then Poet Laureate, Ted Hughes, who told him, 'You will find that the Queen is the most relaxed woman you have ever met.' Once the medal had been handed over, Walcott and the Queen chatted about how Americans speak Shakespearean verse, not necessarily a subject on which one would expect Her Majesty to be expert. They spoke about the American actor Dustin Hoffman who had recently appeared on the West End stage as Shylock and then Walcott proceeded to tell her a joke: 'Ma'am, you know Sly Stallone' (the actor known for his mumbling, monosyllabic roles in *Rambo* and the Rocky boxing films). She nodded. 'Well, his version of Hamlet goes: "To be or what."' Walcott went on, 'She just cracked up. Ted was right; she is one helluva relaxed woman.'

Elizabeth's reign has seen more changes than almost any other period in British history. When she was born television, which has since become an integral and essential part of everyone's lives, had barely been invented, and even in the first years of her reign there was only one channel, BBC, transmitting to a limited audience in black and white. Radio was still the main source of news and entertainment; the majority of homes in Britain did not have a telephone or car and the idea of a man walking on the moon was laughable. Developments in technology have meant a vast increase in mass communication throughout the world, and yet Her Majesty has maintained a simple and effective philosophy which has allowed her to keep to her original course.

It has been claimed that the Queen represents all that was once best in Britain: family values, a highly developed moral conscience and care for the welfare of other people. She has also been accused of living in an ivory tower, isolated from the realities of everyday life, surrounded by sycophants who guard her from the problems faced by less fortunate men and women and who tell her only what they think she wants to hear. But in spite of her privileged upbringing and lifestyle, the Queen is a realist who knows, within the limits of her position, that many people have difficulty in living from day to day. She may not ever have had to worry about paying the household bills but she is aware of the circumstances in which many of the people over whom she reigns have to exist and few doubt that her concern is genuine.

The Queen is one of the richest people in the world. Her personal income, that is, the money that comes from her own investments, is used for her private expenditure. As such the amount is never revealed, but estimates usually start at £100 million and range up to five or six times as much. Whatever the sum, she has the finest financial advice in the world and also the most discreet.

Her circle of true friends is tiny and ultra-exclusive. She has many acquaintances but only a handful of men and women can claim to be real friends, and without exception these are people she has known for over forty years. The royal set is the most difficult in the world to break into and every one of those privileged to be included guards jealously the confidence he or she enjoys. One of her oldest and closest friends, Countess Mountbatten of Burma, says of her, 'She is the easiest person in the world to get on with, but I never for a moment forget she is my sovereign.'

Apart from Prince Philip and possibly Princess Margaret, there is no one in the world who really understands the enigma that is the true Elizabeth. The most regal of monarchs, with a devastating ability to 'freeze' anyone she suspects of undue familiarity, yet when she relaxes, she can be the warmest of companions with a distinct lack of pomposity – and a decidedly unroyal giggle. She is without doubt the most famous public woman in the world, and conversely, its most private. Resisting all requests for interviews, she has managed to maintain the 'magic of monarchy' without confusing aloofness with arrogance. As one of her former private secretaries once declared, 'She may have all the nous of the most experienced political campaigner, but she is not running for election.'

No one doubts the Queen's intelligence. Almost every morning she completes the crossword in the *Daily Telegraph*. Yet she is arguably the least formally educated sovereign of the past hundred years. Her own parents were hardly the best example in academic terms. Her father, King George VI, came last in his class of sixty-eight during his final examinations as a naval cadet at Osborne, a position which would have undoubtedly concerned any other parent but which was a matter of complete indifference to his father, King George V.

Similarly, the young Princess Elizabeth – unlike her own mother, who spent a few months at a select academy in Kensington – was never sent to school. And for the Princess's lessons at Windsor Castle, constitutional history and geography were the subjects in which she needed to shine; everything else was of low priority.

The last half of the twentieth century has witnessed dramatic changes in the monarchy, both in its role and also in the way it is perceived. Gone for ever is the old imperialist tradition of reverence and obsequious devotion. Sycophancy has been replaced by cynicism and even the change-resisting diehards in the royal household are gradually being replaced by a meritocracy. Eton, Oxford and the Guards have given way to lesser public schools, red brick universities and unfashionable army regiments, or even, horror of horrors, members with no military or naval service at all. It's a far cry from 1952 when Buckingham Palace still retained two separate kitchens, one for royalty, the other for lesser mortals.

Through it all, the Queen has sailed on majestically, the only sign of any unease at the anger even contempt for her family, shown by a previously devoted people, being a sense of bewilderment. Elizabeth II genuinely believes that she and her family have served Britain and the Commonwealth well, and even though the events of the last decade may have caused moments of doubt, there has been no real feeling on her part that her people have been let down.

Whatever success the monarchy may enjoy today stems mainly from the Queen's intuitive sense of being able to do the right thing at the right time. Nowhere was this better demonstrated than in the days following the death of Diana, Princess of Wales. Within hours of the announcement of the tragedy, thousands of people were clamouring for some form of demonstration of grief from the royal family. The feeling of loss on a national scale was palpable, with calls for a Union flag on Buckingham Palace to be flown at half mast as a sign of respect, and for the Queen to express her sympathy publicly. She was staying at Balmoral at the time, from where the silence was deafening despite the public clamour.

Five days after the event Her Majesty appeared on live television and spoke movingly and with great feeling about the loss of her former daughter-in-law. The broadcast was not made then because of pressure and mounting criticism, but because the Queen had refused to be rushed into saying something hurriedly. When she did appear, it was as a mother, grandmother and former mother-in-law, and she hit exactly the right note. There was no false emotion; just calm, direct sympathy that struck a chord with everyone who heard her. And by that single act the Queen showed once again that she instinctively knew what she had to say – and, more importantly – when to say it. The criticism didn't disappear overnight but it was stilled, and when she appeared with her family at the gates of Buckingham Palace two days later as the funeral cortege passed by, it was obvious to all that she was deeply moved. This was a moment of private sorrow being shared by the country's most public figure – and she was at one with her people.

Similarly, when there was a massive revolt of public opinion during the eighties and early nineties over the cost of the monarchy, the Queen, realizing the threat that lay underneath, was among the first to accept that changes were inevitable. She did not want to pay income tax – who would? – but she knew that public respect would dwindle and eventually disappear if she was not seen to make this gesture. And when Buckingham Palace was opened to the public it was not the Queen who objected but the true-blue old guard among her household – and her mother – all of whom wanted to maintain the elitist atmosphere they and very few others had enjoyed. Her Majesty realized that royal finances had to be put on a businesslike footing and that the monarchy needed to be seen to be cost-effective. So the loss of the Royal Yacht *Britannia* in 1997, the down-grading of the Queen's Flight, the changes to the Civil List and the removal of many other privileges were accepted as a necessary sacrifice.

If the Queen had been as isolated and reactionary as many of her critics claimed she would not have been able to countenance such dramatic changes, particularly as she entered her eighth decade. It took a woman of remarkable skill, wisdom and spirit to use them to make her own position even more secure and the public attitude to the monarchy more favourable than it had been for twenty years. In an age where anti-elitism is the norm and the class-ridden days of the early part of her reign are coming to an end, the Queen shows perfectly how to combine a closeness with people from all walks of life with, at the same time, the separateness that is essential for a monarch to preserve her dignity.

Throughout her reign, and for five years before, her main support has come from the man who has been at her side all this time. Prince Philip's position as Consort to Elizabeth II has never been fully defined, or understood. He has been described as rude, overbearing, aggressive and self-opinionated. All of which is probably true and yet none of which tells the complete story.

When Lieutenant Philip Mountbatten became a member of the royal family he was disparagingly referred to as 'that penniless Greek', which again was not accurate. He may have been poor but there was not, or ever has been, a drop of Greek blood in his veins. He was born in Corfu, but only because his father, a Dane who became Prince Andrew of Greece, was then living on the island, not because he was a natural-born citizen of Greece. Prince Andrew's grandfather was King Christian IX of Denmark, whose son William (Andrew's father) was invited to take the throne of Greece as King George I of the Hellenes. There was nothing particularly unusual in this; many countries have found their monarchs by inviting in a member of a foreign royal family. Very few sovereigns can claim to be native-born nationals of the countries whose throne they occupy. But the description of the young Philip as a 'penniless Dane' would somehow not have had the same contemptuous ring. And, in truth, although Philip was at one time sixth in line of succession to the throne of Greece, there was no money on his side of the family. When he married Princess Elizabeth his sole income was his salary as a naval officer.

The Queen herself is descended from an 'invited' king. As a direct descendant of George I, the first British monarch of the House of Hanover, she was fascinated to see a letter addressed to him on a 1962 visit to Germany. It came from a group of leading English citizens and urged him to come to England ready to take the throne on the death of the dying Queen Anne, who was the Anglican daughter of James II and reigned from 1702 to 1714. The English feared a Catholic Jacobite succession, so by the 1701 Act of Settlement, George's mother, Sophia, Electress of Hanover, a Protestant and also, like Anne, the granddaughter of James I, was declared the successor. In the event the throne passed to Sophia's son, who spoke no English, only German and French.

In his early days at Buckingham Palace Philip had to fight the establishment of the old household who were antagonistic and dismissive of the young man, perhaps thinking back to the influence which a previous foreign Consort, Prince Albert, had exerted over his wife, Queen Victoria. They did not relish the thought of Philip as the 'power behind the throne'. Nevertheless, he has forged for himself a unique position in the life of the nation. Putting aside his own personal ambitions, he has become the rock on which the Queen is able to lean whenever she feels the need.

A man of great independent spirit, Philip has accepted the need to walk the mandatory two steps behind his wife in public, but in private maintains an unchallenged position as head of the Mountbatten-Windsor family.

The Queen has described Philip as 'the tower of strength I can always rely on', and the present day royal household know how important he is to the stability and well being of the monarchy. Together, Elizabeth and Philip are said to be a 'good team' – but there is only one captain.

When the Queen reached the age of seventy in 1996, it was suggested – but not to her face – that it might be time for her to step down and hand the reins over to Prince Charles. He was then forty-eight and some people felt that perhaps if he did not get a chance to be sovereign while he was still sufficiently young and enthusiastic, a golden opportunity would be missed.

Prince Charles never once, by so much as a whisper, hinted that he wanted the job, but others, who felt they knew his wishes, started a campaign to get abdication placed on the agenda. Newspapers, including the quality broadsheets, carried serious articles by reputable historians and consti-tutional experts, explaining why this was not such an outrage-ous idea. But the plan never gained any real momentum; the man and woman on the street obviously felt there was no need for change; they were perfectly happy with Her Majesty on the throne and wanted nature to take its course.

The truth of the matter was that there was never the slight-est chance that the Queen would abdicate. When she was crowned in Westminster Abbey she took a solemn vow and a sacred oath to serve as sovereign until she died – and there has never been a wavering on her part. Apart from the extra-ordinary events of 1936, when her Uncle David, King Edward VIII, gave up his throne to marry Wallis Simpson, there is no tradition of abdication in Britain. Unlike the Netherlands, where it is not unusual for the monarch to abdicate on reach-ing a certain age, in Britain the sovereign remains on the throne for life. One American observer of the royal scene made the telling point: 'You tamper with institutions at your peril.' Once the position of the monarch is seen to be something that can be changed at will, the permanence that has been the bedrock on which Britain's monarchy has lasted for over a thousand years could quickly become a thing of the past.

Elizabeth II has been the nation's emotional lynchpin for fifty years. She is seen as an integral part of our national identity, the focus of non-political continuity in an ever-changing world. Her role remains vital even though her powers have been reduced to a point where former colonies with republican ambitions now refuse to accept her as their head of state, and where, in Britain, she is seen by the majority of people merely as a figurehead.

All Government work is carried out in her name; she is Commander-in-Chief of all the armed forces. In theory she could sell all the ships in the Royal Navy and disband the Army and the Royal Air Force. Wars are declared in her name and foreign ambassadors are accredited to her Court at St James's. As the fount of honour she confers peerages and knighthoods, and under the Royal Marriages Act 1772 none of her children can legally marry without her permission. The Queen has no direct political power yet one of her Prime Ministers, Lord Callaghan of Cardiff, once remarked, 'No practising politician could possibly hope to be more deeply and widely informed about domestic, Commonwealth and international affairs than the Queen. She has sources of information available to nobody else.'

Her power in Parliament may be constitutionally limited, and indeed she is required to assent to all Bills in Parliament; the sovereign last refused to do so in 1707, when Queen Anne vetoed a Scottish militia bill with the approval of her government; but she does have the right to encourage, be consulted and to warn if she thinks fit. This right to warn was exercised in 1914 to great effect, when King George V threatened to withhold the royal assent on the Irish Home Rule Bill. The bill, which was to provide an Irish parliament in Dublin, was opposed by the Conservatives and the Ulster Protestants, who claimed that it could lead to civil war. Asquith, the Liberal Prime Minister, contended that the King had no right to withhold assent. The King demanded a letter giving all the reasons why he should accept their 'advice'. The outbreak of the First World War meant that the bill was shelved.

As Head of the Commonwealth – a position to which she was acclaimed – the Queen acts as a link between people of vastly different cultures and political opinions. She regards the Commonwealth as a family of nations, herself as its matriarch.

By nature a country woman, whose natural inclination is to solitary rides over her own estates at Windsor, Sandringham and Balmoral, she has been forced to accept a role which means she is constantly in the public spotlight. She has mastered the knack of appearing to enjoy everything she does, when plainly, to use the words of her only daughter when describing duties which are stultifyingly boring, she finds some 'less interesting than others'.

The former leader of the Labour Party, Neil Kinnock, has his own theory about the success of the Queen: 'She may have been brought up in a different age but, it has to be said, it was an age of recovery for the monarchy. The assumption has been made in recent years that the monarchy has been such a fixture, that its existence has never been questioned. The fact is that, for a variety of reasons, for the first forty years of the twentieth century, there were perpetual questions being asked about the monarchy, and its acceptability. The monarchy had a "good war", and the Queen's father, King George VI, died comparatively shortly afterwards, in 1952. Then she, as a young woman, took over at a time when the monarchy was more popular than it had been for the first part of the century, but still not what you would call "locked in" to the admiring oceans of the people generally. The monarchy has always had strong supporters, but while there has never been republicanism as a general consensus, we haven't had an over-whelming tide of great monarchists either. I believe it's a tribute to the Queen's professionalism that she has developed the monarchy to what it is today – a steady fixture in our lives.'

CHAPTER THREE

A Family in Crisis

*'1992 is not a year I shall look back on with
undiluted pleasure.'*
THE QUEEN

Until the tragic death of Diana, Princess of Wales in 1997, one of the most meaningful events in the Queen's reign had been the great fire of Windsor Castle five years earlier. Although a momentous event in itself, destroying much of Her Majesty's favourite residence, the fire seemed to illustrate more clearly than anyone could have imagined the disastrous situation in which the royal family found itself.

The year 1992 had started out badly with the disintegration of the marriage of the Prince and Princess of Wales. Intimate conversations between Diana and James Gilbey, a car dealer, were published in all their gory, if somewhat sentimental, detail. These were actually several years old, having been recorded on New Year's Eve 1989 when Diana, increasingly frustrated by what she regarded as hostile treatment by the royal family, poured her heart out to Gilbey. The *Sun* newspaper censored part of the tape transcript because of its explicit sexual overtones, but the damage was done.

These 'Squidgygate' tapes, so-called after Gilbey's pet name for Diana, were soon to be overshadowed by the discovery of telephone calls made by Prince Charles to his lover, Camilla Parker Bowles. These caused the Queen even more acute embarrassment, with Charles talking in terms normally restricted to soft-porn telephone lines.

Then, to add to the Queen's anguish, Diana demanded a formal separation. Prince Charles did not want it; he was perfectly happy to let things go on as they were, with Diana leading her own life, so long as it was fairly discreet. He could then continue his relationship with the woman he loved. The Queen and Prince Philip both tried to persuade Diana not to proceed with her plans for a separation. They used the arguments of loyalty and devotion to the Crown, and asked her to consider the effects a separation – which was likely to be followed by divorce – would have on Diana's sons William and Harry.

As if these problems were not enough, the Duke and Duchess of York were also going through a sticky patch, again in the glaring light of publicity. In January, a series of photographs of the Duchess and her daughters on holiday in the South of France in 1990 with an American, Steve Wyatt, filled pages of the morning papers.

But damaging as those appeared to be, they paled into insignificance later that year, when the Duchess had to suffer the humiliating prospect of sitting down to breakfast with her in-laws at Balmoral, knowing they had all seen photographs of her topless and having her toes kissed by John Bryan, her 'financial adviser'. Apparently he liked to boast to his friends about making love with Sarah while she was on the telephone to her husband. There wasn't much chance of the marriage surviving after the tabloids revealed that escapade, and in 1993 another royal separation was announced.

Some of the royal household had known about the Duchess's extra-marital affairs for a while, but were content to ignore them until they became public knowledge, thereby embarrassing the Queen. Other members of the royal family had conducted liaisons over the years; everyone knew about them, but as discretion is the watchword in the private lives of royals, a blind eye is turned. Princess Margaret found this out with her unconventional lifestyle. Once her affair with the young Roddy Llewellyn became front page news, it was all over. She knew the rules and played by them, even if she had been brought up spoilt and worshipped by a father who indulged her every whim. She had enjoyed a sheltered upbringing totally at odds with the real world, so was completely unprepared for the torrent of abuse at her openly privileged lifestyle that had marked the early days of her marriage to the Earl of Snowdon. She did not want to risk similar treatment when the Roddy Llewellyn romance was revealed.

Criticism of the royal family often comes down to two things: sex and money, with money beating sex to the number one position. Whenever one of the royals is revealed as having an affair, the story invariably includes a comment about its being conducted 'on the money we pay them'. It is almost as if we wouldn't mind their carrying on as long as they didn't do it while being paid from the public purse.

Over the years critics have called Princess Margaret selfish and self-centred – among other less flattering descriptions. But there is a kinder and much more considerate side to her character, as the writer, the late Quentin Crewe, told the present author: 'When my first wife [the novelist Angela Huth] was pregnant she was having a bad time, which meant she had to remain in bed for several months. We would often hear a knock at the door and then Princess Margaret, who was an old friend, would suddenly appear bearing a tray. She would arrange everything for Angela, serve her lunch or supper, and sit with her for hours keeping her company.' Hardly the behaviour of a woman who never lifts a finger to help herself or anyone else.

Returning to 1992, it was on the morning of Friday, 20 November that Prince Andrew phoned to break the awful news. The Queen was at Buckingham Palace, quietly marking her forty-fifth wedding anniversary alone, before being driven down to Windsor for the weekend, as usual, after lunch. Prince Philip was abroad in Argentina. Shortly before midday, smoke was seen billowing out of Windsor Castle, which very soon became a roaring inferno. It had started near the Queen's private chapel and quickly spread to the State Apartments where St George's Hall, the most magnificent, was seriously damaged.

Prince Andrew happened to be at Windsor and he initially took charge of the recovery operation, directing castle workers and Royal Collection staff in the rescue of many of the treasures that were at risk. He later modestly denied that he had done anything exceptional, but someone had to take charge and he did. Meanwhile the Queen drove straight to the scene, where television viewers saw live pictures of her – a tiny figure dressed in headscarf and raincoat – walking among the debris accompanied by her son. Few would have failed to be moved by the view of Her Majesty standing forlorn in the remains of the home where she had spent much of her childhood and enjoyed many precious years. Nothing could have illustrated more poignantly the despair she must have felt as that dreadful year drew to its conclusion. It was as if her whole reason for being was challenged. Recession in the country, the marriages of two of her sons in tatters, being virtually forced to pay income tax (though the official announcement would not be made in the House of Commons until six days later with the full details released three months afterwards), mounting criticism over the very institution of the monarchy and now this, the destruction of a large part of her favourite home.

To add to the Queen's agony, the initial sympathy which the country showed towards her after seeing her looking so lonely and sad on television was quickly replaced by mounting anger when it was announced the following day that the Government would pay the entire £60 million bill for repairs. The announcement was premature and, as it eventually turned out, unnecessary. The final bill was nearer £40 million and the money was found out of the income from opening Buckingham Palace and the Windsor precincts to the public, plus savings made from the annual Grant-in-Aid allowance paid to the Queen.

But the Queen was totally unused to public hostility. She had been on the throne for forty years, during which her people had generally felt a warm affection for their sovereign. She had never experienced any personal attacks or criticism.

Four days after the fire, on 24 November, she was scheduled to give a speech at the Guildhall in the City of London. It became known as her 'Annus Horribilis' speech and one for which she will inevitably be remembered. Suffering from a severe cold and the after-effects of the smoke at Windsor, the Queen's voice was hoarse and scratchy. Her delivery matched her sombre appearance as, with masterly understatement, she declared the past twelve months 'not a year I shall look back on with undiluted pleasure'. It was the nearest she had come to admitting her sorrow at her children's domestic problems, with the fire on top to seal a disastrous year. And it wasn't just the cumulation of events that caused her unhappiness, it was the feeling of sheer bewilderment that so many people – and the press – were so unsympathetic to her personally. She had not done anything wrong, and for four decades she had worked tirelessly in the interests of her people, so how could they repay her with this unwarranted hostility? If ever there was a moment when she felt like giving it all up, this must have been the one. The Queen has never expected gratitude, but perhaps she did think a little understanding and appreciation of her position would not go amiss.

But even at this lowest point in the Queen's reign until then opinion polls remained overwhelmingly in favour of the monarchy. Any criticism of the Queen and her family did not extend to replacing her with an elected head of state.

Seemingly attacked from many sides, the Queen and her family withdrew into their private world to consider the next moves in their battle to regain the people's respect. They may have appeared a family at war, both with each other and with those outside, but there was no way they were going to admit it – or to surrender almost a thousand years of continuous power and privilege – without a fight. If survival meant paying tax, opening Buckingham Palace to the public and footing the bill for the restoration of Windsor Castle, plus ignoring the inner turmoil within the family as her children's problems became the subject of increasing public debate, the Queen would cope with them all. She was determined that somehow an apparently desperate situation for the House of Windsor would be resolved.

Had she known it, worse was to come: two of her sons divorced, a book, authorized by Diana, which would reveal to the world a sensational version of life behind palace doors, and the huge backlash of public opinion that followed the crash in Paris which killed the woman once chosen to be the next Queen.

This truly was a family in crisis.

CHAPTER FOUR

Lilibet – The Early Days

'Even as a child she had these perfect manners.'
LADY KENNARD

Not many women would welcome the presence of a stranger at the birth of their baby. Even a husband is sometimes considered supernumary at a time when all the mother really wants is to be left alone to get on with the painful and prolonged business of producing a child. So at 17 Bruton Street, in the heart of London's Mayfair, in the early morning of 21 April 1926, the young mother-to-be and her nervous husband did not relish the thought of playing host to no less a figure than the Home Secretary. But the accepted practice at that time meant that this holder of one of the government's highest offices had to attend in person whenever a royal child was born. It was to make sure there could be no substitution.

In fact no law demanded this. It was simply a custom that went back centuries. It dated from the reign of James II (1685–88), when it was claimed that a child had been smuggled into his mother's chamber in a warming pan. Since then a senior minister had been present to authenticate each birth. In 1926, the Home Secretary of the day, Sir William

Joynson Hicks, was entertained by the Duke of York. There was little purpose in his being in the house since he certainly did not witness the actual birth.

The mother in question was, of course, the twenty-five-year-old Duchess of York, whose father-in-law was George V, King and Emperor. The father was his second son, Bertie, Duke of York, who ten years later would become King George VI. The house where the birth took place was the London home of the Duchess's father, the 14th Earl of Strathmore. The Yorks themselves had no permanent London home; they had been given the use of White Lodge in Richmond Park, where Princess Alexandra and Sir Angus Ogilvy now live, but found it too far from all their friends and relations in W1. So they relied on the Strathmores to provide them with accommodation.

The Duchess of York, Elizabeth, was attended by two doctors, Sir Henry Simson and Walter Jagger, and she did not have an easy time. The baby was in the 'breech' position and a Caesarian section had to be performed, an operation that would never be countenanced in a home delivery today. But equally, in those far off days, the idea of a royal child being born in hospital was unthinkable. (Indeed, it wasn't until the 1960s that any member of the royal family was even a patient in hospital. When King George VI had part of his lung removed in a cancer operation in 1951, a room in Buckingham Palace was adapted with all the necessary equipment specially installed.) The Duchess of York was thrilled when she learned she had a perfect baby girl and her husband was overjoyed that everything had eventually gone well.

Looking back on the event after more than seventy years it is hard to imagine the worldwide excitement and interest in the birth. Reporters from all the London newspapers had camped outside the house for hours, and when the news came they rushed to tell their editors so that the early papers could publish the official announcement later that same morning.

It read: 'Her Royal Highness the Duchess of York was safely delivered of a Princess (at 2.40 am) this morning. Both mother and daughter are doing well.' The Prime Minister was informed, as were government officials in every country in the British Empire and Dominions. The Viceroy of India ordered bells to be rung in the country's churches and messages of congratulation flooded in from all over the world. At the time of her birth, the Princess, who was given the names Elizabeth Alexandra Mary, stood third in line of succession to the throne after her uncle David, Edward, Prince of Wales, who later became, briefly, King Edward VIII, and her father.

The christening took place just over a month later on 29 May in the chapel at Buckingham Palace. As with all royal christenings, the service was a private family affair. It was conducted by the Archbishop of York, Cosmo Gordon Lang, and there were six godparents: King George V and Queen Mary, the paternal grandparents; her maternal grandfather, the Earl of Strathmore and Kinghorne; her father's only sister, the Princess Royal; Lady Elphinstone (the former Lady Mary Bowes-Lyon); and her great-great-uncle, the seventy-six-year-old Prince Arthur, Duke of Connaught, Queen Victoria's third son. The infant Princess Elizabeth wore the christening robe of cream Honiton lace which all Queen Victoria's children had also worn. Another royal tradition that was observed was that water from the River Jordan was used for the baptism in the font that was brought from Windsor Castle.

If the child was adored by her parents, she was equally welcomed by the King and Queen who had longed for a grandchild. King George V had been an affectionate but distant father to his children while Queen Mary had been merely distant. She had found it difficult to show any emotion for her sons and daughter, her inflexible attitude towards her royal position forcing her to stifle any maternal instincts. But with the arrival of Princess Elizabeth she unbent to an extent never before seen by anyone in the family or household. Elizabeth was probably the only child she genuinely enjoyed sitting on her regal lap.

The everyday care of the Princess was entrusted to Mrs Clara Knight – the 'Mrs' a courtesy title bestowed on all royal nannies, whether married or not – who had been in service to the Strathmore family for years. As Elizabeth grew older she found difficulty in pronouncing the name Clara so she invented the soubriquet Alla, and that's what Mrs Knight became forever after. Mrs Knight also had an assistant nurse named Margaret McDonald who became 'Bobo' to the future Queen and who remained in royal service for more than sixty years. In her final years, when she was bedridden, Bobo was attended by nurses twenty-four hours a day, in her bedroom immediately above the Queen's own quarters at Buckingham Palace, and where her devoted employer visited her every day.

The Duke and Duchess were doting parents but the King insisted they undertake a strenuous and lengthy Commonwealth tour before Elizabeth was a year old. It was the start of a situation that every royal child had, and still has, to get used to: long absences from parents from an early age. However, there were compensations at the end of the tour when some three tons of toys, given by the host countries, were brought back. Not that Elizabeth saw many of them, most being donated to hospitals and orphanages. Another historical footnote was added at the conclusion of the tour when the fourteen-month-old Princess made her first appearance on the balcony at Buckingham Palace. It was on 27 June 1927 at a welcome home appearance for the Yorks, and Elizabeth was held up by both her mother and grandmother to wave to the crowds gathered in the Mall. It was probably the only time that Queen Mary held a child in public.

During the tour the house that was to become their London home for the next nine years was acquired. It was an elegant four-storey house, with twenty-six bedrooms, just a stone's throw away from Buckingham Palace at 145 Piccadilly.

Destroyed by German bombs in the Second World War, the house has been replaced by a luxury five-star hotel without even a plaque to commemorate the fact that the little girl who was to become Queen once lived there. The site in Bruton Street, however, although the house itself has long been demolished and replaced by commercial premises, does bear a plaque informing visitors that it is the birthplace of the Queen.

Number 145 Piccadilly was a true family home with no rooms sacrosanct and barred to the Yorks' daughter. The only concession the Duke of York made to his daughter being a royal Princess was that he allowed a red carpet in the day nursery. It would have meant nothing to her at the time, of course, but it does give an indication of the style in which the future Queen was brought up. The house itself was no different from its immediate neighbours and during the time the Yorks lived there they employed around twenty domestic staff. Anyone who could afford to live in Piccadilly in the thirties would probably have sustained a similar household.

The fact that the King and Queen were just across the road in Buckingham Palace was a bonus, and the Duke of Wellington, a direct descendant of the original 'Iron' Duke, who occupied Apsley House on the adjacent corner of Park Lane, was another near neighbour and friend.

Elizabeth did not have the company of many other children in her early years because her grandfather insisted that she – and also her sister, Princess Margaret, born on 21 August 1930 – should be taught at home with private tutors. This meant that theirs was a comparatively lonely childhood. But it has also been suggested that this early grounding in self-reliance stood them both in good stead in later life. Later, when they moved into Buckingham Palace, a Palace Girl Guides group was established, with carefully selected members.

One of the extraordinary aspects of the childhood of Princess Elizabeth is the way in which she was able to twist that strict disciplinarian, King George V, around her little finger. Elizabeth Longford, in her biography *Elizabeth R*, says His Majesty would allow Lilibet to play horses with him, getting him down on all fours and pulling him around by his beard. Lady Longford quotes Lady Airlie, Queen Mary's lady-in-waiting, as recalling, 'He used to play – a thing I never saw him do with his own children.' But perhaps it was not altogether too surprising; like many men brought up with parents who were distant and who had a sense of duty thrust upon them practically from the moment they were born, King George V had found it difficult to show affection to his children. It was not that he did not love them; it was simply that he lived by a set of rules that to him were there to be observed. He was quoted as saying, in a phrase that has been repeated time and time again, 'My father was frightened of his mother [Queen Victoria]; I was frightened of my father; and I am going to make damn sure my children are frightened of me.' The true source for this quotation has never been revealed and at least one distinguished biographer has claimed the story is apocryphal. But accurate or not, it certainly worked as none of his children, even Princess Mary, the Princess Royal, had ever been known to answer him back, even when they were adults. So when his first grandchild came along all the repressed affection was focused on her, and she loved it.

It would not have been strange if her own father had followed his father's dictum, but from the moment of her birth Elizabeth was a wanted and much-loved child and the mutual devotion never wavered. The Duke never wanted his children to be afraid of him, and while he did possess a frightening temper at times, neither Elizabeth nor Margaret ever feared facing him. Theirs was a happy home, made even more so by the presence of a mother whose maternal instincts were allowed to flourish and develop freely. The Duchess of York had grown up in a large, gregarious family and was never happier than when she was surrounded by parents and siblings. So she brought to the Windsor family a freshness and spontaneity not seen or experienced for over a hundred years.

And if it is thought that media attention for royal children is a comparatively recent phenomenon, it is worth noting that by the time Elizabeth was just three years old she had appeared on the cover of *Time* magazine. It was also around this period that Hollywood discovered the worldwide appeal of the pretty little girl with the blue eyes and fair curls. As they were unable to get the real thing they invented a 'princess' of their own and Shirley Temple was discovered. Elizabeth grew up accepting as perfectly natural the deference and near adulation that surrounded royalty. Spending lots of time with her paternal grandparents, she quickly understood the reverence with which everyone treated the King and Queen.

Unlike modern children today, or even wealthy children of their own time, the two princesses were not taken abroad for holidays. The Yorks followed the traditional royal seasonal pattern of winters in London, weekends at Royal Lodge Windsor (where the Queen Mother and Princess Margaret still spend every weekend today), Christmas and New year at Sandringham, summers in Scotland with the occasional afternoon spent on the beach at Dunan Bay in Forfarshire where they were allowed to paddle in the icy sea. It wasn't an exciting life for two little girls, but as they had never known anything else, they had nothing to compare it with so had no cause to complain. Not that two such well brought up children would ever dream of complaining anyway. Theirs was a pampered and privileged childhood lived in homes with every comfort and luxury. The only thing missing was the company of boys and girls of their own age.

It may be that this early solitude, apart from the company of adults, is the reason why the Queen turned to animals for companionship. Horses and dogs have always been an integral part of country life for the royals, and Elizabeth – and to a lesser extent, Margaret – made up for their lack of contemporary company by lavishing much affection on their pets. Even today, the Queen is said to prefer to be alone with her corgis and horses than with other people.

The first ten years of Elizabeth's life were spent in this way until the events of 1936, when her beloved grandfather, King George V, died and her uncle David became King Edward VIII. Overnight she moved a step nearer the throne, now second in line of succession behind her own father, who never dreamed that he would be called upon to wear the crown.

The death of her grandfather left a lasting effect on the ten-year-old princess as she was taken to see him in the final hours of his life. She was said to emerge from his bedroom looking very unhappy; hardly surprising on such a sombre occasion. It was also the first experience she would have of seeing someone so close to death. Princess Margaret, four years younger, was not subjected to the same ordeal. The reign of Edward VIII was to last for only 327 days; he was never crowned and much of his time on the throne was spent trying to persuade the government of the day, through Prime Minister Stanley Baldwin, to accept the woman he loved, the American divorcee Wallis Simpson. But it was not to be and Edward abdicated on 11 December 1936, to move to France, marry Mrs Simpson and become the Duke of Windsor.

His mother, Queen Mary, had been implacably opposed to the marriage and she never forgave her eldest son for what she regarded as his ultimate treachery and dereliction of duty. Nor did she ever acknowledge his wife. But the person most affected by the abdication was, of course, the Duke of York, who now took the title of King George VI. On the evening of his accession he went to see his mother and openly wept in her presence. He felt totally inadequate and completely unprepared for what lay ahead, telling his cousin, Dickie

Mountbatten, 'I'm only a naval officer. It's the only thing I know about.'

It was true that he had never been trained for kingship in the way that his brother David had been; second sons rarely were. But what Bertie possessed that David lacked was a woman by his side who was to prove not only his greatest support but also, in years to come, the most popular and best-loved woman in Britain. He also had a stable, happy family life which was to stand him in good stead, especially throughout the dark days of the Second World War.

For Princess Elizabeth, her father's new position meant an end to any hope she might have had for a normal life. From now on she would be trained for the day when she too would sit on the throne. Her every moment would be planned down to the last detail; her private life had suddenly assumed a public dimension. Even at ten years old it was a daunting prospect. Fifteen years later when she became Queen, Elizabeth was certainly the best prepared sovereign of the century, for from the day her father became King, Elizabeth's training for the task ahead began. Constitutional experts devoted hours to instructing her in her future position; her grandmother, Queen Mary, assumed the self-appointed role of tutor in monarchical matters, continually emphasizing Elizabeth's place in Britain's history and stressing how vital it was for her to realize she was different, and, therefore, apart.

In 1939, when she was thirteen, she first met the man who was to become her lifelong partner. She had been taken by her parents on a visit to the Royal Naval College at Dartmouth and while there was introduced to a young, fair-haired eighteen-year-old cadet, Prince Philip of Greece. At the end of the visit, dozens of small boats sailed after the Royal Yacht, *Victoria and Albert III*, as it headed out to sea. Gradually they all fell back, except one. The King, standing on deck, shouted out to the youngster to go back as the sea was getting choppy and it was obviously dangerous for such a small craft.

The Princess was waving madly to the sailor, who was, of course, Prince Philip, and she was greatly impressed by his daring – and romantic – gesture.

Elizabeth's introduction to public life began at an early age. She was just fourteen when she broadcast to the nation for the first time, on 13 October 1940. It was on BBC radio's Children's Hour and she spoke to the children of Britain and the Commonwealth, encouraging them to keep up their spirits during the war. She said, 'We know, every one of us, that in the end all will be well.' The ten-year-old Princess Margaret sat beside her and joined in at the end, saying, 'Goodnight and good luck to you all.' A year later Princess Elizabeth became the youngest ever Colonel-in-Chief of a British regiment when, at fifteen, she was appointed to head the Grenadier Guards. On her sixteenth birthday she inspected her regiment for the first time; it was also her first official engagement. Unlike today's royal family, where education comes first and public duties do not start until that has been completed, Elizabeth's father believed in duties for his family beginning very early in life. In addition, the pressures of war meant that every member of the royal family had to be seen to be active, so the Princess was launched into a round of engagements and appearances which has never ended.

By the time of her eighteenth birthday, in April 1944, Elizabeth had been given her own private sitting room at Windsor Castle so that she could receive official visitors, and she had also appointed her first lady-in-waiting. Lady Mary Palmer was the twenty-three-year-old daughter of the Earl of Selbourne, a close friend and colleague of Elizabeth's maternal uncle, David Bowes Lyon. Lady Mary, who married shortly after her appointment and became Lady Mary Strachey, combined the roles of lady-in-waiting and private secretary for several years.

At the time of Elizabeth's eighteenth birthday, a movement began to have her created Princess of Wales. The Queen was unlikely to have any more children, so a number of people felt that Elizabeth should be awarded this unique title as the heir presumptive. But the King was firmly against the idea. In the first place he loved the name Elizabeth, and didn't want to change his elder daughter's title. The Prime Minister, Winston Churchill, was in favour of the plan but the King refused, writing to his mother, Queen Mary, 'How could I create Lilibet the Princess of Wales when it is the recognized title of the wife of the Prince of Wales? Her own name is so nice . . . and what name would she be known by when she marries?' So there the matter rested, and it was as well. There would have been uproar if the title had been granted and then, three years later, when Elizabeth married, her husband had been called the Prince of Wales.

At the age of eighteen Princess Elizabeth became eligible to be a Counsellor of State, acting as an official representative of the sovereign in his absence. Her first duty in this capacity took place on 23 July the following year, when the King paid a lightning visit to Normandy to see his troops in action. The other Counsellors of State on that occasion were the Queen, Prince Henry, Duke of Gloucester, the Princess Royal and Princess Arthur of Connaught. Among the historic documents that the newest Counsellor had to sign was a reprieve of the death sentence on a convicted murderer. It was a sobering introduction to the lawful business of constitutional monarchy.

In 1945, shortly before her nineteenth birthday, Princess Elizabeth volunteered for military service. She was accepted into the ATS (Auxiliary Territorial Service) and commissioned as a subaltern with the serial number 230873 which, like every service man and woman before and since, she says she will remember for the rest of her life.

The King was not enthusiastic about his daughter joining the army. He felt it would undermine her future position and remove part of the 'mystique' that was so essential to royalty. She lobbied him for months before he finally agreed – on one condition. She was not to live in the Officers Mess at Camberley, the transport depot where she was stationed, but return to Windsor Castle every night (where she and Princess Margaret still occupied what was known as the Nursery Suite), so he would not have to worry about where his daughter was during any possible air raids. There was very little risk so near the end of war in Europe, but the Princess, who did not want to add to her father's anxieties, reluctantly complied with the request, and she began a brief army career in March 1945.

There were also other concessions to the new recruit's royal status. On the day she joined the ATS, her company commander, Commandant V. E. M. Wellesley – a direct descendant of the Iron Duke himself, the great Duke of Wellington – turned up at Windsor to welcome the Princess personally and accompany her to the training centre at Camberley. Not many other young officers have enjoyed a similar introduction to military life. However, her fellow junior officers treated her almost as one of themselves, although they addressed her as Ma'am and never by her Christian name as they did with one another. And when they exchanged family news from home, chatting about 'Mummy' and 'Daddy', the Princess always remembered to use the formal terms when referring to her own parents. They were invariably 'the King' and 'the Queen', just as royal children today, when speaking in front of non-royals, always talk of 'Her Majesty' or 'His Royal Highness'.

During her service career, which was brief as the war in Europe ended just three weeks after she had finished her training course, Second Subaltern Her Royal Highness the Princess Elizabeth learnt how to drive and to service heavy lorries. Many years later Her Majesty said she could still change the carburettor on a five-tonner if required. She also achieved another military objective with ease; a pass in marksmanship. In the early years of the war, the King had had a rifle range built in the garden at Buckingham Palace where he, the Queen and their two daughters regularly practised firing pistols and sub-machine guns. In the event of an invasion His Majesty did not intend his family to be taken prisoner. The King introduced other wartime measures at the Palace. He insisted on having his own ration book and declared that none of his, or his family's, meals should exceed the allotted amount. He did not, however, go as far as his father during the First World War, when, in 1915, King George V ordered that no alcohol was to be drunk in the royal household until the cessation of hostilities. He kept to his word and on the evening of Armistice Day, 11 November 1918, opened a bottle of brandy which his ancestor, George IV, as Prince Regent, had set down in 1815, to celebrate the victory at Waterloo.

VE Day, 8 May 1945, was probably the last occasion when Princess Elizabeth was allowed to be 'one of the people', even if only for a few hours. A couple of hundred thousand men and women, many of them serving in the forces of the Allied countries, had massed along the Mall and in front of Buckingham Palace singing, dancing and shouting for the King and Queen. Swept up in the excitement of the moment, Elizabeth and her sister Margaret asked permission to join them. At first her father refused, worried that she might be crushed in the mêlée. Eventually their pleading was successful and together with their uncle, David Bowes Lyon, 'Crawfie' their childhood governess and a protective group of young officers, they left the Palace by a side door, worked their way around the back of St James's and finally found themselves linking up with the crowd in front. They shouted for the King, who eventually came out onto the balcony with the Queen and Prime Minister, Winston Churchill. No one recognized the royal girls or if they did, they took no notice, and Elizabeth later claimed it was one of the most exhilarating moments of her life. It was a brief moment of freedom that was over all too soon. The King wrote in his diary that night, 'Poor darlings, they have never had any fun yet.'

The next significant date was the Princess's twenty-first

birthday, 21 April 1947, which she celebrated in South Africa, and on which she made an important broadcast to the world. She demonstrated the future pattern of her life and dedicated herself to the service of the people over whom she would shortly reign:

> I declare before you that my whole life, whether it be long or short, shall be devoted to your service and the service of our great Imperial Commonwealth to which we all belong. But I shall not have strength enough to carry out this resolution unless you join in it with me, as I now invite you to do; I know that your support will be unfailingly given. God bless all of you who are willing to share it.

The Princess was in South Africa with her parents, and there was unconscious irony in the location of the speech with its reference to 'our great Imperial Commonwealth', as South Africa later severed all connections with the British monarchy, until the end of apartheid in 1994.

The year 1947 was one of the great moments in Britain's history. After years of discussion, fighting and lobbying, India was finally given independence and with it all future British sovereigns would lose the right to be called Emperor or Empress. Appropriately, it was a member of the family, Earl Mountbatten of Burma, who, as the last British Viceroy, handed the reins of power back to India itself.

In the same year Princess Elizabeth became engaged to Lieutenant Philip Mountbatten, and on 20 November they were married in Westminster Abbey.

CHAPTER FIVE

Elizabeth and Philip

*'You must remember it is always a bit of a
blow to a father when his daughter marries.'*
COUNTESS MOUNTBATTEN OF BURMA

It was still a time of austerity in Britain. The war had been
over for two years but severe rationing remained, of everything
from chocolate to clothes, and the winter of this year, 1947,
was one of the worst in living memory.

Yet for Princess Elizabeth and her fiancé, Lieutenant Philip
Mountbatten, life could hardly have looked rosier. He had
had a good war, served with distinction in the Royal Navy
and looked set to marry the most eligible girl in the world.
The royal family were enjoying a period of unmatched popularity. The King and Queen had remained with their people
throughout the six years of conflict and their two daughters
shared the adulation of a people to whom the royal couple
had endeared themselves. Nothing could have pleased the
nation more than the prospect of a royal wedding.

As far as Elizabeth was concerned, there had never been
anyone but Philip. He was her first and only boyfriend and
there was never the slightest chance that her feelings would

change. Philip it was and Philip it has remained for over fifty years. In many ways theirs has been an old-fashioned marriage, but not in any conventionally royal sense. It was not a union brought about by monarchical expediency; indeed, Philip brought no material gain to the marriage, and Elizabeth could not have cared less. There was no fortune and no combining of two great regal houses as was often the case when European royalty wed. It truly was a love match. They had actually become unofficially engaged in 1946, some nine months before the news was announced on 10 July 1947. Only the royal family and certain members of the household were told, though nearly everyone in Britain realized that something was up and there was great speculation in the press all that summer.

Marion Crawford, the Princesses' former governess, revealed in her biography of Elizabeth, *Elizabeth II*, that a crowd shouted at the Princess, 'Where's Philip?' when she was making a private visit to the theatre in London in 1946. Elizabeth, she reported, was neither flattered nor amused, calling the attention 'horrible'. Princess Margaret, who would years later attract similar attention with her first love affair, was suitably sympathetic, saying, 'Poor Lilibet. Nothing of your own. Not even your love affair.' The situation between Elizabeth and Philip became such a target of public comment that the King's most senior aides advised that there should be either an official engagement or a break. Elizabeth's grandmother, Queen Mary, in a conversation with one of her ladies-in-waiting, Lady Airlie, as early as 1944 had also revealed her feelings, saying, 'They have been in love for the last eighteen months . . . but she's not yet nineteen, and one is very impressionable at that age.' She herself had become engaged to Prince Albert Victor, the Duke of Clarence, in 1891 when she was twenty-four. He died before they were married and she subsequently became the wife of his brother, Prince George (later King George V), in 1893.

Nevertheless, Princess Elizabeth, who had always given the

impression of being pliable and unwilling to go against her parents' wishes, stood up for herself on this issue and had accepted Philip's proposal of marriage without reference to her father or mother.

And there is no truth whatever in the rumour that circulated at the time that Philip did not propose but waited until he was asked by Elizabeth as royal protocol dictated. He never was that sort of man. He might have been well used to naval discipline and authority, without which life on board ship could not continue, but in personal matters he was as much his own man then as he proved to be in later years. He did, however, seek an audience of the King to ask formally for his daughter's hand, which was given somewhat reluctantly. Not because of any particular objection to Philip as a prospective son-in-law, but his inclusion in the royal family would extend the 'Firm', as the King liked to call the cosy unit of himself, the Queen and their two daughters.

On one thing, however, the King was adamant: the timing of the announcement of the engagement. Elizabeth wanted it made immediately. The King felt it would distract attention from their visit to South Africa and he insisted that it should be delayed until they returned. Privately he was hoping Elizabeth might change her mind. He was supported in this by the Queen and, even though His Majesty was unhappy about causing his daughter sorrow, he stood by his decision – and she accepted it. There was nothing that she could have done about it anyway. It would have been impossible to announce an engagement without his consent.

There were many stories circulating that King George VI was at first reluctant to give his permission. Countess Mountbatten, one of the Queen's oldest and closest friends, who was on the scene at the time and knew exactly what was going on, agrees: 'It was perfectly natural. Any father would have felt the same. After all she was only just twenty at the time, and not only that, but compared to her contemporaries she was much less experienced, of course. She had had much less opportunity to meet young people unchaperoned – to make up her own mind – so I think it was a very sensible idea for the King to take her to South Africa. Anyway, she and Prince Philip corresponded a great deal and when she came back their feelings were unchanged, so it was a good move. You must remember that it's always a bit of a blow to a father who is very close to his daughter, when she marries. There is great happiness, of course, at the prospect of her being happily married but also a little sadness because they are losing them from their own family.'

When Princess Elizabeth and Lieutenant Philip Mountbatten announced their engagement on 10 July 1947, many were horrified. He was a penniless young naval officer, relying on his £11 a week naval salary, without a home of his own – and a foreigner at that – while she was the girl who would one day be Queen. The 'Old Guard' at the Palace shook their heads and forecast that it would never work.

Philip was not in fact a 'foreigner'. On 18 March that year Philip renounced his Greek citizenship and became legally a British subject. The move had been instigated to appease those who might object to the heir to the throne marrying a foreign

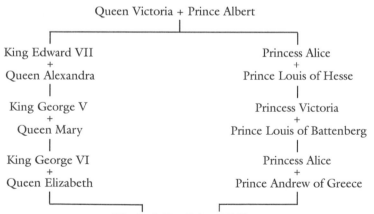

Queen Victoria + Prince Albert

King Edward VII	Princess Alice
+	+
Queen Alexandra	Prince Louis of Hesse
King George V	Princess Victoria
+	+
Queen Mary	Prince Louis of Battenberg
King George VI	Princess Alice
+	+
Queen Elizabeth	Prince Andrew of Greece

Elizabeth II + Prince Philip

prince, but Philip, like Elizabeth herself, was a direct descendant of the Electress Sophia; and this meant that according to
the Aliens Act of 1705, designed to ensure the Hanoverian
succession, he had been a British subject all along. The couple
were in fact distant cousins, both great-great grandchildren
of Queen Victoria. Elizabeth was of course descended from
Victoria's son Bertie, who became Edward VII; Philip's great-
grandmother was Victoria's second daughter Alice, who married Louis of Hesse.

Just before the wedding day, the King's private secretary, Sir
Alan (Tommy) Lascelles told a friend that Philip was 'rough,
uneducated and would probably be unfaithful'. Indeed, there
were many who predicted that the marriage would never last.

The wedding was to take place on 20 November 1947, and
eight weeks before, Philip was received into the Church of
England by the Archbishop of Canterbury. He had been baptized into the Greek Orthodox Church as a baby, and it was
thought in some quarters that it would not be necessary for
him to change. But Philip decided that the easiest course
would be for him to adopt the faith of his future wife. Then
two weeks before the wedding, Philip was created a Knight
of the Garter, on 9 November, exactly one week after Elizabeth had received the same honour from her father, who was
determined that in all things royal his daughter should have
precedence over her husband-to-be.

Philip and his best man, his first cousin David Milford
Haven, stayed at Kensington Palace on the night before the
wedding, in the Grace and Favour apartment occupied by
David's grandmother, the Marchioness of Milford Haven.
Philip's mother, Princess Andrew, was also a guest, but for
the bridegroom and his best man the major part of the evening
was spent at the Dorchester Hotel where the stag-night party
was held. Philip's godfather and uncle Dickie Mountbatten
had returned from India to see his nephew married and to
organize the party with naval efficiency. Nothing was left to

chance; the entire evening was planned like a military operation, and if there were any special surprises in store for Philip,
they were kept secret from the waiting press corps and photographers who staked out the Dorchester hoping to get a
few revealing shots. Mountbatten showed his devious side
when he offered to get the guests to take some pictures with
the photographers' own cameras. They handed them over and
he removed all the flashbulbs before giving them back. It was
some time before the press forgave Mountbatten.

The day of the wedding was grey and cold. The King conferred the titles of Duke of Edinburgh, Earl of Merioneth and
Baron Greenwich on Philip. But it was noticeable that he did
not make him a Prince of the United Kingdom. In fact, it
was not until ten years later, when Elizabeth II was on the
throne, that she elevated her husband to the rank of Prince.
He did, however, become a Royal Highness on the day of
the wedding. The King had given no advance indication of
his intention to give Philip his titles and deliberately held back
the announcement until the morning of the wedding so there
was no opportunity for the official order of service to be
altered. It remained:

Marriage of
Her Royal Highness
THE PRINCESS ELIZABETH
and
LIEUTENANT PHILIP MOUNTBATTEN
Royal Navy

If Philip woke with a hangover he gave no sign of it. He
had coffee and toast for breakfast, but just before he left for
Westminster Abbey he did have a gin and tonic to help him
through the next couple of hours. The wedding was described
by Winston Churchill as 'a flash of colour on the hard road
we travel'. But the Prime Minister, Clem Attlee, refused the

King's request to make the occasion a public holiday on the grounds that there was so much trouble, industrial unrest and severe weather that it would be 'inappropriate'. He did, however, allow the bride 100 extra clothing coupons for her wedding dress – designed by Hartnell – with 23 for the brides-maids; and the couple received 1,347 gifts from all over the world. Princess Elizabeth was given 100 pairs of nylon stock-ings – this was years before tights made their appearance – but when one of the new electric food mixers was sent to the kitchens, none of the royal chefs knew how to work it.

Philip's Uncle Dickie gave the couple a complete cinema, while the Government of Canada sent a priceless collection of Georgian silver – and a mink coat for the bride. Winston Churchill, predictably, gave a set of books which he had writ-ten himself. The Aga Khan gave the couple a racehorse which the Princess named Astrakhan. West African troops were each ordered to give a penny for a regimental present. Most of them had no idea what it was for, or even who Princess Elizabeth was. The Girl Guides of Australia sent the ingredi-ents for the wedding cake and Mahatma Gandhi gave a tray-cloth he had woven himself. Old Queen Mary, the bride's grandmother, who gave no fewer than twenty magnificent presents, hid her gaze from it. She had mistaken it for a loin-cloth.

The royal presents were headed by those of the King and Queen and included sapphires, ruby and diamond necklaces, diamond and pearl earrings, and a pair of Purdey guns for Philip. Princess Margaret gave a dozen champagne glasses and a fitted picnic set. Forty-seven other close members of the royal family clubbed together to buy a Hepplewhite mahogany breakfront bookcase.

The great and the good, the humble and unassuming all sent their gifts, every one of which was recorded in the official list – and eventually acknowledged. Unfortunately, not all the presents, however well intentioned, could be found a place in the young couple's new home and many are to this day stored, in perfect condition, in a building in Windsor Home Park. But before this happened they were all displayed in an exhibition at St James's Palace, with the proceeds going to a number of charities.

Gifts were sent by Philip's German relations, including a gold fountain pen from his three older sisters, Margarita, Theodora and Sophie, with which he signed the marriage register. Philip's fourth sister Cecilie had been killed with her husband and children in an air crash in 1937. But the fact that Philip's sisters were married to Germans, two of whom were known to have Nazi sympathies, while the first husband of Sophie, Prince Christopher of Hesse, had been killed flying as a pilot in the Luftwaffe, meant that none of them was invited to the wedding. But while it was true that part of Philip's family could be rightly accused of Nazi sympathies, a brother-in-law, Berthold von Baden, had been kept under surveillance throughout the war, and the wife of Philip's cousin, Philipp of Hesse, had died in the Buchenwald concentration camp. Prince Philip's only surviving sister, Sophie, known as 'Tiny', whose correct title is Princess George of Hanover, explained to me how it was that one of their family came to be in a concentration camp: 'The wife of our cousin, Philipp, Landgrave of Hesse, was Mafalda, daughter of the King of Italy. When Italy surrendered, Hitler personally ordered that Mafalda, together with her sister, Maria, should be arrested and sent to Buchenwald concentration camp. He also ordered that Mafalda should be particularly harshly treated. Towards the end of the war, when Allied bombing raids were becoming more frequent, she was moved into the SS barracks at the camp because they knew this would be a specific target. However, although she survived the bombing, she died before the camp could be liberated. But her sister, Maria, did survive.' Berthold von Baden had taken over as headmaster of Salem school in Germany when its founder

Kurt Hahn was allowed to emigrate to Britain before the Second World War. Hahn then founded Gordonstoun in Scotland on the same principles of equal opportunity as had prevailed at Salem, and the school was attended by Philip and all his sons. At the time of the wedding Princess Elizabeth was very angry at this treatment of her fiancé's family and she protested to her father, but he, realizing the strength of feeling in the country, refused to do anything to change the situation.

There was comment from some quarters at one omission, however. Elizabeth's favourite uncle, the exiled Duke of Windsor, was excluded. This was not because of any anti-Windsor feelings on the part of the British people, but because the royal family knew the Duke would not accept unless his Duchess was also invited, and no one, including his own mother, Queen Mary, would receive her at any time.

If Elizabeth felt any sorrow at her uncle's absence she managed to conceal it brilliantly. On the day itself she was woken by her old friend and nurse Bobo McDonald, who brought her her early morning cup of tea. Bobo later accompanied her while she was being fitted with her wedding dress and then her private secretary, Jock Colville, had to rush across the road to St James's Palace to retrieve the pearl necklace her parents had given her as a wedding present. It was still on display with the other gifts. As with all royal occasions this one had been timed to the minute, and at precisely 11.16 am she left Buckingham Palace, sitting beside her father in the Irish State Coach. For the watching thousands lining the route it was a brilliant splash of colour in an otherwise grey year. Troopers of the Household Cavalry were permitted to wear full ceremonial dress for the first time since before the war and, as was the custom of the day, the lady guests inside Westminster Abbey all wore full-length evening dresses with gloves and hats or tiaras.

Both Elizabeth and Philip performed impeccably, neither stumbling over their vows, which were of the traditional variety with the bride promising to obey. Elizabeth's wedding ring was made from the same nugget of Welsh gold that had been used for her mother's wedding, and which has since been used for all royal brides up to, and including, the Countess of Wessex when, as Sophie Rhys-Jones, she married Prince Edward in 1999. The King was noticeably moved, and during the signing of the marriage registers was seen to be very close to tears, remarking, 'It is a far more moving thing to give your daughter away than to be married yourself.' His Majesty had always been a sentimental man and a loving father to Elizabeth, and there was no doubt that he viewed the symbolic giving away of his elder daughter as the beginning of the breakup of his small family. Back at Buckingham Palace 120 guests sat down in the State Supper Room for the wedding breakfast. The remainder of the 2,000 who had been invited to the service had to make their own arrangements.

The King was determined to show his people that, even for his daughter's wedding, he was not prepared to step beyond the strict limits imposed by rationing. The menu was a far cry from the sumptuous feasts of Victorian and Edwardian days, when wedding breakfasts were rarely less than fifteen courses. This time they made do with four simple courses and every ingredient came from the royal estates.

The meal began with Filet of Sole Mountbatten – named obviously in honour of the bridegroom. This was followed by a casserole of partridge, the birds having been shot on the Sandringham estate, while the green beans, potatoes and salad were all grown in the royal gardens at Windsor. For dessert, they were served with Bombe Glacée Princesse Elizabeth followed by coffee. There was champagne for the toasts and the Yeoman of the Royal Cellars had unearthed a couple of dozen bottles of his finest wines and a very special vintage port. The next day's newspapers remarked favourably on the frugality of the fare, mentioning that it would have been possible to have a similar meal in any decent restaurant in London. But one paper reported that at another wedding held the same day the guests had sat down to spam and chips.

Throughout the wedding day, thousands of people had remained outside the Palace waiting to see the couple, and once the bride had changed into her going away outfit of a blue velvet hat and coat, she and Philip drove off in an open carriage to Waterloo Station, where the Royal Train was to take them to Broadlands, the Mountbatten family home in Hampshire, to start their honeymoon.

The weather was freezing and to make sure the young couple did not suffer on their carriage drive, the Crown Equerry had installed a number of hot water bottles and two thick rugs. But even in those days the royal family realized the value of good public relations so personal comfort was sacrificed for a short time so that everyone could get a good view. One extra passenger in the carriage was Princess Elizabeth's favourite corgi, Susan. She was bundled into the landau at the last minute.

Elizabeth spent part of the honeymoon writing thank you letters to her family and close friends, and reading the first letter that was waiting for her at Broadlands. It was written, predictably, by her father, surely the only parent in the world who would think of writing to his daughter on her honeymoon. He wrote: 'I am so glad you wrote and told Mummy that you think the long wait before your engagement and the long time before the wedding was for the best. I was rather afraid that you had thought I was being rather hard-hearted about it . . . Your leaving us has left a great blank in our lives but do remember that your old home is still yours and do come back to it as often as possible. I can see that you are sublimely happy with Philip which is right but don't forget us is the wish of your ever loving and devoted – Papa.'

Elizabeth's apparent agreement with her parents that the 'long wait' had been for the best, appears to be an early example of her efforts to appease them in all things. It had already been recorded that she was impatient to be engaged to Philip months before the official announcement, but once the deed had been done she had nothing to lose by telling her mother she and the King had been right all along.

For Philip the honeymoon, or at least the part spent at Broadlands, gave him a taste of what life in the royal family was going to be like. The press besieged Lord Mountbatten's home and when the couple attended morning service on their first Sunday together at Romsey Abbey, there was an unseemly scramble by members of the congregation to secure the best view. Chairs, tables and ladders were strategically placed among the gravestones in the churchyard and Elizabeth and Philip, to give them their due, took it all in good part. When they left Broadlands they issued a statement which showed a nice touch of irony. 'Before we leave for Scotland tonight we want to say . . . the loving interest shown by our fellow countrymen and well wishers has left an impression that will never grow faint. We can find no words to express what we feel, but we can at least offer our grateful thanks to the millions who have given us this unforgettable send-off in our married life.'

There was a brief interruption to the honeymoon when they made a secret visit back to Buckingham Palace. It was said they went to retrieve a lead for Susan the corgi but it could hardly have been necessary for the Princess and her husband to make the journey when a servant could easily have been despatched. The real reason was that the King was missing his daughter badly and she too wanted to see him, so an excuse was found for her to spend a few hours in his company before they left to complete the honeymoon in Scotland.

Balmoral in November is not the warmest place on earth. There was snow on the ground and fierce winds blowing. The Castle is full of draughts at the best of times. In the bleak winter of 1947 it was like Siberia. Philip caught a severe cold; romance was put on hold as Elizabeth did her wifely duties and nursed him back to health. The royal family have never been very tolerant of ill-health and they were well used to discomfort. The Queen Mother is famous for saying, 'If you ignore illness it will go away.' Princess Elizabeth had grown up in spartan surroundings so the idea of mollycoddling oneself was completely foreign to her – and still is. Even today, in her seventies, if the weather becomes too extreme she will put on another sweater rather than have the heating turned up. Philip himself had hardly had a comfortable upbringing, with cold showers an integral part of his schooldays at Gordonstoun. But even he found Balmoral that November to be uncomfortable and hardly conducive to the romantic interlude he had anticipated.

The honeymoon over, the couple returned to London where, because they had no home of their own, they took up residence in the Princess's three-room apartment at Buckingham Palace. The King and Queen were delighted. It meant they could see their daughter every day.

But both Philip and Elizabeth knew that for their marriage to get off to a decent start they would need their own separate establishment. Initially, Sunninghill Park was considered. This was the original house, not the £5 million new building which subsequently became home to the Duke and Duchess of York in 1986. But investigation showed that the house was too far gone and would need far too much money – several hundred thousand pounds, even in 1947 – to make it habitable. Marlborough House, a traditional London home for the heir to the throne, was occupied by Queen Mary, Princess Elizabeth's elderly grandmother. She had already said, 'When I die, Lilibet, you will have Marlborough House.' To which Elizabeth replied, 'We don't want Granny to die. We hope she'll be here for a long time. We must have a London home before that.' As it happened, Elizabeth was never to live in Marlborough House. By the time Queen Mary died in 1953, her granddaughter had become Queen and Marlborough House was given on permanent loan to house the headquarters of the Commonwealth Secretariat in London.

Prince Philip flatly refused to consider Kensington Palace, the 'Aunt Heap' as he called it because of all the ancient family widows who lived there and in parts of St James's Palace. York House, the 75-room residence inside St James's Palace at present occupied by Prince Charles, would have made a suitable home, but the sitting tenant was the King's brother, Prince Henry, Duke of Gloucester. There was no way he was going to move out and neither would the King – or the Princess – have dreamed of asking him. The only other alternative was Clarence House, adjoining St James's Palace.

The house had been named after an early Duke of Clarence, later King William IV, a son of George III, who had lived there as a bachelor but felt it was unsuitable for his wife, Princess Adelaide of Saxe-Coburg-Meiningen, whom he married in 1818. Accordingly the architect John Nash was commissioned to redesign the house, which he did at a cost of £13,000. Subsequent tenants included the Prince and Princess of Wales (later Edward VII and Queen Alexandra) and the Duchess of Edinburgh, Queen Victoria's mother. Its last royal occupant had been one of Victoria's sons, the Duke of Connaught, who had moved in in 1901, with his wife and three children. The Duchess had died in 1917 and on her death the Duke ordered that her favourite sitting room should be preserved exactly as she had left it. The doors were locked and the only persons allowed to enter afterwards were maids, who came in to dust, and the Duke himself, who liked to sit there alone with his memories. When he too died in 1942, at the age of ninety-one, the building was handed over to the Red Cross as emergency headquarters during the Second World War and later used by the Central Chancery of the Orders of Knighthood.

By the time Elizabeth and Philip came to see it, Clarence House presented a sorry spectacle. Part of the roof had been damaged in an air raid, the plumbing was still as it had been in the nineteenth century, the only bathroom hidden in a cupboard. Some of the rooms were still lit by gas and the wiring in other parts of the building was in a dangerous condition. Obviously thousands must be spent to bring it up to anything like the standard required for a royal residence, but neither Philip nor Elizabeth was disheartened. They realized the potential of the place and accepted the King's offer of it immediately. The problem was who was going to pay and where were they going to live in the meantime?

Parliament came to the rescue about the money, voting £55,000 out of public funds to help put the house to rights. The grant was enough to pay for new central heating, installing a new kitchen, having the house rewired and other basic structural repairs, but there was still a great deal to be done for which the money had to be found from private royal sources.

In the meantime, a more substantial temporary home than the apartment at Buckingham Palace was needed. Princess Alice, Countess of Athlone, came to the rescue. She and her husband lived in a beautiful house adjoining the Clock Tower in Kensington Palace and they were going to be abroad for the remainder of the winter. So she offered the house to the newly married couple until their own home was ready. Philip, although he had doubts about living in Kensington Palace, agreed that it was better than the cramped accommodation they were using and they moved in. It was the first time Princess Elizabeth had had the opportunity of being an 'ordinary' housewife and she thoroughly enjoyed the experience. Philip had an office job at the Admiralty in Whitehall, so he was home every evening. They were able to entertain friends like Lord and Lady Brabourne, Lord Mountbatten's daughter and son-in-law, and the Earl of Carnarvon's son, Lord Porchester (who eventually became the Queen's racing manager and remains one of her closest friends).

The King and Queen brought Princess Margaret to dinner and set their elder daughter a small problem of royal protocol. Wherever he dined the King always took precedence and sat at the head of the table. At Kensington Palace, Philip had become used to being head of the family and sitting at the head of his own (or at least the borrowed) table. Princess Elizabeth sought the advice of the Master of the Household. He advised her that as her father was visiting in a private capacity, and not as sovereign, it would be in order to seat him as a guest.

The work at Clarence House took longer than expected and when Princess Alice and her husband were due to return from South Africa it was still not ready for occupation. It looked as if Elizabeth and Philip would be homeless again – or have to move back into Buckingham Palace – so they began house hunting once more. They heard about a property near Windsor called Windlesham Moor which was available to rent. It stood in a fifty-acre park and was in excellent condition, the lady who owned it having spent considerable sums on decoration and maintenance. When the Queen viewed it she remarked that it was 'more palatial than the Palace'. The rent wasn't a problem but under the terms of the lease the tenants were responsible for the upkeep, and it was a large house needing servants and a number of gardeners for the spacious grounds. Philip's naval pay, plus his allowance of £10,000 a year from Parliament, all of which was taxable, didn't leave much surplus. He wanted to be seen as the man of the house, paying all the bills, but secretly Elizabeth knew he could not afford to do so and instructed her Comptroller, General 'Boy' Browning, to settle the bills out of her private account. There was also a practical side to her generosity as many of the couple's creditors declined to cash her cheques, preferring to keep them, with the royal signature, as souvenirs. Then, as now, royalty had a one-sided view about money. While they are quite happy to accept expensive gifts themselves, they do not, as a rule, indulge in acts of largesse to others. This is not regarded as meanness, just good Hanoverian housekeeping.

Among their first guests at Windlesham Moor were Lord and Lady Brabourne. 'We would visit them at Windlesham Moor where the butler rejoiced in the name of King. Princess Elizabeth loved to go around the house shouting out "King" much to everyone's amusement.'

Eventually Clarence House was ready but the cost had escalated well above the £55,000 allocated by the Government. The final cost, without furnishings, totalled some £78,000.

In May 1948 Elizabeth and Philip undertook their first official overseas tour together when they visited Paris for four days. The couple were both fluent in French but unfortunately for the Princess, who was pregnant, the visit coincided with some of the hottest weather the French capital had seen in years. Both Elizabeth and Philip felt the heat and suffered accordingly. He had a stomach upset, but refused to cancel any of his engagements, while she too soldiered on despite the oppressive attentions of an unruly press which at times threatened to get out of hand. On one occasion they found hidden lenses pointing at them in a restaurant which caused Philip to explode with what was to become his characteristic bad temper when journalists are around. It was this attitude to the media which caused the first, slight, rift between the couple. While Elizabeth had grown up used to being in the spotlight and accepted it as part of the job, even if she disliked it, Philip made no effort to conceal his hatred of the constant publicity and consequently Elizabeth felt uncomfortable at his behaviour.

But the overall effect of the visit was favourable, particularly towards the Princess, and the feeling among the Royal Household was that, once her baby had been born, Elizabeth should take on many more public duties. The King was delighted at his daughter's success. Not only would it relieve him of part of the burden he had previously shouldered alone, it also meant that she would still be an integral part of the 'Family Firm' and he would see more of her.

But all this was in the future as the immediate concern was the imminent birth of Elizabeth's first child. Charles Philip Arthur George was born at Buckingham Palace on 14 November 1948, just six days before his parents' first wedding anniversary. He arrived at 9.14 in the evening when his father was playing squash.

Even before the birth there had been serious discussions about protocol and precedent. For centuries a government official had been in attendance at the birth of royal babies, and the King felt it unnecessary for the practice to continue. His private secretary wrote to the Home Secretary, James Chuter Ede, informing him of the King's wish. Chuter Ede discussed the matter with the Prime Minister and together they approached the King saying they felt this outdated practice should cease. On 5 November His Majesty agreed to an announcement ending the custom.

Next to be settled was the question of the child's title. Under Letters Patent issued in 1917 by Elizabeth's grandfather, King George V, only the children of the sovereign, the children of the sons of the sovereign and the eldest living son of the eldest son of the Prince of Wales could be styled as Royal Highness. No thought had been given to the possibility that the heir to the throne might be a daughter. If things had remained as they were, a son born to Princess Elizabeth would not have been automatically either a prince or a Royal Highness, although he would have received the courtesy title of his father's subsidiary rank, Earl of Merioneth. A daughter would have been known simply as Lady (whatever her Christian name was) Mountbatten. The King would have none of this. He was determined that his first grandchild would be recognized with a full royal title. Accordingly, on the advice of his private secretary, Sir Alan Lascelles, he issued new Letters Patent stating: 'The children of the Heir to the Throne shall have and at all times hold and enjoy the style, title or attribute of Royal Highness and the titular dignity of Prince or Princess prefixed by their Christian names.' At a stroke of the pen the question of titles for all Princess Elizabeth's children was settled, and as she produced a boy first there was great rejoicing all round, especially at Buckingham Palace where the child was born. The royal doctors had wanted Princess Elizabeth to go into hospital in case of any complications but the King insisted that the birth should be in the Palace. Royal babies had always been born in palaces or castles and he refused to listen to the pleas of his medical advisers.

The infant was christened in the Music Room at Buckingham Palace on 15 December as the chapel, destroyed by enemy bombs in 1942, had not been replaced. The Queen's Gallery now occupies the site where the chapel once stood. Among the godparents were the King, Queen Mary (the child's great-grandmother), King Haakon of Norway, Philip's cousin Prince George of Greece (neither of whom was able to be present), Princess Margaret, the eighty-five-year-old Dowager Marchioness of Milford Haven (Philip's grandmother), Lady Patricia Brabourne (Earl Mountbatten's elder daughter) and the Queen Mother's youngest brother, David Bowes Lyon.

Patricia Mountbatten recalls her reaction to her invitation. 'I was absolutely delighted and genuinely very surprised. The thought had never entered my head that I would be asked. I just thought it would be lots of Kings and Queens.' In fact, there were two Kings, one Queen, one Prince, one Princess, a Duchess and an Honourable, so as Lady Mountbatten says, 'I was in rather good company.'

Charles was dressed in the christening gown of Honiton lace made in 1841 for the baptism of Queen Victoria's eldest daughter, also named Victoria and used by royal babies to this day. According to Bobo McDonald, who was present with her sister, Ruby, he 'behaved impeccably'. The baby was held by the youngest godmother, the eighteen-year-old

Princess Margaret, who handed him to the Archbishop of Canterbury for the baptism.

Six months later the Edinburghs were able to move into their new home at Clarence House. This was in June 1949, eighteen months after they had first viewed the place and just four months before Philip was posted to Malta. He supervised the move and arranged the furniture and many of the wedding presents which had been in storage. Having spent a nomadic existence in other people's homes since he was rescued from Corfu as a baby at a time of Greek civil unrest, when his parents became exiles and later separated, he was delighted with Clarence House and expected to make it his base for many years. But only three years later the young family was forced to move across the road into Buckingham Palace, which Philip has never liked, and never concealed the fact.

Like most people of their class at the time, the couple had separate bedrooms; they still do. But there was a communicating door which was often left open so they could chat together while they were dressing. Many years later, when it was revealed that an intruder, Michael Fagan, had been found sitting on the Queen's bed when she woke up, there was some comment about the fact that she and Prince Philip did not share the same bedroom. What would have been more surprising to people of their generation and class was if they had been together.

Lady Mountbatten was absolutely right when she described the death of King George VI as 'a disaster' for the Queen, and not only because of the sorrow it naturally caused. Nothing could have caused a bigger upset in Her Majesty's private married life. Elizabeth and Philip had settled down to domestic bliss, and when he was posted to Malta in 1949, it was even better. They were free of many of the restrictions imposed on them in London, and for the first – and only – time could enjoy each other without the constant attention of servants, courtiers and advisers. The absence of their first child, Charles, who remained behind in England, was apparently not a great problem. Like all royal children, he would grow up used to the prolonged and frequent absences of his parents. Philip's Uncle Dickie, Lord Mountbatten, was also stationed on the island – as a Vice Admiral – and living in the sumptuous Villa Guardmangia, where his nephew and wife joined him for a time, before finding their own quarters.

Mountbatten was thrilled, as he never tired of strengthening his ties with the royal family. He was genuinely fond of Elizabeth, but the fact that she was heir to the throne no doubt added to her attraction in his eyes. And Malta had everything the young couple could ask for. At first, Philip, still a Lieutenant, was second-in-command of HMS *Chequers*, but in 1950 he was promoted to the rank of Lieutenant Commander and given his own ship, HMS *Magpie*. For him, life could not have been better. Elizabeth too found the easy-going Mediterranean lifestyle to her taste. There was plenty of polo to watch – and for Philip to play – and apart from the constant presence of an armed bodyguard, security was at a minimum.

When they went to the local cinema in Valetta, they sat in the back row and held hands (surely the only time a future Queen would be able to do that), and at dances Philip invariably asked the band leader to play Elizabeth's favourite tune, Duke Ellington's A–Train. Prince Philip, who had always loved the Mediterranean and its climate, was happier than he had ever been – before or since. He had a job he loved, he could sail, swim and water-ski, whenever he wanted, and if he and his wife fancied a picnic, they simply jumped into their car and Philip drove to a quiet spot where they knew they would not be interrupted or spied upon. The local people treated them with respect but they were not held in awe by the islanders.

So for a few short years they were able to live almost, but not quite, like any other couple, and as Patricia Mountbatten explained: 'It would have been so much better if they had been able to have just a few years more without the responsibilities that came with dramatic suddenness on that misty February morning in 1952.'

The Queen has never revealed her feelings about those early years of her marriage but Prince Philip has openly conceded that he regards them as being of the utmost importance in establishing them as a team. Just like his father-in-law, King George VI, all Philip ever really wanted was to be a successful naval officer. And, in the same way, it was not to be. Both had to sacrifice personal preferences for the sake of public duty. Five years of married bliss, followed by over fifty years of having their every waking moment organized by others and subject to the scrutiny of the world. But at least they had known, for an all too brief period, what life outside the confines of palaces and castles could be like.

Philip has been the Queen's staunchest supporter and the only man she has ever loved. And, contrary to his public image, he is also something of a romantic who still loves to surprise his wife with bunches of her favourite flowers (lilies of the valley). And he rarely returns from one of his frequent trips abroad without a little present he has chosen personally. Throughout the marriage there have been rumours of Prince Philip's relationships with other women, without a single piece of concrete evidence to support the stories. No one has been able to a point a finger and say categorically that he has slept around. And in the fifty-odd years they have been married, he has never been allowed to travel anywhere in the world without the constant attention of his personal police bodyguard. With more than thirty officers attached to him during this time, it is inconceivable that he would have been able to indulge in extra-marital activities without a single leak. Human nature being what it is, someone would have been bound to tell – and no one has.

That he has always enjoyed the company of beautiful young women had never been denied, and his reputation as a flirt is legendary. But nothing has ever threatened their marriage, and the Queen, supreme realist that she is, has invariably paid no regard to his roving eye.

As patron of a particular charity, Philip attended its annual dinner and dance at the Dorchester Hotel one year. The wife of the Chairman was an attractive thirty-something with a deep cleavage which she obviously enjoyed displaying. Throughout the evening, she and Philip carried on a mild flirtation, and during one of their dances she said to him, 'I can't keep on calling you Sir, can I?' To which he replied, 'How about Sir darling?' Philip has always known how attractive he is to women and revels in it. And the Queen, realizing her husband's fascination, has usually taken a sly satisfaction in knowing that no one else has had the slightest chance of stealing him away. This confidence in the married state has been disturbed only by the marriages of three of their children ending in divorce. Both parents found it hard to come to terms with the realization that Anne, Charles and Andrew did not regard the married state with the same degree of permanence as they do themselves.

Countess Mountbatten and her husband, Lord Brabourne, know the problems the Queen and Prince Philip have had to face. 'I think it's rotten luck on both of them,' she says, 'that three of their children have had disastrous marriages and you are bound to start asking yourselves some questions.' The Brabournes are able to sympathize with the Queen and Prince Philip on this subject, as they too have three children who have divorced.

There is no official position for the husband of a Queen Regnant, so Philip has had to carve a life for himself. He has done so brilliantly, managing to fulfil an active and important role in the life of the nation. But whereas the Queen keeps clear of all controversy, the Duke seems to court it deliberately. He says what he feels, come what may, and his 'gaffes' – such as comments about Chinese slitty eyes – have earned him a reputation of using his position to voice opinions with which few will dare to disagree. It is as if he has assigned himself the role of aggressive member of the royal family, the one who is not afraid to speak his mind.

'He has been a wonderful support to her,' Lady Mountbatten says. 'She could not have done it all without him and she has said so publicly. Within the Palace he's been a tremendously modernizing influence. He hasn't gone overboard but it is through him that things have run smoother, more economically, more sensibly. Of course, he has upset one or two people in doing it, that's quite natural. He speaks his mind too much at times and he can come down a bit too hard occasionally, forgetting that most people feel they can't answer back. Strangely enough, if they did, I don't think he'd mind too much. He likes people to stand up for themselves. I really do feel that he is one of the most misunderstood people in the country. I'm also quite sure that the Queen would still have made a tremendous success as sovereign because she is that sort of person, but it has certainly been made that much easier because of Prince Philip. She has had him at home to talk things over with and she knows she will always get an honest opinion from him. If he thinks something could have been done better or has gone drastically wrong, he will tell her so. He has been a great help and support to the Queen throughout their married life.'

Another, perhaps surprising, supporter of the Duke of Edinburgh is his former brother-in-law, Lord Snowdon. There have been many unsubstantiated accounts of their incompatibility, based mainly on their apparent lack of anything in common: Philip enjoys the physical outdoor pursuits such as shooting and stalking, while Tony Snowdon apparently prefers more artistic activities associated with his profession as a photographer. Yet Lord Snowdon once told the present author of an incident when they were both at Balmoral. 'Prince Philip knew I had difficulty with my leg [Snowdon had suffered polio as a boy], so whenever we had to climb steep hills, he always made sure a Land-Rover was there for me to use, and he never made any fuss over it. He really was very thoughtful.'

Another old friend says, 'What many people assume is arrogance in Prince Philip, is really just supreme self-confidence. He never has any doubts about himself or his ability to do anything. It's a family trait he's tried to encourage in his children, but with the exclusion of Princess Anne, with a marked lack of success.'

Patricia Mountbatten feels that while Prince Philip has made an enormous contribution, both to the monarchy and the country, he may still have a few regrets: 'I think he must be a bit frustrated. After all, he gave up what would have been a brilliant naval career. He could even have ended up as First Sea Lord himself. But it wasn't to be. But I think he can look back on his career in public life with great satisfaction. I'm quite sure that he never looks back thinking, "if only" – he's not that sort. I don't believe he would change anything. He's done so much for the monarchy, and whatever some people try to pretend, he and the Queen have remained devoted to each other. I know they admire each other and enjoy each other's company tremendously.'

The Queen once said, 'If marriage is an institution, I am all for it.' In the fifty-odd years they have been together she and Prince Philip have proved that, in spite of difficulties that would have split almost any other couple, this is one institution to which they are both very happy to belong. Her Majesty may occupy one of the loneliest positions in the world, but both she and Prince Philip know that they can always count on each other. Nothing will change that. Rumours of rifts, separation and even divorce have followed them throughout much of their married life. Half a century on it must give the royal couple a sense of quiet satisfaction to be able to prove them all completely wrong. Theirs is an enduring partnership that has lasted.

CHAPTER SIX

Buckingham Palace – The House

'Philip was the first royal this century to
actually venture into the kitchens.'
A FORMER PALACE STEWARD

Before Buckingham Palace was first opened to the public in 1993, the Queen walked through every room deciding which ones she would let the people see. Her private apartments were strictly off-limits. No one would be allowed anywhere near. Nor could they wander through her home when she was there. Eight weeks were allocated, during the summer when she was safely up in Balmoral, and even though suggestions were made to open the Palace for a short period at Christmas, she turned them down. In the end the State Rooms to which the public were to be admitted were the ones that official visitors see. Even then, the State Ballroom was ruled out and not included in the tour until the summer opening of 2000.

While the State Rooms that are open are magnificent, some of the more interesting rooms are seen only by the royal family and their guests. The Chinese Dining Room, with its unique decor, and the India Room next door, containing a superb collection of weaponry, are two which are forbidden to the public as they are next door to Prince Philip's suite. The Audience Room is too close to the Queen's private sitting room – and the special room allocated to the corgis – but the reason why the Belgian Suite on the ground floor cannot be viewed has never been explained.

The Queen Mother and Prince Charles had always been against the idea of opening the Palace, and the rest of the family were not keen either, but as an economic measure it proved to be an amazing success. The souvenir shop in the grounds was especially successful, with annual profits running to hundreds of thousands of pounds. The original idea was just to open for a couple of years and then quietly forget the whole idea. But the Palace tour has become such an integral part of the London tourist scene that it would be quite unacceptable to stop the openings now.

Buckingham Palace is the official London residence of the sovereign and is regarded as the very symbol of British monarchy. Yet it bears the name of a nobleman – John Sheffield, Duke of Buckingham – and has been in the possession of the royal family only since 1762. It was bought by George III in 1762 for £28,000 as a private residence for his wife, Queen Charlotte, and was never intended to be the monarch's principal home.

Both George IV and William IV used Carlton House as their official London residence. George IV commissioned the rebuilding of Buckingham Palace to be his principal home, but he died on 26 June 1830 before it was finished and never lived there. William IV was not enthusiastic about the Palace but continued the work, intending to offer it as a replacement for the Houses of Parliament, which had burnt down in 1834. So Mo Mowlam's comment in 1999 – for which she later apologized – that Buckingham Palace should be handed over to the people, was not exactly an original thought. The Palace was eventually completed in May 1837,

The nine-year-old Princess Elizabeth crouches down for a better view as she attends the celebration service for King George V's Silver Jubilee in St Paul's Cathedral. With her are her sister, Princess Margaret, her parents, the Duke and Duchess of York, and her uncle and aunt, the Duke and Duchess of Kent.

The family with six of the Queen's corgis and her then only grandson, Peter Phillips, on holiday at Balmoral, where they all say they can truly relax.

but William died a few weeks later. His niece, Queen Victoria, moved in on 13 July 1837 and since then every monarch has lived there.

Nobody would describe Buckingham Palace – or The House, as Prince Charles calls it – as cosy. It is a mausoleum of a place which has been universally disliked by almost every monarch. Most lived there reluctantly and spent as little time as possible under its cavernous roof. Still today there is not much comfort, even in the private royal quarters, and the Buckingham Palace to which the young Queen and her husband moved in 1952 had barely changed from the days of Queen Victoria. Edward VII had made few alterations, calling it 'a sepulchre', and George V saw no reason to do so, describing it as 'merely a house. Sandringham is where I have my home,' though his Consort, Queen Mary, grew to love the place and left with great reluctance 'these lovely comfortable rooms which have been my happy home'. George V's successor, Edward VIII, made only one domestic change in his ten months' reign when he installed a shower in his own bathroom. His successor's sixteen years covered a time of stringency during and immediately following the Second World War, and again the Palace remained much as it had been for the previous half century. In any case George VI hated change, as does his elder daughter.

In 1952 Buckingham Palace still had over two hundred open fires, each one requiring up to five people to get going: an outside worker delivered the coal and firewood to the back door where a kitchen porter carried them to the green baize door that divides 'below stairs' from the Palace proper. There a footman accepted the load and took it to the doorway of the Queen's bedroom, but he was not allowed to enter. One of Her Majesty's personal housemaids had to lay the fire with paper, sticks and coal but then another footman was brought in to set it all alight. And this was repeated throughout the Palace as there was only minimal central heating which rarely worked efficiently. The Queen's parents had often envied friends with houses that were fully heated. King George VI was once heard to remark: 'How lucky you are to be able to move from one room to another. We have to stay together in one corner of a room huddled around the fire.'

Although the Queen saw no reason to change this state of affairs – why should she when she had known nothing else? – Philip was horrified at the waste of manpower and the general inefficiency that characterized the running of the most famous house in the land. Four hundred men and women were employed, of whom only a handful actually worked directly for the royal family. The rest spent their days fetching and carrying for members of the household who still lived as they had in the early part of the century. Within weeks of moving in Philip, with his abundance of energy, decided that he was going to take the whole thing in hand. This was much to the horror of the old guard, confirming their original opinion, that this was an upstart foreigner who didn't know how to behave at Court. He moved through the Palace like a whirl-wind, issuing orders and barking at flunkies who didn't answer his questions quickly. (My own first encounter showed me something of the energy that flows from the Prince. I was sitting in the office of the Queen's private secretary – where the door is always left open – when His Royal Highness marched in. When he saw me he said, 'Who are you and what are you doing here?' Without waiting for an answer he turned and stalked out of the room, searching for the private secretary.)

When Philip discovered how many people worked at the Palace and what they did he immediately got rid of over a hundred, many of whom had reached retirement age. The policy had been to leave servants where they were until they voluntarily retired – or died. Dozens had no job at all; they simply spent their days wandering about the Palace or sitting in their rooms on the third floor waiting for the next meal.

Their wages where laughable: two pounds a week for a house-maid, plus a room and board, when the average weekly wage in Britain was around £6. But the cost of this labour force didn't bother the Keeper of the Privy Purse; it didn't come out of his pocket, and as he had been in the post since 1936, he saw no reason to concern himself with such below-stairs matters as domestic wages and conditions.

Philip did earn the gratitude of every footman in the Palace though when he dispensed with the requirement, which had existed since Queen Victoria's day, that they had to powder their hair. It was an antiquated and unhygienic custom which they hated and which Philip knew was ridiculous, so out it went.

The Queen didn't interfere with any of Philip's plans even if, privately, she did not always see the need for them. She had grown up surrounded by flunkies, housemaids and nannies. Until her brief spell in the armed forces, she had only travelled on public transport when her governess, Crawfie, took her on the underground as a special treat; she had never carried money or done any of her own shopping. Her knowledge of what it was like to live an ordinary existence had been limited to excursions with her grandmother, Queen Mary, to the Tower of London to see the Crown Jewels and to Madame Tussaud's, when the trips were organized down to the last detail months in advance. And until she married Philip, Elizabeth had never entered a kitchen in her life. Her sister, Princess Margaret, said later that it wasn't until she grew up that she realized that everything outside Buckingham Palace did not smell of fresh paint and new-mown grass.

Part of Philip's enthusiasm to change things at the Palace evolved from the frustration he felt at his treatment by the Palace household. In constitutional terms Philip did not exist. There was no role for him; he was not even officially named as Consort to the Queen. He saw no State papers; he still doesn't; and while it might be reasonable to suggest that the

Queen would normally discuss with him some of the items she had seen in her red boxes, officially his opinion counts for nothing. Unofficially, his influence is greatly felt. There was no contact with government departments and he had not then decided which organizations he would support. In effect, he had no job, for he had given up active service in the Navy in 1951. His wife was busy learning the business of monarchy. He had to try and find some way of occupying himself. He chose to modernize the Palace. It certainly needed it and he was the right man to do it. Perhaps this also explains his abrupt manner to Palace servants and more senior members of the royal household. He became a figure of terror to some of the younger staff, who would hide if they saw him coming down a corridor. His language was not the sort they were used to from the royal family either. Four-letter words flowed from his lips, and when he was really furious, which seemed to be most of the time, he let go with a vocabulary more familiar with the lower decks than the upper reaches of the Court. Lord Charteris, who was in a better position than most to observe what was happening, commented, 'I think Philip might have tried a little harder to accommodate the views of the royal household . . . He sulked quite a bit.' While Commander Michael Parker, Philip's old Australian shipmate from his Navy days, who was to become his private secretary, remarked, 'I felt that Philip didn't have many friends or helpers in the Palace . . . some of the British Establishment were hidebound and prejudiced.'

Nevertheless, Philip got things done. Even if there was a great deal of antagonism towards him, few dared to challenge his plans openly and in a remarkably short period many improvements began to appear. Not that many were noticeable from the outside. A number of rules govern the external appearance of the Palace which no one, including Prince Philip, could, or can, change. The Department of the Environment is responsible for the upkeep of the fabric, and to do this a workforce of over fifty is based there permanently. They decide when the stonework needs cleaning, how many of the 2,000 lightbulbs should be replaced – nearly always 40-watt strength to save money – and who washes the windows and sweeps the courtyard. One aspect of the Palace that has not changed in over ninety years is the familiar front view where the balcony is located. You will never see a window opened at the front of the Palace, nor are the curtains allowed to be fully drawn, and the white net has to be left undisturbed at all times to preserve the frontage's pristine 'chocolate box' appearance. All this is on the orders of the Department of the Environment whose budget pays for the maintenance and decoration.

The Portland stone façade of the front of the Palace was installed in 1913, and took only three months to complete, at a cost of £60,000. The craftsmen worked night and day, with 350 employed in daytime and 170 at night, and every block of stone is numbered so that, should any need repairing or replacing, the architects can refer to the original drawings and act accordingly.

The major part of the reconstruction of Buckingham Palace as we know it today dates from the beginning of the reign of King George V. In 1911, the most important improvements were new water mains – the Palace had been troubled by inefficient plumbing and water supply for generations. But problems emerged the following year when work was started on the new centre gates leading from the Mall. When the workmen began digging the foundations for the support pillars, they discovered that the new water main passed directly beneath the spot where the pillars were supposed to go. So, in true public works spirit, the brand new water main was dug up and diverted so that the gates could be installed.

If the Queen wanted to change the wallpaper in her bedroom – almost unimaginable anyway – there would be no question of her despatching a lady-in-waiting to the local decorators and making a personal choice. She would have to consult the Department officials first, get their permission and allow them to engage the craftsmen. The whole process for something as simple as this could take months of planning and involve several dozen people. The Master of the Household, who is considered to be the 'hotel manager', would need to talk to the Keeper of the Privy Purse, the accountant, to see if there was enough money in the kitty. He in turn would discuss the matter with his opposite number at the Treasury, since they provide all government funds for the upkeep of public buildings, who would need estimates from the Department of the Environment. Letters would be exchanged between all these before being sent to Her Majesty's private secretary, as direct access to the sovereign is impossible; everything has to go through her private office. Then the Royalty Protection Department – the Palace's private police force – would need to check the credentials of the men who would carry out the work.

Prince Philip constantly came up against this sort of bureaucracy when he was trying to improve efficiency. That he managed to get anything at all done is a tribute to his determination – and in many cases, his sheer bloody-mindedness. But today the private rooms of the Queen and Prince Philip are much more comfortable than when they first moved in. Central heating throughout has made the Palace more bearable in winter, but they still do not have air-conditioning, so some summer days and nights can be suffocating.

The Queen takes many of her meals in her apartment and at least these days she is able to eat hot food as the serving procedure has been streamlined. Forty years ago it could take twenty minutes for food to be carried from the kitchens in the basement to the first-floor rooms, by which time everything was usually stone cold. Now they have hotplates – but no microwave ovens – and the food reaches the Queen piping hot and takes only five minutes or so to reach her table. In addition the Queen's Page has a small pantry across the corridor from her sitting room where he can boil a kettle and serve drinks. It was here that Michael Fagan was taken, on the Queen's orders, to be given a whisky, on the morning he broke into the Palace in 1992.

Philip also set about renovating his own apartments, installing a brand new bathroom with power shower. His valet once said that Prince Philip could arrive back from an engagement, undress, take a shower and change into evening clothes in under five minutes at a push. And in those early days, everything he did was at the double. It was as if there were not enough hours in the day for all he wanted to do. His favourite response when asked when he wanted something done was 'Yesterday'.

Staff conditions have also improved immeasurably, even if the wages haven't kept pace. Palace salaries are still amongst the lowest in the land, particularly among the domestics. But today there is no sense of fear among the servants. They do not have to hide if they see a member of the royal family approaching, and when the Queen or Prince Philip passes one of them in a corridor, they will still bow or curtsy, but will invariably receive a greeting. This would have been unheard of thirty years ago.

It was Philip who raided the 'treasure house', as the Palace storerooms are called. He found priceless articles of furniture and works of art that he used to decorate the private apartments, but he also allowed some of the lesser pieces to be used in the rooms occupied by the domestic staff. As wages were so low, why not let Palace folk have the joy of being surrounded by beautiful objects when they were off duty?

One of his first tasks when Prince Philip and the Queen became tenants of the Palace was to get rid of unnecessary waste. He was the first member of the royal family in the century actually to go below stairs. (Queen Victoria's Consort,

Prince Albert, had been the last.) What he found horrified him. In the early days of Elizabeth's reign there were two separate kitchens: one exclusively for royalty; the other for lesser beings, with the royal chef resolutely refusing to handle any food not intended for the royal family. Had it not been for Prince Philip, it probably would have been many years before anyone woke up to this ridiculous state of affairs. He ordered one of the kitchens to be dismantled and all meals – for both royalty and commoners – to be prepared in the same room and by the same people. Like many of his reforms, it wasn't universally popular, even with those who actually carried out the work, but he pushed it through and the Master of the Household and Keeper of the Privy Purse eventually saw the economic sense.

Prince Philip didn't win every battle, however. During one of his whirlwind tours of the kitchens he found a priceless collection of old copper moulds, some of which dated back to before Queen Victoria's time. There were scores of them, in all shapes and sizes, each one bearing the royal cypher of the reign in which they were made. As none had been used for generations, Philip decided to sell them off. He knew they would realize thousands of pounds from collectors. He eventually persuaded the Master of the Household and the Keeper of the Privy Purse that the jelly moulds should be sold, but they agreed to the sale on one condition – the royal cypher must be removed first. Philip knew when he was beaten. The moulds are there to this day.

Buckingham Palace is not a noisy place, in spite of being at a junction where traffic never seems to stop. The atmosphere of quiet and calm tranquillity strikes you as soon as you enter its doors. It has been described as a village, but few villages of just 300 inhabitants can boast a Post Office which handles over 100,000 items a year, and even has a special three-man security team equipped with a fluoroscope to examine every piece of mail that is delivered. Then there is the police station manned twenty-four hours a day, three hundred and sixty-five days a year, with the latest state of the art technology, and a private laundry which can process five thousand articles every day. The Palace kitchens can be called upon to provide up to 600 meals a day if necessary and there is accommodation for an army of gardeners, upholsterers, seamstresses, carpenters, plumbers, mechanics, engineers, cooks, kitchen hands, maids, footmen, cleaners, chauffeurs, coachmen, police officers, soldiers and two men whose task is to wind the three hundred clocks.

There is even a serving soldier who sits on the roof to make sure the Royal Standard is flying whenever the Queen is in residence. It is his responsibility to ensure that the moment she leaves the Palace the Standard is lowered, and the very second she takes up residence again, the Standard is hoisted. When the Royal Standard is flying everyone can see that the Queen is residing at the Palace. It is also the only flag in Britain that is never flown at half-mast, for at the death of a sovereign the cry is: The King [or Queen] is dead: Long live the King [or Queen]. Because in Britain, monarchy never dies. This tradition is deeply embedded in Buckingham Palace life and in part explains why, when Princess Diana died, there was such reluctance on the part of Palace staff to defy custom and fly a flag for her at half mast. However, the flag in question was not, of course, the Royal Standard, which was flying at Balmoral at the time, but the Union Flag. But until Diana's death even this was not flown over the Palace when the Queen was not in residence; the flagstaff remained bare when she was away. It was because of the public outcry that the Union Flag was flown at half mast some days after Diana's death, and from that time the Union Flag has continued to be flown above the Palace when the Queen is not in residence.

If you ask any visitor to London what they most want to see the answer will be Buckingham Palace. It's where all the tourists, from Tokyo to Tennessee, congregate. They have their photographs taken and watch the daily changing of the guard. For this is, quite simply, the most famous house in the world.

CHAPTER SEVEN

Friends – The Inner Circle

*'Even if she wasn't who she is, she is still
someone I would want for my best friend.'*
LADY PATRICIA MOUNTBATTEN

If the Queen can be said to be able to count the number of her close, intimate friends on one hand, then Countess Mountbatten of Burma would occupy the position of the index finger. Nobody has known Her Majesty longer or had such a lasting relationship. Patricia Mountbatten, elder daughter of the late Earl Mountbatten of Burma, who is also Lady Brabourne as the wife of Lord Brabourne, is a little over two years older than the Queen and there has never been a time when they didn't know each other. Similarly, Patricia Mountbatten has known her cousin, Prince Philip, all their lives. As she recalls, 'We have a marvellous old photograph in the family album of my father holding two very small children by the hand. One was Prince Philip, aged five, the other was me at two. I can also remember Princess Elizabeth, as she was then, coming to tea at Brook House [the Mountbattens' London home on the corner of Park Lane and Upper Brook Street] when we were all children, so the relationship does go back rather a long way.'

Throughout their childhood and adolescent years, Patricia Mountbatten and the two princesses saw each other frequently, so when Patricia and John Brabourne were married in Romsey Abbey in October 1946, at what Lady Brabourne described as 'the first non-austerity event since the war outside London to which the King and Queen came', the royal family were there in force and it was quite natural for Princess Elizabeth, then aged twenty, to act as a bridesmaid. 'The press first became aware that something "interesting" might be happening between Princess Elizabeth and Prince Philip at our wedding,' Lady Brabourne told me. 'She was a bridesmaid and he was an usher and when he took her coat at the door of the Abbey it sort of alerted people that they were interested. The photograph appeared in the newspapers the next day and that started the media attention.'

Lord Mountbatten had long enjoyed a reputation as a royal matchmaker and although there is no evidence that he was responsible for putting the Princess and his nephew together, his daughter has no doubts that he was thrilled: 'Of course, he naturally thought it was an excellent thing – and how right he was! He was very pleased.'

Patricia Mountbatten is unequivocal about the comparatively short time that Princess Elizabeth and Prince Philip had together before the death of the King. 'From the Queen's personal point of view it was a disaster that it all happened so soon. It was a tragedy that they couldn't have had perhaps another five years, which would have given them ten years of living a relatively normal life. They had enjoyed their early days together so much. We saw a lot of them in those days. They would come to us in our tiny cottage on the estate.'

The first time Princess Elizabeth and Prince Philip visited the Brabournes at their estate at Mersham near Ashford, Kent, the Princess was fascinated by the cottage they were living in at the time because the main Adam house was far too large. It had only three very small guest rooms and must have seemed rather like a doll's house to the Princess. Her maid, the redoubtable Bobo McDonald, was not so impressed. Her first words when she saw the place were, 'I don't believe it.' There are none so snobbish as the servants of royalty and the aristocracy. However, the Princess loved it, and by the end of the week even Bobo relented, saying, 'Why can't we have a little cottage like this?'

Patricia Mountbatten remembers with affection some of the antics they would get up to: 'After dark we would take a jeep and drive around with headlights blazing and shoot rabbits. Something you would never dare do today.' Her younger sister, Lady Pamela Hicks, was with Princess Elizabeth in Kenya on the day she learned that her father had died and she was now Queen. Almost everything changed dramatically, but not their lifelong friendship. Indeed, the Princess Royal has said that Patricia Mountbatten and her sister are the closest friends her mother has and really the only people outside her own immediate family with whom she can truly relax. It is a unique compliment.

As both families grew, the children became close. 'We saw a lot of Princess Anne when she was at Benenden as our girls were there also and it wasn't too far from our place in Kent so she used to come over for tea occasionally.' Lady Mountbatten and Prince Charles have also always been close, and for much of his life Prince Charles regarded Patricia Mountbatten's father, Lord Mountbatten, as a surrogate grandfather and the Queen also relied on him considerably. Lady Mountbatten witnessed her father's devotion to the Queen. 'He absolutely adored her. She could do no wrong in his eyes. It was a wonderful relationship. He could say things to her that no one else could have got away with – things that needed to be said, but only he could do so. He also had this way of allowing Prince Charles to unburden himself where he didn't really feel comfortable doing it at home.'

Unlike most people who only see the royal family from a

distance, Lady Mountbatten and her husband know them well and see them when they are not 'on show'. So she is able to testify personally to the other side of Prince Philip's character: 'He's got a very sensitive, thoughtful side. Quite one of the nicest, more thoughtful letters I received after the bomb was from him. [On 27 August 1979, Lady Mountbatten and her husband were with their family on board their small fishing boat in southern Ireland when an IRA bomb exploded, killing her father, one of her twin sons, her husband's mother and a fifteen-year-old Irish boy. She, Lord Brabourne and their surviving twin son were badly injured.] And he [Prince Philip] was describing – not my father's ceremonial funeral in London – but my son's and my mother-in-law's in Kent. He wrote, "It was a most beautiful day, the sheep were bleating and there's that lovely view over the marsh . . . and we did this and we did that." It was very touching; it really was. That's just one example of his thoughtfulness. He's at heart a sensitive person but he has had to grow a hard shell to survive.'

Another perhaps surprising aspect of Prince Philip's character she reveals is his fondness for children, 'He loves small children and he's very good with them – even sweet – I've seen him with ours when they were younger and he couldn't be more patient or understanding.'

A common perception of the Queen is that she is totally non-confrontational and refuses to acknowledge any personal problems. Lady Mountbatten tends to agree. 'That's quite true really. You see, if you are brought up to live your life in the eye of the world, you can't afford to be seen to be terribly sad, or in tears or even cross or unwell. You have to have such total control over yourself at all times that it then becomes quite difficult to show your emotions, even in private. I think this is a particular thing with the royal family – they cannot be seen to be other than totally composed and in control of the situation in public, and that spills over into their private lives.'

On a happier note, Lady Mountbatten is able to testify to the Queen's sense of fun: 'The thing that most people miss about her is how fun-loving she is. Everyone thinks she is serious all the time but she can be very amusing and she laughs a great deal. She is also very intelligent and tremendously well-read.'

That the Brabournes and the Windsor-Mountbattens are extremely close is exemplified by the fact that they have been together on most of the occasions when the royal family has been in crisis: the divorce of Princess Margaret and Lord Snowdon, the break-up of the marriages of the Prince and Princess of Wales and the Duke and Duchess of York. Lady Mountbatten remembers the occasion of Princess Margaret's separation: 'The Queen and Prince Philip were staying with us at Broadlands [the Mountbatten family home in Hampshire] and she was certainly pretty shattered by the news. It was terribly sad when she told us.'

The Queen and Prince Philip have been guests of Lord Brabourne and Lady Mountbatten throughout their married lives. 'She is a wonderful guest, always punctual, not in the least demanding and always willing to fall in with whatever is happening. It's just a nice weekend with friends and the routine rarely changes.' The main difference today is that when Princess Elizabeth and her husband first stayed with the Brabournes, 'The village bobby used to wander up and sit in the kitchen at night. These days it takes a battalion of police with all sorts of sophisticated equipment. A sign of the times I'm afraid.' And Patricia Mountbatten never forgets for a moment the identity of her special guest: 'I was brought up in a traditional manner, so when we meet I always kiss her hand. I always have and I always will. It may be slightly old-fashioned by it's something I'm used to and there's nothing strained about it. We also make sure we are down before her for lunch and dinner and I keep up the old tradition of seating the Queen at the head of the table, with Prince Philip at the other end. Wherever she is, she is still the Queen and it's simply good manners to treat her as such.'

Lady Mountbatten's grandmother had the perfect expression to sum up one's attitude to royalty: 'She used to say, "There are only two beings who can automatically go through a door first – one is an Emperor and the other is a dog," because neither would look around and see if there is anyone else who should be going through first!'

Patricia Mountbatten admits that with the Queen Christmas and birthday presents can be something of a problem. After all, what do you give the woman who is supposed to have everything? But she has the answer: 'It's usually something fairly useful and never too expensive. That would simply be embarrassing. The easiest way is to get hold of one of the ladies-in-waiting who has a little list of what might be suitable. One year I found out that the Queen really wanted one of those transparent see-through umbrellas, so I bought one for her which was a great success. A couple of years later, I found the same item was on the list again. So I told the lady-in-waiting I had already given one to Her Majesty. "That's right," she replied, "but she liked it so much she wants one for Sandringham and Balmoral." Another year I gave her a kettle which she uses in the little hut they have up in Balmoral where they often have picnics.'

If there is one emotion the Queen inspires in her close friends it is loyalty, and never more so than in the case of Patricia Mountbatten. In summing up the Queen's character, Lady Mountbatten pays her the ultimate compliment, and it doesn't sound in the least presumptuous: 'Even if she wasn't who she is, she is still someone I would want for my best friend.'

Another member of that exclusive group of truly close friends is Lady Georgina Kennard, known as Gina to those, including the Queen, who really know her. Lady Kennard, tall, erect with the slimmest of figures, is a widow who lives alone in London. She is the personification of elegance and has total recall of events that took place more than seventy years ago. Two of her daughters are Duchesses: Abercorn and Westminster, and her grandfather, Sir Julius Wernher, was one of the creators of modern South Africa. He was the son of an engineer who made his fortune in gold and diamonds and came originally from Darmstadt in Germany. He also owned one of the grandest houses in England, Luton Hoo in Bedfordshire, which eventually was inherited by Gina's father, Sir Harold Wernher, the chairman of Electrolux. Gina Kennard's aristocratic pedigree is impeccable; her mother, Lady Zia (Countess Anastasia de Torby), was the daughter of Grand Duke Michael of Russia, and she was related to just about every European royal family. She and Prince Philip can trace their joint ancestry back to Czar Nicholas I.

A few years older than the Queen, Gina has known her since they were both children. As she recalls, 'In Scotland, Princess Elizabeth and Princess Margaret used to come over to our house for tea with their nanny, who was called Alla, and their nursemaid, who was the redoubtable Bobo. Then in London, we all used to go swimming at the Bath Club and Princess Elizabeth never failed to come across and give me a sweet – not only me but all the other children there as well. Even at that age I used to think "what perfect manners". We also used to go for walks around the "inner circle" and often saw the two little princesses being driven through the park in their horse-drawn carriage. They would always give us a wave.'

Lady Kennard has known Prince Philip even longer than the Queen. 'He spent a great deal of his early life at our various houses. He often spent Christmas and other holidays with us, so he was just like a brother to me, and when they became engaged my family were absolutely delighted.' It is however a myth – repeated over the years by newspapers and periodicals – that Princess Elizabeth and Prince Philip spent part of their honeymoon at her parents' home. 'It's totally untrue. They did not come to Luton Hoo during their honeymoon. It's just a story that the press seized upon years ago and it has become accepted, but it didn't happen. What is true, is that for over twenty-five years they did celebrate their wedding anniversary every November with my parents. It was a fixture in their calendar and we all loved it.'

Lady Kennard, whose first husband 'Bunny' Phillips was very close to Edwina Mountbatten, had a unique insight into the early days of the marriage of Princess Elizabeth and Prince Philip. She was able to observe them at first hand – when they were not 'on display'. 'I'm quite sure that the first five years they spent together were the happiest days of their life. Particularly when they were in Malta. The Princess was able to live just like an ordinary naval officer's wife and it was the only time that she lived such a free life.'

Lady Kennard agrees with her friend, Countess Mountbatten, that in personal terms the early death of King George VI and the accession of the Queen was an absolute disaster. 'It would have been so much better all round if they could have had a few years more without the strains imposed on them both through the Queen's position. It was harder for Prince Philip than for the Queen. In the beginning he had a very difficult time. He was not used to the ways of the Court. He wasn't exactly rough, but he was his own man and never took to the idea of toadying to anyone. The Court was something of a time-warp and Philip was a much more modern man. He had been through a war, and he wanted nothing more than to remain in the Navy. It wasn't to be, of course.'

Even after Elizabeth became monarch, the friendship continued. 'We used to take our children to Balmoral for the shooting, and one of the things that very few outsiders would believe is how wonderful Prince Philip has always been with children. He was so patient and every night he would read to them, and he is a great story-teller.'

The Queen is known as a superb hostess, but few realize

how dedicated she is to the comfort of her guests. 'Whenever we arrived, Her Majesty would always be there to greet us and she would show us to our rooms herself. She really is the perfect hostess who goes to endless trouble to make sure everyone is comfortable and at ease.' When the positions are reversed the Queen is also an excellent guest. 'She loves to join in, she has a healthy appetite and likes to let her hair down and enjoys party games. She is more comfortable with country people, because she has such a lot in common with anyone who loves dogs and horses and, it may surprise some people to learn, she is an excellent mimic.'

There was only one occasion when things didn't go quite as planned. 'It was Halloween, and Princess Elizabeth (as she then was) and Philip brought the young Charles and Anne to stay. We all dressed up in the weirdest costumes and when they came down to tea, there we all were waiting to shock them. It worked, but not in the way we thought it would. We thought it was frightfully funny, but they didn't react at all, there wasn't even a giggle. It was a complete flop. In fact I don't think they even knew what Halloween was all about.'

And does the Queen ignore personal problems, even those involving her own family? 'I suppose it could appear that way to some people, but in her position she has to be so careful. I think when she came to the throne she made a conscious decision that the country and the Commonwealth had to come first – before her family, before her own happiness, everything. And I believe she was right. Most of us can afford to put our families first. She cannot. She has been proved right because she has now arrived at that stage in her life when nobody can point a finger at her and say she has neglected her job. It's a remarkable achievement for any head of state.'

What about Prince Philip's position? 'He has been a wonderful support to her. I've seen them together in all sorts of situations – country weekends and so on, and they are always terribly affectionate and loving. Everyone knows Prince

Philip's reputation for plain speaking, but he never makes a joke at the Queen's expense. He is respectful at all times without ever losing his authority as head of the family.' Lady Kennard is godmother to the Duke of York. At the time of the christening she was Mrs Harold Phillips, the only untitled godparent, the other godparents being Prince Henry, Duke of Gloucester, Princess Alexandra, Lord Elphinstone and the Earl of Euston, 'I was very surprised and honoured to be invited, and these days, whenever I see Prince Andrew, he always greets me with the words, "Hello, Godmother, how are you?"'

Lady Kennard is also close to the Prince of Wales, but less so to the Princess Royal. 'I think Prince Charles has a heart of gold. He's a very feeling man with tremendous qualities who I know has it in him to be a great leader.'

Other friends of the Queen have said that she has difficulty in expressing her feelings, unlike her sister, Princess Margaret. 'I think that is true.'

After a lifetime of true friendship, the Queen and Gina Kennard remain in touch, sharing the occasional cup of tea. 'There is no one in the world I admire and respect more than the Queen,' Lady Kennard sums up her feelings. 'She has a wonderful disposition and an instinctive tact. I cannot imagine her ever deliberately hurting anybody, and there are not too many people you can say that about.'

Lady Myra Butter is the younger daughter of Sir Harold and Lady Zia Wernher and, like her sister Gina, has known the Queen for most of her life. 'My earliest recollection is of a birthday party when we were about six or seven at a hunting lodge used by the then Duke and Duchess of York. We played with Princess Elizabeth in the garden. She particularly enjoyed a little game where one of us was locked in the garden hut and had to shout the loudest to be let out. Then when they [the Duke and Duchess of York] lived at 145 Piccadilly, we used to go out into a little private square at the rear – and at our house in Regent's Park, she liked to play Kick-a-Tin. There was never any question of her being thought of as any different from us. It simply didn't occur.' In fact their association goes back even farther, though both were too young to remember. When Princess Elizabeth was just two and a half she was taken to a birthday party at Thorpe Lubenham, near Market Harborough in Leicestershire, the Wernhers' country house.

Lady Butter was also one of the Buckingham Palace Girl Guide Troop, whose surviving members remain friends to this day. As she recalls, 'Sonia Graham-Hodgeson, whose father, Sir Harold, was the King's radiologist, was another early guide and she has remained a friend of the Queen. We were divided up into patrols: Kingfisher, which Princess Elizabeth was in, and Robin, which I joined. The one thing I remember about her was that she could always light a fire first time which most of us couldn't manage without help. Once a year we went camping at Windsor Great Park which was fun, but Princess Margaret wasn't allowed to join us as she was too young, so she became a Brownie. We had a marvellous time coming back in the coach singing at the top of our voices. When the war broke out things got a little difficult but the King encouraged us to continue so we met whenever we could.'

There was one occasion though, in 1940, when Myra was invited to stay at Windsor Castle, that caused Myra extreme embarrassment. The Queen (now the Queen Mother) had asked lady guests not to bring their lady's maids in wartime. However, Myra's mother, Lady Zia, who was considered by many people to be 'more royal than the royals', would not hear of her daughter travelling without a maid and insisted that she was accompanied, to the fury of the Queen.

On other occasions Lady Zia made little concession to the rank of royal guests. She believed in punctuality in all things, including meals, which in her house always started at the appointed hour. Princess Alexandra once arrived at the dinner table after the soup course had been served. All the other guests immediately stood – except Lady Zia, who admonished the Princess, saying, 'You are late.' She was probably also the only person in the world who has knocked on the Queen's door and asked, 'Are you ready?'

Myra Butter, like most young ladies of her class and generation, was taught to ride from an early age and also to swim, which was not so common. 'We had a woman instructor, the renowned Miss Daly, who used to tie a piece of rope around our waists and then she would hold a long wooden pole just in front of us as we splashed along. She would gradually release the rope until we suddenly found we were swimming. She had no failures and the Princess was one of the first to cast off the rope. She had no difficulty in the water and no fear either when it came to diving. She went on to an advanced level, winning a silver medal for life-saving when she was still very young.'

During the final years of the Second World War, a number of young officers from the more fashionable regiments would be invited to Buckingham Palace or Windsor Castle for a dance. The teenage Princess Elizabeth 'absolutely loved dancing and thoroughly enjoyed herself – we all did. It was a splendid opportunity for young people to meet.'

Towards the end of the war Myra had become a nurse while Princess Elizabeth enlisted in the ATS, but they resumed their old friendship when hostilities ceased. 'David [now Major Sir David Butter] and I married in 1946. Princess Elizabeth came to the wedding together with old Queen Mary, Princess Margaret and Princess Marina. There seemed to be a lot of family events just then and we saw a great deal of each other.' The wedding took place in St Margaret's Westminster with Princess Alexandra as bridesmaid and Prince Michael of Kent as Page of Honour.

Then, of course, came the news that Princess Elizabeth was to marry. 'We were naturally delighted that Philip had been accepted. He was practically one of our family and we all thought he was exactly the right sort of man to come into the royal family at that time. He was – and remains – so strong with such an individual personality. I cannot think of any other man we knew who could have been more suitable and I still believe he was the best thing that ever happened to the Queen. He was – and is – a tough man, who had fought a hard war and he didn't change. If he saw something that he thought was wrong, he set out to change it. He was a complete breath of fresh air and while the Queen has always made her own decisions, I believe she listens to him and heeds his advice. At the same time I can understand how some of the 'old-style' courtiers must have been horrified. Philip really was a "goer".'

For the first five years of Princess Elizabeth's and Philip's marriage, they saw their friends as often as they wanted, and often stayed with the Butters and the Phillipses at the Wernher country home. There was one occasion though when things did not go quite as planned. 'As luck would have it, the boiler broke down just as the Princess was going to have her bath so there was no hot water. We didn't find out until much later but she never said a word about having a stone-cold bath.'

Prince Philip was always in evidence in those days, supporting his wife and teaching his children to fish and shoot. 'He was a rather energetic father. There was no question of the young ones sitting about when he was around. He was always organizing them into some new game.'

How did the King's death affect the relationship with her old friend? 'I don't think it changed very much at all on a personal level. Apart from the obvious fact that she was now our sovereign. But we continued to go to Balmoral where, when the Queen worked her dogs, she was exactly the same as she had been before. And they still liked to picnic at a small hut they had in the hills where Philip would cook and the Queen would wash the dishes afterwards. She still enjoyed normal family pleasures when she could, but she knew what she liked to do and you had to be careful not to get in the way. Yet, when she crossed the threshold back into Balmoral Castle itself there was a barely perceptible and very subtle change from housewife to Queen.'

It has often been claimed that the Queen rarely gives any thought to anything outside her constitutional duties. Myra Butter disagrees and can point to a personal experience to strengthen her argument: 'We have five children and when the youngest two were leaving to go to boarding school for the first time we were naturally feeling a little bit down. The Queen, sensing how upset we might be, suggested that we should return to Balmoral and David could go stalking with Prince Philip. It was a wonderfully thoughtful gesture from one parent to another and showed how she knew what we were feeling.' Lady Butter does agree, however, that the Queen never shows emotion in public. 'The nearest I've ever seen was at a memorial service for a very dear friend when she did appear to blink rather a lot. She does have amazing self-control.'

Myra Butter has known the Queen for over seventy years and their lives have been intertwined in so many ways: both married at around the same time, have children of similar age, with the Queen godmother to Myra's eldest daughter, Sandra. She is unequivocal in her praise. 'I respect and admire her more than anyone else on earth. She cannot change now – she is who she is – and I wouldn't want her to change. She is very wise and unique in her wisdom and tact.'

The de Trafford family has been associated with royalty for generations. They share a passion for horse racing which goes back many years. Sir Humphrey de Trafford was one of the wealthiest landowners in the country, having vast estates in Lancashire and Cheshire, including some of the most valuable areas of Manchester. For example, he owned the Old Trafford cricket and football grounds – the home of Manchester

United. He was also a philanthropist and a well-known sports-man, and was pictured frequently with both the Queen and Queen Elizabeth the Queen Mother. His greatest success as a racehorse owner was winning the Derby with Parthia in 1959. Sir Humphrey's grandson, now Brigadier Andrew Parker Bowles, has continued the relationship, becoming even closer than his illustrious grandparent. His association with the Queen goes back to the time when he was a thirteen-year-old schoolboy, and she was approaching the most nerve-wracking ceremony of her life. 'In 1953,' the Brigadier recalls, 'the Earl Marshal, the Duke of Norfolk, was asked by the then Lord Chancellor, a charming man called Lord Simonds, if he knew of a young man of a suitable age to become his Page of Honour at the Coronation. I was suggested and became a page, carrying the coronet of the Lord Chancellor. Just in front of us in the procession was the Prime Minister, Sir Winston Churchill, and immediately behind was the Archbishop of Canterbury, so I was in rather good company.'

This must have been quite an ordeal for a youngster, even one brought up in a family who had known royalty for years. 'I remember going into the Abbey and all of a sudden a fanfare of trumpets sounded just above me, and I nearly dropped the Lord Chancellor's coronet. When the Queen came into view I was struck, even then, by her marvellous complexion and her vivid eyes. The pages were all standing together in a small group and when she saw us she smiled at us, which was wonderful as she must have had other things on her mind just then.'

Andrew recalls an incident relating to the coronation which occurred in 1993, and which illustrates perfectly the Queen's amazing memory. 'The senior page at the Coronation was Duncan Davidson, who attended the Earl Marshal. His job was to stand at the foot of the steps leading to the throne, and when the peers came forward to pay homage, he held their coronets. Duncan went on to found one of the largest and most successful building companies in Britain. At a party in 1993, Her Majesty saw him and asked, "What were you doing this time forty years ago?" To his embarrassment, he couldn't remember, and she had to remind him of his role at her coronation, which she did with some amusement.'

Andrew Parker Bowles was educated at Ampleforth and went from there straight to Sandhurst before being commissioned into the Blues, where he first learnt to ride. He went on to become one of the few amateur jockeys to ride in, and complete, the Grand National – in spite of having broken his back in an earlier racing accident. 'I also started playing polo, and later I got to know Prince Charles and Princess Anne quite well.' He and the Princess are still the closest of friends, in spite of divorces on both sides. They were once rumoured to be romantically involved, but neither took it too seriously. Andrew is Zara Phillips's godfather and also one of her Trustees.

He then started to see the Queen frequently as he had been appointed Staff Captain of the Household Division, based at Horse Guards. 'When we were organizing the Sovereign's Birthday Parade [Trooping the Colour], my job at Buckingham Palace was to get the timing absolutely right so that the procession moved off at exactly the right second. It was vital that the Queen should arrive at Horse Guards and come to halt at the precise moment when the clock struck eleven o'clock. On one occasion, we were in the quadrangle at Buckingham Palace and we were talking about racing. I forgot the time and the Queen looked at her watch and said, "I think I'm a bit late. It's time we went." So instead of me telling her, "Your Majesty, it's time to go," it was the other way around. But, as usual, she was spot on, making up the minute I had lost her, which takes some doing when you are riding side-saddle. The Queen seems to have this inbuilt sense of timing. She knows exactly where she is supposed to be at any given moment and she never gets it wrong.'

By 1981, Andrew Parker Bowles had been promoted to the rank of Lieutenant Colonel and was Commanding Officer at Knightsbridge Barracks. So he was involved in the wedding ceremonial of the Prince and Princess of Wales. 'I was charged with commanding the mounted troops and this meant we also provided a small guard to accompany Prince Charles and the Princess of Wales from Buckingham Palace to Waterloo Station to begin the honeymoon journey. It was a bit chaotic with children everywhere – pages, bridesmaids and people tying balloons on the back of the carriage. The Queen came up to me and said, "Please, please make sure you don't let any of the children get run over, keep an eye on them. Otherwise it will rather spoil the day." She said this last bit with a smile, but I knew she was anxious as the children were running about all over the place.'

Not all the occasions were so happy. The following year, the IRA exploded a bomb killing four of the Queen's Life-guards and several horses. 'I was on duty in the barracks when it happened. That evening, my Orderly Officer came into my office and said, "Colonel, there's a call from the Queen." I went to the telephone and indeed it was Her Majesty herself.

'She said, 'I've heard all about it and I'm terribly sorry. Will you please pass on my condolences to the families of all those killed and injured." Her Majesty then added that she knew as soon as the bomb went off that we were the target. She said, "I was sitting here [in her room overlooking Consti-tution Hill] and I heard the bang and I knew that they had had a go at the Queen's Lifeguards." It was a terrible blow but the Queen put the whole thing into its proper perspective when I told her about the loss of the horses, which was, of course, very sad. She said, "Just remember we can always buy more Army horses, we can't buy more soldiers." It was exactly the right thing to say, to bring one back to what were the right priorities. After the attack, around 98 per cent of press and public attention was centred on the horses and just two per cent on the actual boys who were killed – one officer and three soldiers. How right she was.'

As Officer Commanding the Household Cavalry, Andrew Parker Bowles also automatically assumed the position of Silver Stick in Waiting. This is a ceremonial role that dates back to Tudor times, but the holder of the office is also charged with being nearest to the sovereign, to protect him (or her). The Silver Stick had originally been a member of the royal household, but since Queen Victoria's reign, had been attached only for State Occasions and was not included in the Royal Household List. Colonel Parker Bowles decided it was time to address the matter. 'I had a word with the Queen's private secretary to ask whether Her Majesty would consider reappointing Silver Stick as a member of the royal household. I thought it would be a great honour for the Household Cavalry. The Queen agreed and told me, "That's right, you are a part of the royal household." This meant I could wear gold epaulettes and the royal cypher EIIR. The wonderful thing about the Queen is her ability to take a decision quickly. Once she's made up her mind, there's no messing about.'

The opposite number to Silver Stick in the Foot Guards is known as the Field Officer in Brigade Waiting. Each year at the Garter ceremony, held at Windsor Castle, the Queen and Prince Philip are attended by the two officers. Andrew Parker Bowles describes what happened on one such occasion: 'I was walking behind Her Majesty with my brother officer in the same position behind the Duke of Edinburgh. His Royal Highness was wearing a very long cloak which trailed some way behind him. My opposite number managed to tread on it, not once but twice, jerking Prince Philip's head back. The first time he just turned around and glared, the second time it happened, he said, "You bloody fool." The Queen just smiled and calmed him down, saying, "Don't worry, it will be all right." She was right, of course. Her knowledge and management of ceremonial is second to none.

'The Queen notices everything about State Occasions and ceremonial parades. And as an experienced horsewoman, she knows instinctively when something is not right. In the past she has drawn the attention of her Silver Stick in Waiting to a lapse in military detail saying, "I think that officer opposite is riding a little short [with too short a stirrup] – he should ride with a straight leg." And she's perfectly correct. Old cavalry hands think there are fewer uglier sights than soldiers riding too short.'

Andrew Parker Bowles is the first to admit that many royal doors have been opened to him because of his family connections and his military service, and this has given him an insight denied to many others. He has been invited to stay with the Queen on a number of occasions when the social whirl requires a certain degree of stamina. 'I was invited to stay at Windsor Castle during Ascot Week, which is fascinating. You are guests of the Queen for the whole four days and nothing is too much trouble for her and her staff. Every morning we would ride with the Queen, with a race around the Ascot racecourse on the final day. It was a sight to behold – about twenty horses, all shapes and sizes, with people of all ages galloping up the course. It was the greatest fun. Then you would hurry back to the Castle, change and have an excellent lunch and then off to the races in the afternoon. If you were lucky you would be asked to take part in the carriage procession, which in my case was a great experience. In the evening there would be a formal dinner followed possibly by a dance. The only problem was that timing was vital and as the royal family have perfected the art of getting changed in about three minutes flat, you were sometimes running down the passage fixing your black (or white) tie as you went. If your rooms were in one of the towers far removed from the State apartments it was sometimes a neck and neck finish to get there before the Queen. But a marvellous experience which I will never forget.'

The Brigadier now lives in a tiny hamlet in Wiltshire where pride of place is given to a signed photograph of one of his greatest friends – and an admitted heroine – Queen Elizabeth, the Queen Mother, congratulating him after he won the Grand Military Gold Cup in 1974. 'She has been a wonderful friend and has been very good to me. Back in 1965, I was thinking of leaving the Army, and somehow Queen Elizabeth got to hear of it. She summoned me to lunch at Clarence House and said, "I think it would do you good to go to New Zealand for a spell."

'Before I knew where I was, I was being interviewed by the Governor General, Sir Bernard Ferguson, and a month later I was in New Zealand, which in a way rather changed my life. If that had not happened, I suspect I would have come out of the Army, so it was very lucky for me. There again, I've been asked to stay at Royal Lodge at Windsor, Birkhall and the Castle of Mey in Scotland with Queen Elizabeth, so together with Sandringham, Windsor Castle and Balmoral, I really have been very fortunate. It's been great fun, as all my visits have been happy and great experiences.'

The film star Douglas Fairbanks Jnr, who died at the age of ninety in May 2000, was a member of Hollywood's 'Royalty' as his father, Douglas Fairbanks Snr, and step-mother, Mary Pickford, were the undisputed king and queen of the movie capital for over twenty years. He became a friend of both Prince Philip and the Queen, but his connections with the royal family went back to the years before the Queen was born. As a wealthy and well-connected young man-about-town, he became an early friend of Prince George, Duke of Kent, in the thirties, and also the Duke and Duchess of York. But it was his close relationship with Lord Louis Mountbatten that brought him into close contact with the Queen and the Duke of Edinburgh. Fairbanks was one of the first Americans to volunteer to serve in the Navy during the Second World War – in which he was decorated many times – and his self-confessed hero worship of Mountbatten drew him into the Sea Lord's close circle. Mountbatten introduced Douglas Fairbanks to Philip and they found they had a number of things in common – in particular they both enjoyed the company of good-looking women.

Fairbanks's standing with the royal family was never better illustrated than at the funeral service at St George's Chapel of the Duke of Kent, who had been killed in a flying accident on 25 August 1942. As the actor told me: 'I was given special permission by the Navy to accept Princess Marina's invitation to attend, and I believe I was the only "private" foreigner there. All the others were either diplomats or high-ranking service officers with "official" invitations. It was quite an occasion, even in the darkest days of the war.'

After the war, Fairbanks continued his friendship with royalty and, having a splendid house in The Boltons, one of London's most fashionable addresses, set about consolidating his reputation as a superb host. 'We used to give dinner parties for twenty people and even though there was still rationing, we always managed to provide something decent for our guests to eat. But when Princess Elizabeth and Prince Philip came, after they had married in 1947, we were always careful not to be too ostentatious because they were determined not to be seen indulging themselves while others were on bare rations.'

In 1949 King George VI conferred an Honorary KBE (Knight of the British Empire) on Fairbanks for his efforts in strengthening Anglo-American relations. It was an honour he cherished above all the others he had received. 'On the day I went to Buckingham Palace to be invested, I was more nervous than going on the set for the first time of any of the movies I've ever made. The King told me how pleased he was to give me the award. It was all very formal, but as I rose and walked away I detected the slightest wink and a faint twitching of his lips as if he was trying to hide a smile.'

Once Princess Elizabeth became Queen, Fairbanks felt it

would be presumptuous to invite the couple to his home. But word came via Princess Margaret that Her Majesty and Prince Philip would be delighted to accept the occasional dinner invitation. 'Naturally, I was thrilled and with things getting easier in the fifties I was able to offer much better hospitality than previously. Remember this was in the days of little security, so the Queen and Prince Philip, sometimes with the Queen Mother and Princess Margaret, would turn up accompanied only by a single bodyguard, who, after seeing them safely into the house, would go into the kitchen, where he would eat his dinner while we were having ours. And we would make sure that he ate the same food as we did. Occasionally these evenings went on quite late and once we all saw the dawn coming up. Conversation was never a problem. The Queen can talk on any subject under the sun, and we didn't have to wait to be asked a question, we just jumped in whenever we felt like it. And she always wrote a witty and courteous "Thank you" note the following morning. Such exquisite manners.

'There was one occasion when the Queen and Prince Philip came to dinner and Maurice Chevalier was also a guest. After dinner I asked him to sing one of his famous songs, so he obliged with *Louise*, his theme tune. Then he said to me, in French, 'I know a couple of others, but they are a bit risque. Should I sing them in front of the Queen?' I told him to wait a moment and I would find out. I repeated what he had said to Her Majesty, and she replied: "I am free, white, over twenty-one – and married to a sailor, please ask him to continue." And she and Prince Philip thoroughly enjoyed themselves. That was an evening when the entire proceedings were carried out in French. The Queen went out of her way to make Maurice feel at home.'

Throughout his long life, Douglas Fairbanks kept up his friendship with the royal family. Whenever he came to London he was invariably invited to Clarence House to have a drink or a meal with Queen Elizabeth, and during his final illness both she and the Queen insisted that they be kept informed of his condition. When he was buried, he was dressed in his trademark immaculate evening dress, with a black tie given him by his oldest friend and bearing the legend: Lord Louis Mountbatten.

If there is one bond that links those closest to the Queen, it is their loyalty. They never disclose what she has said to them in private and the fact of their total discretion means that she can relax in their company. The Queen greatly appreciates this faithfulness and repays it with equal consideration to the small group of men and women she has known for most of her life. She values her friends, loves to chat with them on the telephone and to drop in on them when she can. It might surprise many people to see one of the royal cars – not a limousine – pull up outside a block of flats in central London, not a million miles from the Royal Hospital at Chelsea, in the late afternoon, and a petite figure who strongly resembles the Queen step out. It happens more often than one might expect. It's just Her Majesty calling on an old friend – a member of the charmed 'Inner Circle' – for a cup of tea and a little bit of harmless gossip. It is one of the few 'ordinary' pleasures left to her.

CHAPTER EIGHT

Family Ties

'You've got it the wrong way round –
she's been my mother longer than she's been
my Queen.'
PRINCESS ANNE, THE PRINCESS ROYAL

I was once sitting in the drawing room at Gatcombe Park, the Gloucestershire home of the Princess Royal. There were just the two of us present and we were chatting about a book I was writing. Her butler, dressed in check shirt open at the neck and corduroy trousers, came into the room and said, 'Your Royal Highness, Her Majesty the Queen is on the telephone, shall I put it through to you here or will you take it in the study?' The Princess replied, 'No, I'll take it here.' I asked her if she would like me to leave the room, but she declined the offer and then something occurred which I found quite extraordinary. When she picked up the telephone to talk to her mother, she stood up. I walked to the other end of the room so as not to listen in to their conversation, which was fairly brief, and when it was over we resumed our talk. What was so unusual to me was that, even on the telephone, Princess Anne paid her mother, the Queen, the compliment of standing while she was talking to her. It appeared to be an unconscious act resulting from an upbringing which instilled good manners towards elders and protocol when addressing the sovereign, and it was somehow symbolic of attitudes within the royal family that separate them from the rest of us. I don't believe she even realized what she was doing, or if she did, it was so unconscious an act that its significance didn't register. Ironically, some weeks earlier, I had asked the Princess if it was difficult having the Queen as a mother, and her reply made it clear how she regarded the relationship: 'You've got it the wrong way around,' she said; 'she's been my mother longer than she's been my Queen. That's how I've always known her.'

The Princess Royal is regarded as the hardest-working member of the royal family, and rightly so if you count the number of engagements she undertakes in a year. But she has never been seen as the most demonstrative member of that regal group. That she is greatly admired and respected has never been challenged, but she is not known to encourage friendliness and she has never gone out of her way to be liked. In fact, those closest to her claim she would positively hate to be thought of as 'greatly loved'. On her own admission, she has never been maternal; she is certainly not the tactile woman that Diana, Princess of Wales was. She hates being touched or having to hold children on any of her visits. As she told me herself, 'I don't do stunts.' She has an icy self-control which has only once deserted her in public. She was on one of her African tours, shortly after the death of Diana, and the BBC's renowned royal correspondent, Jennie Bond, had the temerity to ask her if she was taking on Diana's work in regard to AIDS. Anne blew up, rounded on Jennie and lost her temper. Whether it was the mention of Diana, whom the royal family had come to detest, or simply that she did not want to be associated with the dreaded disease which she once famously described as 'a self-inflicted wound'. Whatever the reason, it was a rare glimpse of an Anne not too many people realized existed. Her attitude to her staff is correct without, at any time, being cordial. Secretaries who have worked for her for many years rarely hear a word once they have left.

In the 1980s I myself spent over a year working on a television programme with Princess Anne and then writing her biography. I cannot claim to have got to know her very well on a personal level, and we certainly never became close friends. But I was able to talk to her fairly informally and she never vetoed any subjects. On one occasion, I travelled as part of her entourage to Houston in Texas, on an Olympic fund-raising trip. She performed brilliantly and professionally, but never once, during the entire four days, did she speak to me or acknowledge my presence. She knew I was there, of course; without her permission I would not have been allowed to tag along. But I was there only as a chronicler of her journey: to record the events that were taking place. It was off-putting at first until I discovered there was nothing personal in this and that the same rules applied to her permanent staff. The only time she spoke to them was to issue an instruction or to ask for information. Small talk was not her forte. At Gatcombe one of her longest-serving police bodyguards was often seen carrying a young Peter or Zara on his shoulders. When I asked him if he was regarded as an 'uncle' he replied, 'Nothing could be further from the truth. I'm just a piece of furniture. They know that if I went today, by tomorrow someone else would be here to take my place. Even as little kids, they never get too close.'

This obviously applies within the family also. Many of us have seen the pictures taken nearly fifty years ago of the young Prince Charles at Victoria Station meeting his mother when she returned from an extended overseas tour. Instead of the hugs and kisses with which any ordinary Mum would greet her three-year-old son, the Queen actually shook hands with him. It was a distressingly sad and heartrending sight. How could we expect normal behaviour in later life from a family so straitjacketed that they cannot express emotion of any kind, either in public (horse racing excluded), or, even more surprising, in private?

At thirty-four, Prince Edward was single, rapidly going bald and still living at home with his parents. And when he did finally decide to marry, he had formally to ask the permission of his mother under the Royal Marriages Act of 1771. Not many young men of his age are so constrained that when they go out on a date, they instruct their girlfriends that the proper way to address them is to call them 'Sir'. And on his wedding day, when the Queen invariably confers an extra title on her sons, what did she make Edward? Earl of Wessex, a place of legend that has no boundaries on the map.

Prince Charles and Princess Anne, both now over fifty years of age, still call their mother 'Mummy' while the Duke of Edinburgh remains 'Papa'. Perhaps this is not so unusual when one remembers that the Queen, in her eighth decade, still addresses her own mother as 'Mummy'. So too does Princess Margaret, while they both, as small children, used to say good-night to their grandfather, King George V, by curtsying and retreating backwards while wishing 'Your Majesty a peaceful night's sleep'. Such was the imperial dignity of the pre-war Court.

Even today formality is accepted as the norm at private family meetings. If the Duke of York wants to see his father while they are both in the Palace, he would not dream of simply poking his head around the door to see if he was in. Instead, his valet would enquire of the Duke of Edinburgh's valet if it was convenient for him to receive his son. If the answer was yes then an appointment would be made and Andrew would walk downstairs – his rooms are on the floor above – where he would be announced with the following words: 'Your Royal Highness – His Royal Highness, the Duke of York.' Prince Andrew would then give his father a short neck bow and sometimes receive a kiss on the forehead in return. And any of the children going to see either of their parents would have to wear suitable clothing; jeans and sweaters are definitely not acceptable.

However, in an interview Andrew gave, he denied that life at Buckingham Palace as a child was lonely: 'My parents made huge efforts to make sure they were with us a lot . . . I remember my mother would look after Edward and me in the evenings in the Palace, alone, quite happily. It was a proper family.' He did however admit that the geography of the royal residences meant that 'our rooms happened to be quite a long way from where the Queen's rooms were.'

The Mountbatten–Windsors have been described as the most dysfunctional family in the land. In itself this is a nonsense, as they clearly have continued to function as a family. The mother and father are still married after more than fifty years, while the children remain close to their parents, even if their own marriages have broken up. But by dysfunctional most people mean maladjusted or simply difficult to understand. Even ultra-respectful courtiers used to laugh (behind her back) at old Queen Mary's refusal ever to speak on the telephone, an eccentricity she kept up until her death in 1953. And is that so very different from the Queen's sister declining to say anything directly to a domestic servant in this day and age?

If Princess Margaret wants to make a comment or complaint about one of her staff, she makes a note on the silver-edged writing pad she keeps near her at all times. This is passed to her private secretary who then summons the offending servant and passes on his royal mistress's comments. Another idiosyncrasy is that Princess Margaret prefers her own daughter-in-law, Viscountess Linley, to curtsey on first meeting her during the day and again when she leaves at night. She also discourages any familiarity in the form of address used, still demanding the formal 'Ma'am' on all occasions. If the royal family are impossible to understand, is it perhaps the result of having spent their lives in an unreal world? Perhaps it would be more surprising if they were like any ordinary family. From the moment of her birth the Queen herself has been subjected to an unnatural amount of attention. What other child of three would have had her picture on postage stamps, as she did in Newfoundland? Or seen her name featured in thousands of articles in scores of languages, or had a waxwork figure displayed in Madame Tussauds and even had boxes of chocolates named after her. With the amount of publicity that surrounded Diana, Princess of Wales, and which was blamed for much of her troubles, it has been forgotten that this was as nothing compared to the attention focused on the young Princess Elizabeth, who had lists of her birthday presents published in the daily newspapers before the Second World War.

The Queen's children have always known that they are different. Destined to live lives of great wealth and privilege, in the full glare of the media spotlight, they are in a unique position. An extraordinary situation that dictates, in their eyes anyway, that, close as they may appear to their friends and partners, as members born into the royal family they will always be isolated.

The one thing that Charles, Anne, Andrew and Edward have in common is the fact that they are restricted in their outside relationships. And by outside they know this includes spouses who are not royal by birth. The 'semi-detached' royals such as Princess Michael of Kent also know they will never be fully accepted by their in-laws. Indeed, Princess Michael once told Lord Wyatt (as he dutifully reported in his *Journals*, published after his death) that she knew Princess Anne didn't like her, 'and she didn't speak to me even after I went up to her.'

The Queen's three sons and one daughter were brought up in a structured regime that taught them not only obedience and respect for authority – as long as that authority is royal – but also suspicion of anyone outside their immediate family. This wariness has meant that for much of their lives the four children have relied on one another for true companionship and support. And the fact that three of the four have been through painful divorces has given them a shared understanding that has brought them even closer. Not that this has blinded them entirely to one another's faults or prevented the usual sort of sibling rivalry that one finds in any family.

Princess Anne has often criticized Prince Charles over his dedication to some of his more 'worthy' causes, which she finds irritating in the extreme. While she likes to think of herself as the practical face of royalty, Charles is subject to sudden and sporadic enthusiasms which do not suffer the inconvenience of needing to be realistic. Even when they were small children in the nursery, the relationship was volatile. Charles was the quiet one, given to day-dreaming and gentle pastimes, while Anne was headstrong, obstinate and always itching for a fight. But even then there was a definite pecking order. Charles was the one whose future was mapped out and on whom the attention was focused. Princess Anne told me many years later, when we were discussing her position in the family, 'I've always accepted the role of being second in everything from quite an early age . . . You start off in life very much a "tail-end Charlie".' However, in her case, being second in line did not mean second best, as she was determined to prove.

As they grew older, Anne and Charles grew closer, and their harmonious relationship has never been threatened, even by Charles's capricious behaviour during his separation and divorce. Anne was never a fan of Diana; she declined to accept the friendly overtures her sister-in-law made in the early days, while Diana got her own back by refusing to allow Anne to be a godmother to Harry – despite the Duke of Edinburgh's pleas. But if Anne was privately dismayed by Charles's unseemly – and unnecessary – public confessions of marital discord and his own infidelity, there has never been one word of censure. She now occupies an apartment next door to Charles in St James's Palace, where Camilla Parker Bowles is frequently seen. If Anne has any reservations about the heir to the throne entertaining the woman who is blamed by many as the cause of his marriage break-up, nobody would ever guess. Similarly, when her own first marriage was in difficulties and she announced to the family that she and Mark Phillips were to divorce, it was Charles who gave unqualified support and encouragement to his sister.

When Anne told the Queen of her decision to separate from Mark, her mother, with her well-known attitude when confronted with personal problems, pursued her policy of non-interference, saying, 'I think it's time to walk the dogs.'

The one area where Charles and Anne do disagree is on the subject of their father. Princess Anne will not hear a word said against the Duke of Edinburgh; he is the blind spot in her make-up. He can do no wrong, even when he is blatantly at fault. Members of the royal household know they must never voice the slightest criticism of the most argumentative and abrasive senior royal in her hearing, and the same applies to her siblings. Privately, they may hate some of the things Prince Philip says and does, but none of them would say so when Anne is around.

Prince Charles's rows with his father have been well documented for years. On one occasion he was heard to shout at his father, in the middle of a blazing quarrel, 'Don't you realize you're speaking to the next King?'

But where Anne and Philip are concerned neither has any faults. She has often been described as the son he wished he had had, and he was once reported to have said that she would make a better sovereign than his eldest son. Similarly there is nothing about Prince Philip that she would change. To see them together is to realize how alike they are. The relationship is happy, relaxed and easy-going, in sharp contrast to that between the father and his sons. While Charles, Andrew and Edward could honestly claim that their father has never spoilt them, he has, on occasions, found himself being twisted around his daughter's little finger. Theirs is a mutual admiration society and Anne's devotion to her father is returned in full measure. Anne showed her respect for her father in a subtle way on the marriage documents for her wedding to Mark Phillips on 14 November 1973. In 1960 the Queen had declared that members of her immediate family who were not entitled to the designation HRH Prince or Princess should take the surname Mountbatten–Windsor. Anne was, of course, both HRH and Princess but signed herself Mountbatten–Windsor on this important day.

The Queen's only daughter has also always been closer to her mother than her brother Charles has been. Sharing a deep love, bordering on passion, for horses, when Anne was young, she and her parents would spend hours discussing various aspects of equestrianism, often to the discomfort of Charles. And they were not above laughing at his clumsy attempts to join in their conversations, which is said to be one of the reasons he turned at an early age to the Queen Mother for the affection he was denied at home. She would never ridicule him and offered the spontaneous love and support he needed.

Prince Charles's fondness and admiration for his grandmother is well known throughout the family and elsewhere. It is not however generally understood outside that these feelings are not always shared by Princess Anne. She has never looked at her majestic grandmother through the rose-tinted spectacles used by every other member of her family. The word 'manipulative' was once heard to be uttered by Anne when speaking of the Queen Mother and the manner in which she gets her own way in most things.

If Anne resembles any of her forebears it is the last woman to hold the title of Princess Royal, her great-aunt Mary, sister of George V. The physical similarity is uncanny and many other features of their characters can also be compared: both 'no-nonsense' women, both undertaking engagements considered unglamorous for royalty, and the phrase 'did not suffer fools gladly' – or indeed at all – might have been coined for them.

Anne is determined, totally without fear and easily the most intelligent of the Queen's children. She also has the ruthless streak that all winners seem to need, and she doesn't care too much if she is liked or not. In a poll held in 1998 to find out who would be the most popular choice as president if Britain abolished the monarchy and became a republic, Princess Anne came top. It's not a post she would ever want, but the poll was an interesting indication of where she stands in the public's opinion.

The Queen showed her appreciation of her daughter's hard work and loyalty by awarding her the Order of the Thistle, Scotland's highest order of chivalry. She made the announcement, appropriately, on St Andrew's Day, 30 November 2000, and that evening Her Majesty and Prince Philip hosted a reception at Windsor Castle, as a belated 50th birthday tribute to their only daughter, for 500 representatives of the many charities with which Anne is associated. It was an informal occasion and when the Princess Royal replied to her mother's toast, in a brief off-the-cuff speech, she acknowledged the debt she owed both to her privileged accident of birth and to her parents, saying: 'Parents: very fortunate. Residences: pretty fortunate. Hobbies: that was pretty good.'

In times of stress the royal children really value one another's support, and at no time was this more clearly demonstrated than when Prince Edward decided to resign from the Royal Marines in January 1987. He did so in the middle of his training course and many people assumed it was because he couldn't take it. Prince Philip is Commandant-in-Chief of the Royal Marines, so naturally he was disappointed at his son's action. But, contrary to what was written at the time, he did not shout and rave as expected. He knew his youngest son would not have taken such a momentous decision without great thought so he kept quiet. It was the Queen who expressed her anger at Edward, for she felt he had let down the family. Many assumed that Princess Anne would also disapprove but they could not have been more wrong. She lent a sympathetic ear to Edward's troubles and offered him a room at her home, Gatcombe Park, away from the prying attention of the media. She didn't lend a shoulder to cry on – that's not her style – but she was there for him, as she's always been, when it mattered.

Anne has always found it difficult to refuse her baby brother, so when he asked her to take part in his ill-fated 'It's a Knockout' television show in June 1987, she agreed, even though she had severe reservations. Prince Andrew also took part along with his then wife, the Duchess of York. Of them all, she was the only one who seemed to enjoy the humiliating experience. Charles and Diana wisely declined. But even though the show was panned by critics and public alike, the young royals didn't blame their brother for involving them, and he raised £1 million for charity.

Edward's foray into the theatre, working for Andrew Lloyd Webber's Really Useful Company – where he asked to be known as plain Edward Windsor but expected everyone to stand up when he entered a room – was also encouraged by Charles, Andrew and Anne. It might have been easier for them to point out that he had responsibilities in public life, and that a more conventional role was expected of him, but they realized his heart was set on it, so they gave their support. Edward's more recent television enterprises, in which his most successful programmes have been about royalty, while at the same time denying strenuously that he is exploiting his connections, have attracted huge public criticism, but not from his family, apart from an alleged protest from his grandmother.

My personal impression of Prince Edward was of a pleasant, interested and well-informed young man who certainly did not go out of his way to emphasize the difference in our status. We met in the Deanery at Windsor Castle, when I had been invited to meet the Dean, the Very Reverend Michael Mann, to discuss the then Lord Chamberlain, Lord [Charles] Maclean, about whom I was writing at the time. Prince Edward came into the room and we spent around half an hour talking about rugby. He was still at Cambridge University and was having a rough time at the hands of some of the opposing teams who had started a 'Get Edward Club', the intention being to inflict the most harm on the Queen's youngest son.

Andrew and Edward were once seen as the 'other family' when Andrew was born eleven years after Anne, with Edward two years later. But the two groups did not 'pair off' with the older brother and sister closer to each other than to their younger siblings. But this never happened. All four have been remarkably close and interdependent to a large extent.

When Prince Andrew's marriage broke up, he retreated into a private shell, not wanting to share his feelings with anyone, including his family. This was rather surprising, for Andrew is perhaps the most outgoing and gregarious of the Queen's children. He was the one most likely to shoot his mouth off, saying how angry and disappointed he was. When eventually the time came for him to confide, he naturally turned to his brothers and sister. The idea of talking to anyone outside the family would have been unthinkable.

Prince Andrew has the most unconventional domestic arrangements of all the royal family. Although divorced from his wife Sarah, they remain living under the same roof at Sunninghill, the house the Queen had built for them as a wedding present. He has never spoken publicly about the situation, but on the occasion of Sarah's 40th birthday, in October 1999, they were photographed together with their two daughters, Beatrice and Eugenie, in a pose that would have graced any family album. Theirs must be the most sophisticated and civilized understanding of their generation. While the rest of the family refuse to have anything to do with Sarah, Andrew is her staunchest supporter, refusing to join in the general criticism of his ex-wife even when confronted with irrefutable evidence of her erratic behaviour. His loyalty is steadfast and without question.

The Queen's relationship with her children remains a mystery to those outside the confines of the Court. When they were small she appeared to favour Prince Charles. After all, he was her first-born so there was naturally a special bond. She never seemed to be particularly close to Anne or Andrew, but Edward, as the baby of the family, occupied a special place for many years. However, as they grew older and had families of their own, Princess Anne has become closer to her mother. The Queen is a practical woman who recognizes in her daughter the same forthright approach to her public duties she herself adopts.

On a personal level, the grandchildren have now taken over the place of the Queen's children to some extent. Anne's children Peter and Zara were the first and they have an affectionate, if slightly distant, relationship with their royal grandparents. The Duke of York's two daughters Princesses Beatrice and Eugenie are trotted out periodically to be inspected and entertained, but it is on the sons of the Prince of Wales that most of the Queen's attention is focused these days. They are the future of the monarchy and in her eyes nothing is more important.

Prince William, and to a lesser extent, his younger brother, Harry, carry the hopes of the Mountbatten–Windsors into the twenty-first century. William's education and training for his eventual role is supervised personally by the Queen, with constant advice from the Duke of Edinburgh. Although Prince Charles went against his father's wishes by sending his sons to Eton rather than Gordonstoun – which he hated – every aspect of their instruction in matters royal and constitutional is programmed by Buckingham Palace. For Charles realizes that independence can only go so far. He may be bloody-minded, indecisive and occasionally curt to the point of rudeness, but when it comes to the future of his sons he knows he dare not go against the wishes of the Queen.

The four children of this the most public family, whose every movement, relationship and attitude is captured in the spotlight of media attention, have managed to retain a comparatively stable relationship with their parents and with one another. Perhaps it is the fact that they are totally non-judgemental about their own tiny group that allows this affinity to continue and prosper. It is, by any standards, an extraordinarily self-protective group, which is one of the main elements of their collective strength.

Mainly uncritical, certainly never in public, they seem to know that, whatever happens outside, in the final analysis they can always rely on one another. If they appear neither to need nor to want anyone else, it is because they have learnt to trust only their immediate family. Spouses may come and go; after all, they are only strangers who have been brought in – and in three cases, despatched when they didn't meet the requirements of royalty. Charles, Andrew, Edward and Anne regard themselves as the backbone of the royal family and consider it their sacred duty to ensure its future.

CHAPTER NINE

The Impact of Diana

*'I don't think it's any secret that Diana could
be very difficult.'*
ROBERT RUNCIE, ARCHBISHOP
OF CANTERBURY 1980–1991

'I was an outsider and let's face it I never had a chance.' These
were the words of Diana, Princess of Wales, shortly before
her death in August 1997.

About seven years earlier Diana was at Bridgend in South
Wales, where she was to open a scanner at a hospital named
after her. She had invited me to attend and even arranged for
an official car to collect me from my home about ten miles
away. As she walked along the line of local dignitaries she was
animated, polite and friendly to everyone. At the end of the
line there was someone who had not been included in the
official programme because of uncertainties about his health.
This was the late Viscount Tonypandy (the former Speaker of
the House of Commons, George Thomas). He was an old
friend of the Princess, having read the lesson at her wedding
in 1981. He had also just been released from hospital after treatment for cancer. When Diana saw him, she threw her arms

around him, kissed him on the cheek, crying: 'George, how wonderful to see you.' All protocol was forgotten as she tucked her arm through his and led him on her round of the wards. It was obvious that nothing could have pleased him more.

Towards the end of Diana's visit the party arrived at Cardiff Airport, and as usual on these occasions she had been given hundreds of bunches of flowers. Before she boarded the Queen's Flight aircraft, she called all the police, security men and airport workers towards her and said: 'Tomorrow is St Valentine's Day. I want you each to take one of these bouquets and give them to your wife or sweetheart with my love.' Such a spontaneous gesture is unimaginable from any other royal, even today.

This informality was in sharp contrast to the occasion when I was working for the BBC in Wales and Prince Charles was on one of his visits to the Principality. Then everything was planned down to the last detail. Questions were submitted in advance and vetted by his staff with no deviation permitted. Nevertheless, when we met subsequently, he was courteous enough to pretend he remembered me; no doubt it was because a member of his household, when presenting me, used the words: 'And Mr Hoey you already know, Sir.' It is a ploy used by the royal household whenever someone is presented to a member of the family. They ask beforehand if you have met them before.

Prince Charles proposed to Lady Diana Spencer on 4 February 1981 and was immediately accepted, though the official announcement of the engagement was not until three weeks later, on 24 February. He had just returned from a skiing holiday in Klosters with his close friends the Palmer-Tomkinsons and those nearest to him were of the opinion that he proposed, not because he was madly in love with Diana, but because he was resigned to providing the country with an heir. His relationship with Camilla Parker Bowles was an open secret in royal circles. Even Diana knew of it, and later said she believed she could overcome the problems and force Camilla out of her husband's life. But the truth was that Camilla had pushed Charles towards Diana, for she realized that the younger woman would not threaten their friendship.

The Queen and Prince Philip were said to be 'delighted' at the prospect of Diana as a daughter-in-law, but members of the royal household, and friends of the Queen and Philip, acknowledged that their principal emotion was relief that at last their son had done his duty. Charles had been under considerable pressure to marry for some years; he was, after all, thirty-three, well past the age when most of his generation had married. Prince Philip was said to have despaired of his eldest son ever finding the right woman, mainly because of his inability to make up his mind. And it was because of the constant urging of his father that Charles finally proposed. He knew that marriage was inevitable if not entirely welcome, and Diana, who had been subjected to intense vetting, was the safest candidate.

Though the Queen's feelings towards Diana were never of the warmest, she didn't dislike her or make her feel unwelcome. It was just that they had little in common apart from the fact that Diana's family had served the Crown for generations. The Spencers received their earldom from Charles I, and Diana's father, the eighth earl, had been an equerry to Her Majesty, while her maternal grandmother, Lady Fermoy, was not only a lady-in-waiting to Queen Elizabeth the Queen Mother, but also one of her closest and oldest friends. In fact, Lady Fermoy was the one member of her own family who did not welcome the idea of Diana marrying Charles. She was reported to have warned Diana against joining the royal family, saying, 'I don't think it would suit you.' She might also have quoted the words of Rudyard Kipling to the new royal bride-to-be: 'Yet not look too good, nor talk too wise.'

The bride-to-be should have had the advantage of 'knowing the form', so important in any relationship with the royal family.

After all, she had been born at Park House on the royal estate at Sandringham and had grown up familiar with the Queen's children, particularly Andrew and Edward, who were nearer her own age than Charles and Anne. It wasn't as if she was coming into a strange environment. But Diana was not quite the sort of young woman the Queen was accustomed to, unlike, say, the Knatchbull girls, the granddaughters of Earl Mountbatten, whose relationship with the royal family was easy, relaxed and informal without being in any way too familiar.

However, in spite of the Queen's supposed coolness towards Diana – and there was never any outward sign of it – efforts were made both to make her aware of her new position and to include her in the family. The difficulty was that the royal family – that is those who are born into it rather than those who join it by marrying – is incapable of complete closeness with anyone not defined as royal in its own peculiar terms. The Queen Mother is the exception that proves this particular rule (though even in her case, King George V and Queen Mary had initial reservations about their son marrying 'a subject'). Almost every other outsider, in other words, commoner – Antony Armstrong-Jones, Mark Phillips, Angus Ogilvy, Sarah Ferguson and even those who appear to be assimilated such as the present Duchesses of Kent and Gloucester – know that they are there on sufferance.

When Princess Margaret announced that she was to marry a society photographer, Princess Marina, widow of the Duke of Kent, was horrified. As the daughter of Prince Nicholas of Greece, and therefore a first cousin of Prince Philip, she believed that 'royals should marry only royals' on the grounds that they can be relied upon not to rock the regal boat.

If there is one thing at which the British royal family has been totally successful it is survival. Queen Victoria guarded her powers assiduously, even when she retreated into virtual seclusion after the death of her beloved consort, Prince Albert, in 1861. Edward VII's unconventional private life, with its succession of mistresses, did little to harm his position as monarch, and his wife, Queen Alexandra, accepted his extra-marital liaisons. His son, George V, survived the violent anti-German feelings aroused throughout Britain during the First World War by the simple expedient of changing the family name to Windsor. He also forced all his relatives to abandon their German titles and become British aristocrats overnight. So the Saxe-Coburgs, Schleswig-Holsteins and Battenbergs became Edinburghs, Cambridges, Connaughts, Albanies, Athlones and Mountbattens. Even the cataclysmic events of 1936, when Edward VIII abdicated because of his refusal to give up Wallis Simpson – and when the soldiers guarding Buckingham Palace were issued with live ammunition for the first and only time in case of attacks by his supporters – is seen with hindsight as a mere hiatus. True, it wasn't quite a seamless transition, and the rows within the family were never fully resolved, but soon after the reluctant succession of George VI the monarchy was as secure as ever.

But none of these events had as much impact on the royal family as the arrival of Diana. Single-handedly she transformed the public's perception of royalty and her influence is still felt.

Within months she became one of the most glamorous and photographed women in the world. When she went among handicapped and disadvantaged people she displayed a compassion that was unprecedented in one of her generation and unheard of among royals of any age. She captivated huge crowds and became more popular than even the Queen Mother, until then the unchallenged darling of the people. Her style was distinctive and eventually her influence became immense. And as this happened, her position within the royal family grew more and more precarious. Not because she was seen as competition for the established members, though certain royal noses were certainly put out of joint, but because, as she became more confident in her new role, she also became more demanding.

Until he married Diana in 1981, Prince Charles had been regarded as the most eligible bachelor in the world. He was adored by millions of women of all ages and he revelled in the adulation he came to regard as his right. He was not used to being upstaged, and he didn't like it. Newcomers to the royal family are made painfully aware by its more senior members, by both birth and marriage, that they are expected to defer to those born to the purple. If they do not do so quickly enough – as for example, Princess Michael of Kent, who in her early days was a little too flashy and flamboyant – they are firmly put in their place.

With Diana it was slightly different. It all happened so quickly. She became the star of the family almost before they realized there was competition, the ultimate royal icon, acclaimed by the world, including two women as far apart as it is possible to visualize: Margaret Thatcher, who described Diana as a 'beacon of light', and Mother Theresa, who claimed she could see the 'faith in her whole personality'.

From the moment Diana emerged she, and Prince Charles, became the focus of intense media attention. Diana coped impressively though her early days as Princess of Wales were not always easy. She had a mind of her own, refusing to be seen as merely a pretty accessory, and she displayed a remarkable sense of duty as she came to realize that from now on she would have very little private life.

Diana had star quality, of that there was never any doubt. And she thoroughly enjoyed her celebrity. It was not long before she was being described as one of Britain's greatest assets. Almost single-handedly she restored a moribund fashion industry. Her beauty, style and elegance made her the most sought after woman on earth, and thousands of women, from Tokyo to Tennessee, tried to copy her way of dressing. For example, shortly after the wedding, Diana wore a tiny, Robin Hood type of hat. Almost immediately replicas were sold in thousands. As her popularity grew, so too did Charles's bewilderment. He could not understand the adulation that was poured on her. And, as he quickly found out, she was not the girl he had thought.

Charles had grown up surrounded by people who shared his interests – or if they didn't certainly pretended that they did. Diana was different. As she had been born on the royal estate at Sandringham and her father had been a typical upper-class countryman, Charles expected his daughter to be one of the 'huntin', shootin' and fishin'' set. He proposed, Diana said, in a ploughed field. But what he got was a young woman who detested the country, preferring the city with its delights of shopping, dancing, pop music and gossiping with girl-friends. He was clearly mystified and had no idea how to cope with his modern and much younger bride. Nor did any of his immediate relations. They completely failed to understand that they and their surroundings were very intimidating to an outsider. The Queen, Prince Philip and their children were all well used to Buckingham Palace and Windsor Castle. They had known little else, and they could not understand why anyone should be apprehensive at the thought of having to live within those walls.

Diana once said that she was given no job description when she became Princess of Wales. Neither were Antony Arm-strong-Jones or Mark Phillips, but they were never intended to be consort to the monarch; their royal duties were merely supporting roles. For Diana it was different. She was expected to behave as a future Queen, but no one gave her any instruc-tion as to what that involved. Perhaps the Queen's only daughter, the Princess Royal, might have been the right person to advise Diana, but she would never dream of offering such advice without being asked. And Diana never asked.

Had Charles been more understanding, he might have seen the need for help. It wasn't that he was unsympathetic, it was simply that he didn't realize there was a need. And in those euphoric early days there were few who imagined that Diana would one day be the cause of the greatest threat to the monarchy since the Abdication. In the early years the Queen herself was completely unaware of any problems with her. If she had known the extent of the difficulties, there is no doubt that she would have acted to resolve them. The Queen is a kindly woman who would not have set out to isolate Diana deliberately. She is also pragmatic, so that if she had realized the seriousness of the marriage problems, she would have moved heaven and earth to prevent a breakup, because of the effect it would have upon her own position and that of her eldest son.

The marriage hardly had an auspicious start, though few outside the royal circle knew it. It wasn't until 1992, when Charles and Diana had separated, that both revealed doubts about going through with it. Diana said that on the evening before the wedding Charles told her he was not in love with her. She added that even when she was walking down the aisle at St Paul's Cathedral, she was in two minds about whether or not to turn back. Charles himself said that he wanted to call the wedding off but that he was under great pressure from his father to 'do the right thing'.

Diana also knew her duty – to provide the House of Windsor with a future heir to the throne. She accomplished this on 21 June 1982, when she gave birth to Prince William in the private Lindo Wing at St Mary's hospital in London. She completed her royal maternal duties two years later when Prince Harry was born on 15 September 1984. She had produced an 'heir and a spare'.

As a life-long friend of the Queen, Myra Butter is well qualified, among few others, to comment on the relationship between Her Majesty and her former daughters-in-law. 'The Queen was very supportive with them both. Sarah and she got on very well. They had a fine relationship, but unfortunately things got out of hand but she is still very sympathetic. Diana was very strong-willed and determined to do things her own way. When she took Prince William to Australia as a baby, the Queen understood her feelings about not wanting to be parted from her child. She could never have done it herself because of her position when she had her first child, and travel and communication were so much improved in 1981 compared to 1948. But she sympathized. The big problem was that Diana was too young when she married. If she had been twenty-five, it would have been very different. She was thrown into this very structured family where discipline and punctuality were taken for granted and for her it was a distinct culture shock. Add to that the fact that she and Prince Charles were rarely alone in the early days of their marriage. He was used to it, she never adapted.

'The Queen did everything she could to help Diana. On one occasion I was at Windsor when the Queen had included some young people of Diana's own age so that she would be more comfortable. Suddenly she said, "I'm tired and I'm going to bed." It was unheard of for anyone to leave before the Queen, but Diana did. The problem was that we had been brought up very strictly and Diana wasn't. It clearly was not her fault but neither was it the royal family's. The media attention didn't help either. Can you imagine what it would have been like if Princess Elizabeth and Prince Philip had married today? He would have been described as a "Viking Prince" by the newspapers. He was as much a superstar in the forties as Diana was in the eighties.'

In 1984, the Prince and Princess of Wales accompanied the Queen to the State Opening of Parliament. That day Diana had a new hairstyle, a dramatic, swept-up, formal look designed to set off her tiara. The following morning every newspaper, including *The Times*, had front page pictures, with comments about Diana's hair. It completely overshadowed the Queen's speech, and there were even leaders in the newspapers days later. Her Majesty was said to be 'less than pleased' – the phrase the Palace uses when she is absolutely furious –

not because she objected to Diana changing her hair, but because, by doing it on that particular day, the gravitas of the occasion was lost. Diana had, knowingly or not, reduced one of the most solemn and dignified state occasions to the status of a film première. She later expressed her remorse at causing any embarrassment to the Queen, but privately told friends she couldn't see what all the fuss was about.

Inside the household, they refer to time as BD and AD – Before and After Diana – though never in the presence of the Queen. Until Diana came along royals were seen as figure-heads. After Diana, they were under pressure to become celeb-rities. For generations they had grown used to an unrelenting, tedious and often downright boring round of public duties that many see as the sole justification of a monarchy. The Princess Royal is known as the hardest-working member of the 'Royal Firm' because of the number of engagements she carries out. Prince Philip has attended thousands of functions in an official capacity, some of which he privately admits are 'bloody boring'. It's the work they do for the positions they occupy.

Diana changed all that. Not only did she accept the leader-ship of scores of organizations, she actively supported them, involving herself in their activities and making her public duties seem a pleasure. She spread compassion like honey, hugging sick children and geriatric men and women with equal enthusiasm. Her warmhearted involvement with causes as disparate as AIDS, handicapped children, the Deaf, Blind and Rubella Association, Mencap, the Malcolm Sargent Cancer Fund and any number of charities involved with the elderly, soon meant that she was being asked to take on hun-dreds of different active roles.

She gave the impression that she loved meeting people and had the gift of being able to identify with everyone. Not surprisingly, the rest of the royal family found it difficult to accept that this inexperienced newcomer had superseded them. However, Prince Charles was the only one who came close to expressing any resentment, when he remarked during one of their joint walkabouts. 'I know it's my wife you have really come to see, not me.' It was true. Diana had eclipsed her husband as the star attraction. She had upstaged the royal family and made them look dull and out of date. Adulation which they had taken for granted was transferred to the young newcomer who developed a knack of being able to judge exactly the public's mood.

Over the years different members of the royal family have taken on roles with various organizations which have brought real satisfaction to themselves and to those they work with. The Princess Royal found her niche at the age of twenty-one when she agreed to become Patron, later President, of the Save the Children Fund, the charity with which she has since become totally identified. The Duke of Edinburgh has worked equally tirelessly for the Worldwide Fund for Nature. Prince Charles's causes tend to be more aesthetic: inner city regeneration, English architecture and the state of the language. Diana took a more modern 'hands-on' approach to subjects everyone could understand.

When she was pictured holding a baby suffering from leprosy or hugging a young girl maimed by a landmine in Angola, the impact was immediate and shocking. It also had a startling and surprising effect on many of her own generation. Here was a young mother, like themselves, who didn't mind touching the untouchable; didn't object to being handled by dirty and diseased people. Where previously the royals had always stared straight ahead and never showed either sorrow or happiness, Diana allowed her feelings to be seen by all. She shed tears, laughed and cried in a natural reaction to what she had witnessed, and so displayed a vulnerability that was the secret of her success. Young people in particular felt that she alone knew what they were going through and identified with her because of it. This was how she earnt a unique and adoring affection from people in many different walks of life. She had an instinctive ability to communicate with ordinary people, and it was this very characteristic that set her apart from every other member of the royal family. Diana became the acceptable face of a modern monarchy. It's often been said that Princess Anne would have made good in any field she entered, without the advantages of birth and privileged background, because of her tough determination, her iron will and her single-mindedness. But had Diana not been royal she could never have succeeded as she did. She needed the mystique and magic of the monarchy just as much as the monarchy needed her.

Then, once the separation and divorce occurred, she took off into the stratosphere. The infamous BBC television interview with Martin Bashir, broadcast on 20 November 1995, when she admitted her own affair with James Hewitt and uttered the phrase 'There were three of us in the marriage. It was a bit crowded,' referring to Camilla Parker Bowles, brought her even more attention. The perfectly phrased soundbites she used were obviously the product of professional tutoring. All the same, Diana made a serious error in agreeing to that interview. It did not show her at her best, and she later told friends that she regretted doing it. It was a gamble that didn't come off, and when she said that she believed Charles didn't really want to be King, she made implacable enemies at Court. She had challenged the Palace – and she lost.

It was not, however, that *Panorama* TV interview that was the beginning of the end for Charles and Diana but Andrew Morton's book, *Diana, Her True Story*, which was published in 1992 after serialization in the *Sunday Times*. It proved to be the start of many of the troubles. At first she denied to Robert Fellowes, the Queen's private secretary, that she had cooperated with the author, and when it later emerged that she had, he offered his resignation to the Queen – who refused it. The authority of Morton's book lay in its provenance. All his sources were named and quoted and his later version included the tapes she had made available through an intermediary, Dr James Colhurst, a mutual friend. Diana never admitted it was her intention to harm the monarchy. Indeed, in one interview she said, 'Why should I try to destroy an institution my son will one day inherit?' But her independence and wayward behaviour were guaranteed to be divisive, and with them came a need to place the blame on anybody but herself.

Lady Kennard felt sympathetic to the Queen's problems, not only with Diana, but with Sarah also: 'She was always kind to both Diana and Sarah. They could never claim anything else. Sarah, in particular, got on well with the Queen as she enjoyed many of the same things: riding, shooting and most country pursuits. The trouble with Diana is that she wouldn't listen, even when the advice was well meant. She played the part of the Princess of Wales brilliantly and, like the Queen Mother, she had the common touch. When the marriage broke up, the Queen must have been desperately worried and unhappy, but you would never know it because she has this iron self-discipline.'

As the man who performed the marriage services of both the Prince and Princess of Wales and the Duke and Duchess of York, the late Lord Runcie, former Archbishop of Canterbury, was better placed than most to gauge the reaction of the Queen to the divorces that followed, and he told me he agreed with Lady Kennard: 'No one would ever know because she is in a league by herself in terms of rising above calamity or changing fortune. She's very much in control of her emotions about these things, just as she is about almost everything. With her, duty comes first, even above family problems.'

So what about the behaviour of her two daughters-in-law and their effect? 'I think her first reaction may have been of bewilderment. How are we going to handle somebody who is clearly getting out of control? How are we going to help them to become part of a family that must be the target of daily attention? A common factor in all my relationships with the Duchess of York and the Princess of Wales lay in their respect and indeed affection for the Queen, who was always distanced from any criticism they might level against the whole courtier culture. The Duchess of York may have been critical of the Palace and the household, indeed highly critical at times, but never of the Queen herself . . .

'The difference between Sarah and Diana is that Diana was two different people and never came to terms with either one. The suggestion in some quarters that the Queen would think "Here is somebody who has become a superstar overnight, I've got a thing or two I can learn from her," is quite ridiculous. The Queen would never be in the slightest bit influenced in that way at all. I think she would have been more puzzled and hurt – I don't think it's any secret that Diana could be difficult.'

Within the Palace the Duchess of York and the Princess of Wales were known as 'the terrible twins' because of their unpredictable behaviour. A senior courtier told me, 'They were timebombs waiting to go off. The Princess of Wales was very like the Queen Mother in that inside she was a very determined woman who gave the outward impression of being totally soft-centred. She also learned quickly how to do and say the right thing – and when not to say the wrong thing, at least at first. I don't think anybody has made a bigger impact in such a short time. The mistake she made was that she listened to the wrong people. She took the wrong advice when there were plenty of people at the Palace who wanted to help her. She wouldn't keep her head down. It was very sad and all so unnecessary.

'The Duchess of York didn't have the guile of Diana. She was much more open and friendly to everyone. I remember on one occasion when the family were all at Balmoral. The

Yorks were staying at Craigowan House on the estate. I used to bump into her quite a lot and she would always stop for a chat. Anyway, on the day the Queen was leaving, the Yorks were remaining, so everyone lined up for the formal farewells and then just as the car pulled away, up runs Fergie shouting, ''Bye-bye'' at the top of her voice. It was harmless; the Queen looked daggers, but what could she do?'

Many people, including experienced observers of the royal scene, were of the opinion that Sarah was the sole cause of her own downfall, while Diana was a victim. But any sins that might be laid at the Queen's door were surely sins of omission. It was a lack of foresight that allowed the Diana situation to get out of hand. By the time Charles brought the problem to his mother's attention as late as the summer of 1992 it was already too late.

And when Diana spoke on television about her unhappy marriage, and admitted an affair of her own, the Queen realized that a divorce was not only inevitable but necessary. On 21 November 1995, the day after the TV interview, she wrote to Charles and Diana telling them that an early divorce was the only solution to their problems and that both she and the Duke of Edinburgh believed this to be the sad but essential next move. This was Elizabeth writing as sovereign, and when the contents of her letter were deliberately leaked, allegedly by the Prince of Wales's office, Prince Charles confirmed that he took the 'same view' as his mother. Diana was taken completely by surprise. Friends revealed that she thought the Queen would do anything to avoid the scandal of a divorce. But when it came to a confrontation between the personal happiness of her family and any possible damage to the monarchy, there was no contest, duty would always come first.

When the divorce was finally granted, ending fifteen years of marriage, it appeared at first that Diana had emerged as the winner in the War of the Waleses. Her financial settlement of £17 million was hailed as a victory for women everywhere.

However, the Queen decided to remove Diana's right to be called Her Royal Highness, which was seen in some quarters as a mean-spirited and spiteful gesture reminiscent of her parents' treatment of the Duchess of Windsor sixty years before.

During what was to be the last year of her life, Diana became close to someone more than twice her age, whom she had known professionally for some years, and whom she came to rely on for his honesty and experience of the world. Lord Deedes, better known as the distinguished journalist W. F (Bill) Deedes, is one of the few – possibly the only – reporters still working who was around at the time of the Abdication. A well-known figure, as a former editor of the *Daily Telegraph*, a commentator and one-time government minister, Bill Deedes became even more famous as the companion of Diana during their campaign to assist the victims of landmines. 'I was heavily involved with her for only the last eight months of her life, mainly because of the mines issue, but they were eight very significant months,' he recalls. 'In January 1997, we went to Angola – I was with the "Rat-Pack" and she made a really big impact. Here was the mother of a future King showing enormous compassion; the first time any of us had seen anything like it. After that we kept in touch.

'She made a speech to the Royal Geographical Society which I drafted for her,' he says. 'She actually wanted to go everywhere, but I knew that would be impossible. She was restricted on security grounds from certain areas. For example, she wanted to see Cambodia, which was obviously out, so we settled on Bosnia.

'One of the conditions she laid down was that none of the people she was going to speak to should be given less than half an hour. She knew that if you'd had your leg blown off by a mine you couldn't tell the whole story in a couple of minutes. And the people wanted to tell their stories to someone. We travelled in the same car and saw some terrible sights but she never flinched. Naturally she didn't speak the language, so she communicated through a sort of baby talk. At first, none of the people knew who she was: they had been told a general was coming – all they really knew was that she was very, very important. What was so remarkable was her attitude. She was more like a nurse. There was one man with terrible injuries. He had lost both feet and said to her, "You ought to see what the results look like." Then he lifted his trousers and showed her his stumps which were truly hideous. She didn't recoil an inch.'

Bill Deedes is not a man easily influenced by the behaviour of public figures. He's seen too many and realizes that for most of them it is a performance, as it was even with Diana. 'You cannot be a member of the royal family without having an element of the actor in you. She had it – they all have it. In Bosnia, there was a young widow who met Diana while visiting a cemetery to see her husband's grave. Diana went to her and they stood together in silence for a while. It was a bit of an act, but the point is it made a huge difference to the widow. Diana was a natural performer, but I've often wondered how much my presence turned this naturalness into an act. She was always fully aware of what she was doing and the effect she was having.'

Although Lord Deedes's closest relationship with Diana was during the period he has just described, his association with her had started some years earlier when his nephew, and godson, was Diana's last boyfriend before she began her relationship with the Prince of Wales. He was also one of the group of newspaper editors who were summoned by the Queen to Buckingham Palace in 1981, shortly after the couple had moved into Highgrove, when she tried to persuade them to leave Diana alone. This was the famous occasion when Barry Askew, then editor of the *News of the World*, in reply to the Queen's remark that Diana could not even go into a shop to buy a bag of sweets, said, 'Surely, Ma'am, she could send a footman?' To which the Queen, in a devastating put-down, replied, 'That is the most pompous statement I have ever heard.'

In 1968 Lord Deedes had helped to form the Institute for the Study of Drug Dependency (amalgamated into Drug Scope in 2000), and Diana accepted his invitations to their annual lunches. Then came a much more personal occasion. 'I was asked to lunch at Kensington Palace with Diana and Prince Charles, just us. After the meal she said, "I'm worried that when William goes into the park with his nanny and needs to wee-wee, a photographer will jump out of the bushes and catch him on film." Charles shook his head as if it could never happen. Not that the photographer would be there but the thought of one of his children "spending a penny" in public – it simply wouldn't occur. But that's exactly what did happen.' Just a few months later William was 'caught in the act' when out walking with his nanny and a photographer, by chance, was on the spot to record this momentous event for posterity.

After that Diana and Bill Deedes became good friends. 'She once asked me to see if I could arrange for the *Daily Telegraph* crossword to be made easier, "Because my butler thinks it's too difficult."' Bill Deedes has thought deeply about the impact that Diana made on her in-laws. 'When she first came into the family, the major influence was her ability to persuade the Queen to accept change. It wasn't that the Queen herself was against it but the Queen Mother hates change and there's always been this feeling in the Palace that "You mustn't upset Grannie."'

Lord Deedes also sees a lot of similarities between Diana and the Queen Mother. 'Her smile, like that of the Queen Mother, concealed an iron will. Had she and Charles stayed together, her strength would have bolstered him in the same way that the Queen Mother shored up her husband. They both needed strong women.'

On the question of the threat to the monarchy following

Diana's death, Bill Deedes is dismissive. 'It was merely a temporary hiatus. Republican sympathies in Britain are no stronger now than they were a hundred years ago in Victoria's time. The Queen has a conscience and diligently does her homework, and she genuinely has a wish to keep herself in line with public opinion. Added to which, of course, she has this exquisite sense of propriety. She would never retaliate and the reason why Prince Philip takes out his frustration on the press is because of the raw deal he believes his wife has had from them.'

Others have said that Diana could be difficult at times. Bill Deedes is more emphatic: 'She was difficult all the time – immensely difficult. But the period I'm talking about was when she was alone. Her original role had disappeared and she was rebuilding a life of her own which was why she felt so insecure. At the same time, I liked her enormously – we got on. We shared the same jokes and we were at ease with each other. I've come to the conclusion that there are very few people who could have the same effect on people that she had. True, she could be manipulative, but so can we all at times. The difference is that with most of us it doesn't matter. With her, it meant that she usually got a favourable press, but that wasn't the entire object of the exercise. The cause did well out of it too. For instance, her legacy in Angola is still being felt. You still see people wearing Diana T-shirts and they still talk about her. She did more in eight months than the rest of us had been able to achieve in five years.' And what about her lasting effect on 'That Family'? 'Her impact on the royal family was that she made them think. They had seldom had to do that before – but they do now.'

At the time when Lord Deedes's association with Diana began, opinion polls proved she was more popular than ever. But when it was revealed that she was seeing other men, in particular the unsuitable Dodi Fayed, the climate of opinion gradually changed. Prince Charles began to be seen as not the totally guilty party. His long-standing relationship with Camilla Parker Bowles slowly became more acceptable and Diana was no longer seen as the innocent victim she had claimed to be. Although she was now wealthy in her own right, she was still fascinated by the super-rich who could provide her with private aircraft, luxury yachts and every extravagant amenity. The highly publicized romance with Dodi Fayed tarnished her image badly in the summer of 1997.

But all this changed overnight when she, along with Dodi, was killed in a car crash in a Paris underpass after they left the Ritz hotel, owned by his father. The sanctifying of Diana had started to crumble shortly before her death, but the fact that she died in such an unexpected and violent fashion, at the peak of her beauty and fame, meant that she would be remembered as the blameless princess deserted by her unfaithful husband. In the latter days of her life, she wanted the world to see her as an ill-treated martyr; when she died she got her wish.

Her death unleashed an unprecedented torrent of grief. There were scenes of people collapsing in the streets, weeping in public and even (unsubstantiated) reports of suicides by those unable to cope with the tragedy. The hysteria was entirely disproportionate to the event and completely foreign to what most people expected of the British. Far greater catastrophes had been suffered with lesser displays of naked emotion: the Aberfan mining disaster in 1966 when 144 people, including 116 children, died; the Dunblane tragedy in 1996 when a gunman shot and killed 32 schoolchildren; the 1988 Lockerbie aircraft explosion, were all far worse.

There was also an immediate and vast wave of criticism, bordering on hatred, of the royal family. They were blamed as the cause of her death: Charles because of his infidelity, the Queen because of her apparent lack of compassion and the Duke of Edinburgh because of his alleged coldness towards his daughter-in-law. This last accusation proved to be completely untrue when it emerged that Prince Philip had written several times to Diana after the marriage had broken down. His letters were warm and friendly and offered genuine support to the mother of his grandchildren.

But in the days following the tragedy the royal family could do nothing right. No statement of condolence was issued from Balmoral, where the Queen was staying, and no flag above any royal residence was flown at half mast.

The public was incensed at what they considered the Queen's insensitivity. But within days the Palace reacted with the Queen making a superb and moving appearance on national television in which she spoke about Diana in loving and affectionate terms. This did not, however, save her from being savagely criticized by no less a figure than the American ambassador in London, Admiral Charles Crowe. In a despatch back to the United States, later released under the American Freedom of Information Act, the ambassador wrote: 'The royal family, "the Firm", whose aloofness and lack of emotion were criticized by Diana in life, had a rough ride last week. They might have been mourning Diana and comforting her sons. But they were not seen to be doing so . . . Their gestures to public sentiment appeared reluctant and extracted under duress. Only on Friday, when the Queen, Prince Philip, Prince Charles and his sons visited with the crowds in London, did they receive favourable comment . . . For the moment, the royal family seems locked in an unequal struggle with Diana's memory . . . It will be difficult to change the public's perception of the Queen and Prince Charles. In middle to old age, they are what they are, with a strong sense of duty, but styles that lack empathy.' The envoy continued with a paeon of praise for Diana, saying she had a combination of beauty, royalty, good works and star quality and had become an instant legend.

Politicians rarely miss an opportunity for self-promotion, and the Prime Minister, Tony Blair, is a past-master at the art. He has been seen with the Queen on numerous public occasions, and almost invariably manages to insert himself alongside her whenever a photo-opportunity presents itself. His presidential style of leadership grates on many of his colleagues and opponents alike, and infuriates large numbers of the Queen's subjects who think he considers himself her equal. But no one doubts his political acumen, and nowhere was this more apparent than in the immediate aftermath of the death of Diana, Princess of Wales. Blair may well have been genuinely moved by the tragedy, most people were, but the speed with which he assumed the role of the nation's spokesman was breathtaking as he swiftly propelled himself into the limelight. Allied to which the 'siege mentality' that afflicted the royal family, hidden away at Balmoral without a word of condolence or sorrow being uttered, played right into his hands. When the Queen declined, on the advice of her senior household, to be rushed into speaking about Diana, Blair stepped in with professional and consummate ease. Some people charged that he had 'hi-jacked' the entire proceedings, even inviting himself to RAF Northolt as part of the official party that received Diana's body when it was flown back from France, which should have been a purely private affair, restricted to family and the Lord Chamberlain, the Earl of Airlie, representing the Queen. And, in the absence of any word from Balmoral, it was Tony Blair, sounding more like an elder statesman than a newly elected Prime Minister, who spoke to the nation outside Trimdon parish church in his constituency, on the morning the news broke.

Television cameras from every network covered the event live as he said: 'I feel like everyone else in this country today, utterly devastated. Our thoughts and prayers are with Princess Diana's family – in particular her two sons, her two boys – our hearts go out to them. We are today a nation in a state of shock, in mourning, in grief that is so painful for us.' He was brilliant. To the watching and listening millions, it was exactly what they wanted to hear and needed to be told. But intentionally or not, Blair and his team had instantly upstaged the Queen and her family and assumed the role which many felt should have been hers alone. Hers was the voice the people wanted to hear; his was the one they got, and in the absence of the sovereign, they warmed to him. He had also proved that in this age of media immediacy, it is vital for anyone aspiring to political heights to be an accomplished public performer, and able to react instantly. And while his motives may not have been entirely unselfish, no one could fault the accuracy of the way in which he gauged the people's needs. His stock had never been higher, the royal family's never lower.

Later that same week, when the Queen spoke on television, it was said that her speech showed signs of Downing Street draughtsmanship, with phrases such as 'speaking as a grandmother' bearing the hallmarks of the Prime Minister's press office rather than her own. However, it was also claimed to be the invention of one of her private secretaries. Whoever wrote it, it did seem as if the Prime Minister had assumed responsibilities that should have been the Palace's.

Lady Butter believes that the antagonism the royal family attracted in the immediate aftermath of Diana's death was caused by confusion rather than any personal animosity. 'Whenever there's a moment of national crisis or jubilation, we all like to congregate in front of Buckingham Palace. It happens when there is a royal wedding or particular anniversary to celebrate – or in a moment of public grief. When Diana died, the people expected to see the Queen sharing their emotion immediately. It is so easy for us to drop everything and run to the Palace; the Queen cannot do that, especially as she was then at Balmoral. Her first thoughts were to protect her grandsons from any media intrusion, and she was right. When she did arrive in London for the funeral and led her family outside the Palace gates to pay tribute as the cortege passed, she did it with her usual dignity and grace.'

If there is one lesson the royal family had to learn after Diana's death, it is that they needed to be far less remote. And no one learned it faster or better than her ex-husband. Admiral Crowe had been wrong, at least in one part of his assessment: that the public's perception of Prince Charles would be difficult to change.

Prince Charles emerged in the twelve months after the tragedy as a caring single parent who rapidly developed the common touch exemplified so brilliantly by his former wife. His dignified appearances with his sons touched the hearts of the people, and opinion polls showed that public sympathy was now very much on his side.

A year earlier he was seen as the man who had wronged his young wife with his middle-aged mistress, and the majority of the British people had dismissed him as a future king. Suddenly all that changed. His visit to the bereaved families in Omagh in 1998, after an IRA bomb outrage – when his intended two-hour stay lasted all day – showed he could be equally as compassionate as Diana, and if he still did not show an emotional face in public, his genuine concern was obvious. The polls also showed that many people in Britain felt it was time to draw a line under Diana and allow Charles to enjoy a little personal happiness. And his place as a future monarch, only recently so shaky, now appeared to be secure.

The rebranding of Charles as the 'People's Prince' continued apace with successful tours of South Africa and Canada and with his sons helping him to regain much of his lost prestige. The favourable comment he attracted was not lost on the Palace. The caring 'lone-parent' image was carefully nurtured by his staff, aided and encouraged by new political friends such as Peter Mandelson, at that time an influential member of the Government, who had been a personal guest of Charles's at Sandringham.

As we have seen, no single event this century has affected

the sovereign, the royal family and the institution of the monarchy as much as the death of Diana. Beside it even the abdication of Edward VIII in 1936, dramatic as that was, pales into insignificance. At the time of Diana's death the lack of an immediate response by the Queen caused feelings of intense anger and disappointment. The barrage of criticism was bitter and unexpected. People questioned the value of a monarchy if the woman who personified it remained isolated in her Scottish holiday home.

The family were stunned by the ferocity of the assaults. The royal public relations machine made desperate attempts at damage control, with Palace spokesmen trying to mollify the feelings of the people by explaining, when details of the funeral were late in being published, that, 'It is a unique funeral for a unique person.' For all royal occasions the Palace invariably goes by precedent. They have files to cover every eventuality, to which they can and do refer constantly, except the sudden and violent death of a 'semi-detached' member of the family. They were completely unused to handling such an event – and it showed.

In the end the tragedy not only shook the people of Britain and throughout the world, it caused the royal family to reassess its values, its attitudes and its role. It also changed our perception of royalty – possibly for ever. The most immediate change occurred within days of Diana's death when the Queen ordered the Union Flag to be flown at half mast at Buckingham Palace. Before this the flagstaff had always remained bare when she was not in residence. A further consequence is that a Union Flag now flies every day when the Royal Standard is not in use. An even more unusual change in royal protocol took place on the day of Diana's funeral when the family emerged from Buckingham Palace to pay silent tribute as the coffin passed. This truly was a unique event; and much of the public's antagonism dissolved as they saw the former remoteness evaporate.

Another significant result was the announcement, months in advance, that the Queen, Prince Philip, Prince Charles and his sons, William and Harry, would attend a memorial service for Diana in Crathie parish church on the anniversary of her death. It might seem comparatively unimportant, but for the royal family to announce what they would be doing during their annual summer holiday was no small matter. They never make public their private plans during the sacrosanct vacation period, and the fact that the announcement was released so far in advance of the day was a clear indication of how seriously they took the possibility of further criticism. Even the Princess Royal, who was never close to Diana, announced that she was changing previous plans to attend a maritime festival in Portsmouth, in order to join the family at Crathie. Another first for the royal who is notoriously inflexible. Public opinion had been anticipated. No other member of the royal family had ever been remembered in this way: not Kings, Queens, Princes or Princesses.

Diana's death meant that the royal family had to become far less distant. They learned with remarkable swiftness that they ignored public criticism at their peril. Other seemingly small, but quite significant, changes have been made. Men and women are no longer required to bow or curtsy to the Queen if they prefer not to, and she now has her own website which gives thousands of details about family life. Her Majesty has also installed her own spin doctor to supervise all media affairs, for years the sole responsibility of the press secretary. Some say these changes are the result of pressure from 10 Downing Street, and certainly the lines of communication between Downing Street and the Palace have never been more active, even if senior courtiers see the traffic as one-way. Insiders at Buckingham Palace claim that the changes, the openness and the accessibility, were all planned long before Diana's death. But royalty hates change and the royal family had strenuously resisted efforts to modernize – until she died.

Meanwhile the press has become even more adversarial, mainly because, without Diana to provide a never-ending stream of stories, there is a huge gap which has still to be filled. The new Countess of Wessex, Sophie Rhys-Jones, described by Prince Philip as 'the daughter-in-law I always wanted', was intended as the replacement, but it simply has not happened. Not through any fault of her own, though her insistence on continuing with her public relations business while enjoying the privileges of being royal hasn't improved her chances. It's just that Sophie has not got what Diana had in abundance – star quality.

The Palace might deny that Diana's death inspired the new informality at Court, and it is certainly true that the Queen had been quietly adapting to the many changes that have taken place throughout her reign. The difference is in the speed with which it has all happened. Even the decision to fly the Union Jack at half mast in tribute to Diana, a major and meaningful about-turn of royal policy, was made in days, when previously it would have taken weeks.

In her lifetime, Diana became a serious problem to the royal family. Perhaps it is not an overstatement to say that for a time she rocked the monarchy to its foundations, and her death has not solved all the difficulties. She may have been capricious and unpredictable, but she had the common touch. And the royals had to learn that if they were to survive and prosper, they too needed a little of this quality. Diana will be remembered by many as an inspirational woman who once said she wanted to be known as a 'Queen of Hearts'. It was a ludicrous, headline-seeking statement by a woman who had become a success because she possessed precisely the right combination of innocence and guile. It wasn't even her own phrase, one invented for her by a professional wordsmith. But it accomplished what was intended, and was repeated by the media throughout the world.

Of course, she never achieved this ambition in her lifetime, but perhaps in the years after her tragic death, that is exactly what she has become – to some people, if not to those who were really close to her and realized what a manipulative and scheming woman she could be at times.

It may also be that once the memory of Diana settles into its proper place in royal history – without the unseemly and unwarranted emotion that immediately followed her death – the monarchy will emerge a stronger and more potent force. If it does, the royal family will have much to thank Diana for. This could be her true legacy. Instead of destroying the institution she blamed for her own troubles, she may have strengthened it by causing its members to reassess their attitudes and perceptions.

CHAPTER TEN

The Camilla Factor

*'The period of mourning for Diana is over
and life has to go on.'*
A FRIEND OF PRINCE CHARLES

If Diana was seen as the greatest threat to the monarchy this century, then Camilla Parker Bowles must surely have run her a close second. Once her relationship with Prince Charles became public knowledge, in January 1993, she was blamed for just about every ill that affected the royal family, and it was three years after Diana's death before the Queen acknowledged her publicly.

The rift between Buckingham Palace and Prince Charles's separate establishment at St James's Palace had caused deep unhappiness to the Queen and extreme anger in the respective households. The cause of it all was Charles's determination to stand by the woman he loves – and she was blamed for placing him in an impossible situation. If Diana was the ill-treated martyr, Camilla was the wicked witch, whose spell was responsible for the break-up of a fairy-tale marriage and the subsequent condemnation of the future king. To add to the difficulties, neither the Queen nor Prince Charles relish the prospect of personal confrontation. So, amazing as it may seem to any ordinary mother and son, they never once discussed the problem of Camilla, or its possible repercussions on the monarchy.

Camilla is the great-granddaughter of Alice Keppel, who for twelve years and as a married woman was mistress to Prince Charles's great-great-grandfather, King Edward VII. It is a relationship Mrs Parker Bowles mentions frequently. She is fascinated by Mrs Keppel and a portrait of her graces the drawing room at Ray Mill House, Camilla's elegant Regency house set in seventeen acres of rolling Wiltshire countryside. The connection with the royal family extends even further, for Mrs Keppel's brother-in-law, Sir Derek Keppel, was Master of the Household to King George V for more than twenty years (1913–36) and, during his brief reign, also to Edward VIII.

A year older than Prince Charles, Camilla Shand – she was then single – met the Prince when she was twenty-four, and at their first meeting in 1972 she reminded him of the love affair and playfully added the words, 'How about it, Sir?' Over the years Camilla became a fully fledged member of Charles's set and a regular – with her future husband – when he played polo at Smith's Lawn, Windsor on Sunday afternoons. She was comfortable with the Prince from the outset, while he was happier with her than with other, more conventionally beautiful girls. He had never particularly cared for young women who were too attractive – or clever – partly because he found them intimidating and also, according to some of his contemporaries, because he has never welcomed competition, from either sex.

While Camilla could never be described as 'one of the boys', there was an openness about her that made her easy to get on with, and her sense of humour, ironic and at times ridiculous, made her an ideal companion. In other words she wasn't afraid of Charles or overawed by his pedigree. Whether her initial ambitions went beyond being merely a good friend is unclear. What is certain is that she quickly became established as Charles's number one girlfriend with a special role in his life.

Camilla's family background equipped her admirably to be a royal confidante. Her father, Major Bruce Shand, was one of the Queen's gentlemen-at-arms and had held several posts in the public life of his home county of Sussex, including Vice Lord Lieutenant. A distinguished soldier who had served with great bravery in the Second World War, he was awarded a double Military Cross and was taken prisoner of war. With homes in London and Sussex, the Shands had an active social life and were guests at a number of royal functions, but they were never – nor did they ever claim to be – part of the intimate circle that surrounds the royal family. Brought up with one brother, Mark, and one sister, Annabel, Camilla's entry into Society was predictable and conventional. She was given a coming-out party at seventeen, attended all those of her friends, and life consisted of one long round of cocktail parties, hunt balls and weekend country house parties. From an early age she had shown an aptitude for hunting and the countryside – another plus when she came to meet Prince Charles – and her first boyfriends were either minor aristocrats or the sons of wealthy businessmen. At one time she was linked with a member of the Hambros banking family, but nobody serious came along until she met a young cavalry officer in 1966.

Andrew Parker Bowles, at that time a Captain in the Blues, was already known to the royal family as his father often went racing with Queen Elizabeth the Queen Mother. In addition, as an officer in the Household Cavalry, Andrew was comfortable in the surroundings of Buckingham Palace. Indeed, as a young boy, he had had his first taste of royalty when he was a Page of Honour at the Queen's Coronation in 1953.

Camilla had dated Andrew's younger brother, Simon, for a while, but with Andrew it was apparently love at first sight. Like his ex-wife, Andrew Parker Bowles is gregarious, charming, excellent company and has perfect manners. In addition, as has been proved, he is also totally discreet. Not by so much as a whisper has he let it be known how he feels about the behaviour of the Prince of Wales, and none of his friends has ever heard him speak in anything but courteous tones about Camilla. If there is any bitterness, it certainly doesn't show. They have reached an amicable understanding and share the affection of their two children.

Andrew was an early escort of Princess Anne. As he explained to the present author, 'We were very fond of each other.' But there was never any chance of the relationship going any further because Andrew is a Roman Catholic (educated at Ampleforth), and under the Act of Settlement of 1701, no Catholic, or anyone married to a Catholic, may succeed to the throne or retain their place in the line of succession.

At the time that Andrew and Camilla started going out together, he was well aware of her closeness to Prince Charles, as was everyone in their circle. But any suggestion that when they married it was in the full knowledge that the relationship would continue is not true. Their wedding took place at the Guards Chapel, Birdcage Walk, London on 4 July 1973. It was a Catholic ceremony conducted by a Benedictine priest, Father Jerome Lambert. Camilla did not convert to Catholicism, but she did agree that any children should be Catholic. Their son, Tom, was born in 1975 and baptized as a Catholic in the Guards Chapel with Prince Charles as godfather. Although he is an Anglican, the Roman Catholic Church allows non-Catholics to be godparents as long as one of the godparents is a Catholic. The Parker Bowleses' daughter, Laura, was born in 1979. She is also a Roman Catholic.

Once Camilla and Andrew were married – having held their wedding reception in St James's Palace – they attended many royal functions together as official guests of the Queen. Everyone in the royal family had known about the relationship between Camilla and Prince Charles and they accepted her willingly. A female cousin of the Queen once remarked, 'All men need a Camilla at some time and Charles more than most. She has always been the strongest one in their relationship; he needs her more than she needs him.' What is unclear is whether the affair continued once Camilla had married or, if, as Prince Charles has claimed, it stopped on his marriage to Diana in 1981 and did not resume until 1986 when, in his own words, his marriage had 'irretrievably broken down'. In September 1995 Charles and Camilla took their first holiday together. They went to Greece. This was after Camilla and Andrew were divorced, in January of that year.

By claiming that it stopped when he married, Charles seems to be admitting that there was an active relationship in the years leading up to 1981. Friends of the couple have said that, in 1979, Prince Charles tried to persuade Camilla to leave her husband, but she refused, for Charles's sake, knowing that if she divorced Andrew at that time, the constitutional repercussions would prove disastrous for the Prince.

The position of Andrew Parker Bowles, by now promoted to the rank of Brigadier and commanding the Army Veterinary Corps, is also somewhat murky. Did he accept his wife's infidelity until it became public knowledge and he was forced to take action? Or was he completely unaware that the affair was back on, which seems unlikely considering all the circumstances. What does seem apparent is that the Queen and Prince Philip thought it unnecessary to take any action to stop their son seeing his mistress so long as they were discreet and no one outside their immediate circle knew what was going on. But with the publication of telephone conversations between Charles and Camilla in January 1993 – known as Camillagate

– and as Charles's and Diana's marriage problems became more public, it quickly became apparent the monarchy could be harmed. This was something the Palace could not tolerate. Hence the leak from Buckingham Palace: Mrs Parker Bowles was currently not being received by the Queen. Even this was misleading. While it was true that Camilla did not attend royal functions in any official capacity, so there was no chance of the sovereign formally receiving her, there was never any deliberate snub by the Queen. On a number of occasions, Camilla found herself accidentally face to face with the Queen. If that happened, Camilla was not forced to hide behind curtains or run into another room. They would simply exchange greetings in a friendly casual manner and continue on their respective ways. This happened on at least one occasion after 1997. Camilla was staying at Wood Farm on the Sandringham estate when the Queen was in residence in the main house. Out riding one morning, as she invariably does, Her Majesty bumped into Camilla who was similarly occupied. They spoke for a few moments and then went in different directions. Charles had already, many years before, made it clear that the position of Camilla was 'non-negotiable', and that applied as much to his family as to his staff.

The problem was resolved on 3 June 2000, when the Queen and Camilla both attended a 60th birthday party for ex-King Constantine of Greece, given at Highgrove by Prince Charles. The meeting between the two women had taken months to arrange, but it was only in the week before the party that confirmation came from the Palace that the Queen would attend. It was a triumph of public relations for both camps: Buckingham Palace and St James's. For Prince Charles it meant the end of years of frustration; privately being with the woman he loves, but unable to present her to his mother. It wasn't that the Queen had anything against Camilla; they had known each other for years and got on very well. It was that according to strict royal convention, the Queen could not be seen to be receiving her son's companion – a divorced woman whose ex-husband was still living.

Camilla has always had a champion in Prince Philip, who is not in the least censorious about the relationship. He also fully appreciates why his eldest son is so attracted to Camilla's earthy sexiness. The only member of the family who has resolutely refused to acknowledge Camilla is Charles's grandmother, Queen Elizabeth the Queen Mother. But it is not a question of morals or personal animosity. For her anything or anybody who threatens the position of the monarchy deserves little sympathy or consideration. Personal happiness is unimportant when public duty calls.

The Queen Mother was delighted when Charles married Diana; she felt that together they would see the Windsor dynasty safely into the twenty-first century. And while she had some private sympathy for Diana when her early problems emerged, it soon evaporated once the position of Charles and the monarchy was threatened. Similarly, she had no objection to Charles seeking solace from Camilla, until the relationship became public and Mrs Parker Bowles was described as 'the most hated woman in Britain'. From that moment, all mention of Camilla was forbidden in the Queen Mother's hearing and even Charles, who can normally do no wrong in his grandmother's eyes, realized that it would be many years before he would be able to present his close friend. There may, however, have been a slight thawing in 1999, when Prince Charles and Camilla were allowed to use Birkhall, the Queen Mother's house on the Balmoral estate, for a four-day holiday. But another strike against Camilla, so far as the Queen Mother is concerned, is that she has retained a fond affection for her godson, Andrew Parker Bowles. They meet frequently – at Clarence House and when he accompanies her to the races at Cheltenham and Sandown Park – so if her loyalties were to extend in any direction, it would be towards him.

In 1999, definite moves were made by the 'Court' of Prince

Charles at St James's Palace to establish Mrs Parker Bowles's place in the eyes of the public. She was seen in his company, even arriving at functions with him, where previously they had gone to great lengths to make sure they were never photographed together. When Camilla paid a private visit to the United States, as patron of a charity that supports those who suffer from osteoporosis, the disease which afflicted her mother, there were all the hallmarks of an official royal occasion. She was accompanied by Mark Boland, assistant private secretary to the Prince of Wales, and one of the most powerful – and feared – men in the royal household. In New York, Camilla was fêted like royalty and entertained by many of the leading socialite figures, while celebrities clamoured for invitations to meet her. The visit was a tremendous success and Prince Charles was clearly delighted that his companion was accepted so wholeheartedly in the country which had for years been in total support of his late ex-wife.

Later that same year it was revealed that Prince Charles had taken over responsibility for part of Mrs Parker Bowles's expenses. Her horses were stabled at Highgrove (she has two, each costing around £300 a week to keep), she was provided with a car by his Duchy of Cornwall office and other household bills were paid. Newspapers reported that the total amount was around £3,000 a week or £150,000 a year. However, even though there was no denial from St James's Palace, that amount has been greatly exaggerated. Prince Charles may be a generous lover, but he is not that generous. Nor did he purchase Ray Mill House: there was no need. Camilla comes from a wealthy family. Her mother, the Hon. Rosalind Shand, was a member of the very rich Cubitt family – her father was Baron Ashcombe – and Camilla's father, Bruce Shand, was a successful wine merchant. Camilla has a sister Annabel, married and living in Dorset where she runs an antiques business. And there is one brother, Mark Shand, a travel writer who is married to Cleo Goldsmith. The children of her siblings are frequent visitors to Ray Mill House and they all get on well together.

Camilla is a frequent visitor at Prince Charles's apartment at St James's Palace, where the security officers and sentries have grown used to seeing her. So she does not need a special pass to allow her into the precincts. She is also popular with most of Prince Charles's staff, never using her privileged position to 'lord it' over them or order them around. There has only been one report of any disagreement between her and a member of the Prince of Wales's household, which was when she allegedly referred, disparagingly, to the former Tiggy Legge-Bourke (now Mrs Charles Pettifer), one-time nanny to Princes William and Harry, as 'the hired help'. Her attitude to Tiggy is similar to that of the late Diana, Princess of Wales, who thought that her sons' nanny was trying to take her place. So neither Prince Charles's late ex-wife nor his present consort had too much time for the woman he always considered a valuable employee, and of whom William and Harry appear to be very fond. Tiggy finally left the employment of the Prince of Wales in January 2000.

In recent years Charles and Camilla have settled down to a routine which has many of the appearances of a married couple. They now make no effort to conceal their relationship and Camilla is fully accepted at St James's Palace, even joining her companion for his annual staff Christmas parties. They are obviously comfortable together, and their happiness is plain for all to see. To many of his closest friends – and family – Charles has never been more content. He enjoys nights out at the theatre, dining with friends and attending concerts, always with Camilla at his side. There is no longer anything remarkable in seeing them together.

It cannot be all that long before Camilla is accepted once again at Court. The Queen dislikes leaving loose ends; once a situation has arisen, she wants it resolved. She knows that there is nothing she, or anyone else, can do about Camilla's presence in her son's life, and as people throughout Britain appear gradually to accept the position – with Diana's memory fading – she wants to see a solution. The only difference between Charles and Camilla's situation and that of thousands of others, is, of course, his position as heir to the throne. And even that does not now seem to be an insurmountable obstacle. The Church of England is starting to make moves towards allowing certain divorced people to marry in church, and with the Queen looking as if she will reign for many years to come, public opposition to Camilla as consort will inevitably weaken in time. Even if a church wedding in England is not possible, there are few obstacles to their getting married in church in Scotland, as Charles's sister, Anne, did when she married for the second time.

Charles may be a romantic, but his mother is a realist, and she knew that once the people were willing to accept Camilla, then she too must surrender. She also knows that a happy Charles with Camilla at his side means a more effective Prince of Wales, and that is infinitely preferable to a despondent heir whose personal problems weigh too heavily.

Prince Charles has been accused of indecision in the past; at least now he is showing some steel in his determination to stick by Camilla. Her position has definitely been eased by her meeting with the Queen, which, while it may not be taken as a sign of royal approval, is certainly an acknowledgement of the relationship. Marriage is now more of a possibility than was thought feasible until quite recently, but the idea of a Queen Camilla still seems unlikely. Indeed should they marry the question of Camilla's title would raise many problems. The wife of the Prince of Wales automatically becomes the Princess of Wales, and the memory of the last woman to hold that title is still too vivid in the minds of many people. Camilla could adopt one of Charles's secondary titles and become, for instance, Duchess of Cornwall, which would not be nearly so emotive, but the royal family would prefer not to face that problem. Opinion is still divided, but gradually Charles is winning over many previously implacable opponents, and at last the public vilification of Camilla seems to be at an end.

CHAPTER ELEVEN

Mother and Daughter

'I think the Queen Mother may well have
slowed much of the progress the Queen wanted
to make.'
LORD DEEDES

When the Queen was still a baby, her mother started to market
her to the public, and she has never stopped. As Duchess of
York she authorized a first biography of her infant daughter.
It was called *The Story of Princess Elizabeth* and was told with
the 'sanction of her parents' by Anne Ring, who had previously
been attached to the York household. Published in 1930, this
was surely the earliest case of a book written about a child
who had barely learned to talk. No one has grasped the value
of public relations faster or better than the Queen Mother,
and she has used her knowledge to help her elder daughter
in every way she can.

In those early days, favoured authors and photographers
were invited to contribute to the image of the Windsors as
the perfect family, with all the ground rules laid down by
the Queen Mother. She was brilliant in controlling access to
Princess Elizabeth and, in a seller's market, knew the strength

of her position. If any writer published something she didn't like, he was never allowed back. After the war, she appointed the first press officer to supervise Princess Elizabeth's launch into adult life, and she has continued to monitor every aspect of media interest in her family. So in any assessment of the character of the Queen, the influence of her mother cannot be overlooked. No family decisions are ever taken without the views of the Queen Mother being sought. Many times court-iers have made suggestions to the Queen, only to be told, 'We shall have to see what Queen Elizabeth thinks.' It is common knowledge that the Queen will never allow any changes to be made at Court that might upset her mother, apart from those she has to make as sovereign. The subjects she discusses with the Prime Minister or any of the Common-wealth leaders remain sacrosanct, but when it comes to matters of style within the Court of St James's, or private family mat-ters, the Queen Mother is consulted.

Countess Mountbatten says, 'Of course, as the senior member of the royal family, she has this wealth of past experi-ence and she has seen it all, so they would be foolish not to seek her advice. But her influence is not over-riding in all things. Just because members of the family ask for her advice, it doesn't always follow that they accept it.' A former courtier at Buckingham Palace added: 'Queen Elizabeth has enormous charm which she unashamedly uses to devastating effect, not only on outsiders, but also on every member of her own family. The trouble is she makes everything she says sound so reasonable. If one goes to her with a suggestion that she plainly does not like, she will ask, "Do you really think that is such a good idea?" and that's the end of it. You never get her to change her mind, and if the Queen knows her mother is against something, she always sides with her.' The Queen Mother has the habit of ending nearly all her sentences with a questionmark, so that, instead of giving instructions, she appears to be making a request, knowing full well that nobody will deny her. Bill Deedes goes even further, 'In fact I think the Queen Mother may well have slowed much of the progress the Queen wanted to make.'

There are exceptions. One was when Sir William Heseltine persuaded the Queen and Prince Philip to allow television cameras to film them for a year for the BBC documentary *Royal Family*. The Queen Mother felt it was a great mistake – letting too much daylight in on the magic – and she could not be induced to appear in it. She was in fact proved wrong. The film did nothing but good for the image of royalty, and for once the Queen had overruled her mother. The programme was first shown in July 1969 and there were five repeats over the first eighteen months. In Britain alone it was seen by 40 million people and it was also shown worldwide.

Similarly, when the Queen decided to open Buckingham Palace to the public, the Queen Mother objected on the same grounds. She felt that the very exclusivity of the Palace added to the mystique of monarchy. The Queen's argument that opening the doors to visitors showed that the monarchy was trying to pay its way, cut no ice with her. She had never been concerned about the price of anything. And when the Queen decided that she was going to pay income tax she could not bring herself to tell her mother. A senior courtier was despatched to Clarence House to face the music. Apparently it was a painful and one-sided discussion.

During 1996 Queen Elizabeth told guests at several of her luncheon parties that it was totally unnecessary for the Royal Yacht to be decommissioned; her feeling was that for a nation with as proud a maritime tradition as Britain not to have a royal yacht for the sovereign to sail in was the beginning of the end.

When the Queen first came to the throne in 1952, suggestions were made by various politicians, supported by one or two members of the royal household, that the Queen Mother's talents should be harnessed for the country's benefit by sending her to live for a couple of years in one of the Dominions; both Australia and Canada were mentioned. The Queen dismissed the idea out of hand. She did not even discuss it with her mother, saying, 'Oh no, we could not possibly do without Mummy.' Even today Queen Elizabeth still talks to the Queen every morning on the telephone. The senior telephonist at Buckingham Palace connects them with the immortal words: 'Your Majesty, I have Her Majesty for you.' It's a tradition that has lasted since the Queen Mother was widowed in 1952.

Lady Myra Butter says, 'It is very touching to see the tremendous care and courtesy the Queen shows towards her mother. She will always make sure she is comfortable, with everything she needs close to hand.' However, not everything she does to ensure her mother's comfort is fully appreciated. A stairlift installed at Sandringham has only ever been used when the Queen is there to make sure. Otherwise her mother insists on climbing the stairs.

When Prince Philip was introducing his reforms at Buckingham Palace in the early fifties, he did so on the understanding that nothing he did should upset his mother-in-law; in particular this applied to memories of her late husband, and included the 'Brushing Rooms'. These small chambers on the first or principal floor are really more very large walk-in wardrobes, and in them are stored the clothes of King George VI. There are scores of uniforms from every country in what used to be the British Empire, winter and summer outfits, complete with necessary accessories, and all maintained in pristine condition, brushed and inspected every week. The shirts, ties, cuff-links and socks are also kept and shoes polished to a level where you really can see your face in them. They have been stored in this way since the King died in February 1952. Out of respect for her mother, the Queen will not allow any of the articles to be moved even though there have been numerous requests for some of them to be exhibited. A staff member of the Royal Collection has the responsibility of cataloguing this unique assortment which also includes every service medal and foreign decoration His Majesty was awarded.

If during those early years the Queen felt Philip was about to start something that might be a little controversial, she would urge him to nip across the road to sell the idea to Queen Elizabeth. Because if she found out and hated it there would be hell to pay. But the Queen would never put in an appearance herself, shying away from anything that smacked of confrontation. This is not to suggest that the Queen is frightened of her mother; it simply illustrates the consideration she shows towards her, and the older the Queen Mother has become the more concern the Queen has displayed that nothing should upset her.

This is partly why nothing is ever done about the extravagant lifestyle of this oldest royal. I was once invited to Clarence House when Queen Elizabeth was already well into her nineties. She served the most deadly aperitifs with her gin and tonics guaranteed to make anyone's eyes water, but as a hostess she was perfect. She stood for an hour without the slightest sign of tiredness and talked animatedly on a variety of subjects. She was by far the oldest person present, yet we were all wilting long before the time came to leave. It was an exhilarating experience as she effortlessly turned what could have been an ordinary occasion into a spectacular success.

At Clarence House alone there are eighty-three staff to look after Queen Elizabeth's wellbeing. Most of them have been with her for years; the normal retirement age of sixty is ignored here. She dislikes change and, like every other member of the royal family, prefers to see familiar faces around her, so whether it is as footmen and butlers, or higher up the scale as private secretaries and comptrollers, they all remain in their posts. She is not familiar with her servants, who are never allowed to forget for one moment who their employer is, yet they are the most loyal staff. And, like her mother-in-law,

Queen Mary, the Queen Mother has her own network of informers in every royal residence.

She knew all about Camilla Parker Bowles long before Prince Charles came to tell her shortly after his separation from Diana, but she still let him think it came as a complete surprise. She grew up in an age when little was thought about male infidelity among married couples of her class. Wives were expected meekly to accept that their husbands would wander and to be there when they returned. The Queen Mother had anticipated that Diana would be in this mould, having grown up in a similar background. So she was not only amazed but angry at what she felt was Diana's over-reaction to Prince Charles's involvement. As long as Charles and Camilla were discreet, what was the problem? The monarchy had to be protected at all costs, and Diana was rocking the boat. From that moment on, Diana became *persona non grata* with the Queen Mother, who took her grandson's side in the dispute, as she inevitably would with a future sovereign. She is a formidable enemy of anything that threatens to damage the institution. In this she follows Queen Mary, who after the Abdication refused to see her son David for many years.

The Queen Mother has known Camilla for years and knew her parents before her, so she has nothing personal against her. She is non-judgemental about other people's relationships. Her refusal to receive her – which Camilla and Charles fully understand – is again because of the possible damage to the image of the royal family. Charles would not take Camilla to Birkhall if he thought for one moment that doing so would distress the family member he loves most – and who returns his affection in full measure.

The special bond between Queen Elizabeth and Prince Charles has been well documented and has always been accepted by the rest of the family. It was she who first taught him to paint, when he was only seven, and who introduced him to the delights of angling, when she stood alongside him in the icy waters of the River Dee at Balmoral. Because his mother acceded to the throne when he was barely four years old, and duty quickly took the place of maternal sentiment, Charles, even as a child, transferred his feelings to his grandmother. She was only too willing to accept the responsibility, and throughout his life there has never been a time when he did not feel he could turn to her or tell her anything.

This has not caused any feelings of jealousy in the Queen, but it has meant that the closer Charles grew towards his grandmother, the more distant he has become towards his own parents. He once said, 'Ever since I can remember, my grandmother has been the most wonderful example of fun, laughter, warmth, infinite security and, above all else, exquisite taste.'

They share many interests in common, including lifestyles totally at variance with those of any other member of the royal family. As Bill Deedes says, 'The rest of the royal family would like to live in a style that would make them less attackable by the media, but the Queen Mother doesn't care – and why should she?' She also believes Prince Charles's lavish tastes, in furniture, food, pastimes and exotic holidays, need no explanation or justification, as they reflect perfectly her own impeccable values when it comes to gracious living. The Queen and Prince Philip might have private reservations about their eldest son's way of life; the Queen Mother has no doubts and sees no reason to criticize. His apartments in St James's Palace are across the courtyard from Clarence House, so if he wants to pop in and see her, which he does on almost a daily basis, his valet will telephone his opposite number in the Queen Mother's household to warn her and Charles will simply walk over. Which is something he has never been able to do with his own mother at Buckingham Palace or Windsor Castle.

The Queen Mother's influence extends throughout the family. None of them would dream of taking a serious decision without consulting her, and only the Princess Royal has ever been heard to hint that she is not always the soft-hearted romantic she is usually portrayed. That candyfloss exterior conceals an inner steeliness. Or, as Lady Mountbatten has said, 'the iron fist in the velvet glove'. A determined woman who likes her own way, she has various, devious means of getting it. Some of the people she has openly admired give a clue to her own feelings and opinions. Field Marshal Montgomery, the Second World War victor of Alamein noted for his ruthless ambition, was a great hero, whose photographs are displayed prominently in several places at Clarence House; and Queen Elizabeth has made no secret of her admiration for Margaret Thatcher and the way she governed Britain, brooking no interference from either colleagues or opposition – a characteristic that might equally be applied to herself. She is not afraid to voice her opinions on any subject and, unlike her elder daughter, is not subject to the restrictions brought about by being sovereign. Even as consort to King George VI, she let it be known that she regretted the end of Britain's rule in India, when constitutionally he was forbidden to comment.

She spends every weekend at Royal Lodge, Windsor, usually in the company of Princess Margaret, but occasionally with a small party of guests – invariably male – whom she calls 'my geriatrics' but all of whom are a couple of decades younger than herself. The group included octogenarians such as the late Robert Runcie and Lord (Peter) Carrington, and although they no longer roll back the carpet and dance to records, they still listen to some of the old favourites, hers being 'A Nightingale Sang in Berkeley Square'. Then they sit and enjoy a couple of episodes of *Fawlty Towers, Morse* or *Dad's Army*. On Sunday mornings after church, the Queen always joins her mother and sister for pre-lunch drinks, but never stays for the meal. Nor does the Queen Mother go up to the Castle, preferring to eat in her own house and leaving her elder daughter to the privacy of a quiet lunch with her husband.

The Queen Mother knows her strengths and works to them. She has perfected the art of being the world's favourite grand-mother – and great-grandmother. But none of this has come about by accident. It is a combination of determination, skill and an innate knowledge of what 'they' want from her. She knows her public better than any politician and she gives what it demands. She has achieved a unique place in the nation's affections: something that no other member of her family – including the Queen – will ever do to quite the same extent.

A London taxi driver dropping off a guest at Clarence House remarked, when he found out who his passenger was going to see, 'She's a great old girl.' He might also have added, 'And a tough old bird.'

CHAPTER TWELVE

A Woman of Faith

*'Do you think Mrs Thatcher is a
religious woman?'*
THE QUEEN

Early in 1942, a young, rather nervous ensign presented himself at the officers' mess at Codford B Camp on Salisbury
Plain. Lieutenant R. A. K. Runcie had arrived straight from
the Royal Military College at Sandhurst to join the Third
Battalion, Scots Guards.

In June 1944, shortly after D-Day, his battalion crossed
into France and fought their way to Germany, where he would
distinguish himself as a tank commander, winning the Military
Cross before the end of the Second World War. Among his
contemporaries were Major Willie Whitelaw, later to become
Leader of the House of Lords in the Thatcher Government,
Major Sir Charles Maclean, who would go on to become
Chief Scout and eventually Lord Chamberlain of the Royal
Household, and Major Sir Michael Fitzalan Howard, who for
some years was the Queen's Gold Stick in Waiting.

Robert Runcie, though, would eventually outrank them
all when he was appointed the Most Reverend and Right

Honourable Lord Archbishop of Canterbury, residing in Lambeth Palace and only one step behind the Queen herself, Prince Philip and the Princes of the Blood Royal in the order of precedence in England.

Lord Runcie was retired and living back in St Albans, where he was also once bishop, when I spoke to him a few weeks before his death in July 2000. He recalled his first meeting with the Queen: 'The first time was during the war when she was still Princess Elizabeth, but that was very briefly. It was in 1947 that I actually met her properly and had a face-to-face conversation. I was President of the Junior Common Room at Brasenose College, Oxford, when she came to lunch, and it was my job to introduce her to one or two undergraduates. She was obviously enjoying meeting people of roughly her own age, but you could sense even then that at the same time she was sizing us up. None of us knew quite how to react to her but then – we were outside at the time – she dropped her spoon in the mud. I picked it up and cleaned it on my handkerchief and it broke the ice.'

It was to be some years before they met again, by which time the Princess had become Queen and the former Guards officer had been ordained and risen swiftly through the Church's ranks. 'I was due to be consecrated Bishop of St Alban's [in 1970] and there is a ceremony where you have to do homage and the Queen places her hands over yours while you swear allegiance. It's quite long and complicated with the Home Secretary playing a prominent part. Jim Callaghan was then Home Secretary, but he had been called away to deal with an important matter in Northern Ireland, so the Welsh Secretary, George Thomas [later Viscount Tonypandy] stood in for him. He had never done anything like this before and was absolutely overcome with the thrill. As we waited to start he whispered to me, "If only my Mam knew I was introducing a Bishop to Her Majesty!" George made a meal of his part, loving every minute, and all his brilliant Welsh Methodist oratory came out. As a result, the ceremony went on twice as long as usual, but it was rather moving, and when I stood up the Queen looked at me and said, "He did very well, didn't he?" George was delighted.'

From that moment, Lord Runcie would have occasion to meet the Queen from time to time, but it was when he became Primate of All England in 1980 – a position he would hold for eleven years – that his closest association with her began. As Archbishop of Canterbury, Lord Runcie was a Great Officer of State and a Privy Counsellor. He was expected to attend every State Visit, and during his period of office he baptized both Prince William and Prince Henry of Wales. On his retirement in 1991 Her Majesty conferred on him her personal Order of Chivalry, the Royal Victorian Chain.

There is a common misconception among those who come to work for the Queen that any relationship with her depends on rank. They are very quickly disabused of such ideas. It doesn't matter to her if you are a duke or a dustman; her attitude rarely changes. Lord Runcie discovered this early in his career as Archbishop of Canterbury. 'It is very true and it takes a little time to get used to it. I remember a senior courtier – Philip Moore, the Queen's private secretary – saying to me, "You will enjoy a good relationship with the sovereign and the rest of the royal family, if you don't try to rush things." I took it to mean there was a relationship that mingled the official and the personal but if you got it wrong you would never understand its value. There were one or two occasions when there was a breakthrough. I remember at the time of Prince Charles's wedding, and later on the baptism of the children, there was conversation with the Queen about the character of the service and the hymns which would be sung and so on. I particularly remember at the time of the christening of Prince William she asked me if it was possible to have a mixture of the old service and the new. I replied, "Well, strictly speaking . . ." She then said, "Oh, I wouldn't want any special privileges."'

Access to the Queen is what counts in the power stakes at Court. The private secretary controls her diary, and even the Lord Chamberlain, titular Head of the Household, is obliged to ask for an appointment. Lord Runcie did not have regular audiences of the Queen, but he could get to see her if he had good reason. 'There was one occasion when I felt the Church was being misrepresented, and I said to Bill Heseltine [Sir William Heseltine, private secretary from 1986 to 1990] that it would be nice to have a word with the Queen about these matters. He said, "Well, you're Archbishop of Canterbury, you should have an audience," so it was arranged and I went to see the Queen who was very gracious and quite formal. This wasn't a social occasion but a business meeting brought about because of the Church's concern for the casualties of perfectly understandable but rather fierce Thatcherite policies. When we had finished our discussion I was rather surprised when she asked me, "Do you think Mrs Thatcher is a religious woman?" It was a very penetrating question asked in a very inconsequential manner. I replied: "Well, it depends what you mean by religion. I think she has a very high moral sense and I know she reads the Bible, so she does qualify." What was so typical of the Queen, though, was the fact that she could ask such a fundamental question but she never once revealed what she thought. It was absolutely characteristic of her to encourage you but seldom to let you know her own opinions. On occasions like the Falklands conflict [of 1982] or that dreadful *Marchioness* disaster in the Thames [on 20 August 1989; 51 people were killed], one would preach a sermon and Prince Philip would be inclined to say something like, "I don't know how you think of the right words – they're wonderful," whereas the most the Queen would say was, "I'm sure that will be an encouragement to a lot of people." You still didn't know what she really thought.'

The Queen is considered to be a traditionalist in most things: her attitude to family life, her dress, her manners and choice of companions. But the form of worship she prefers is not always the one most commonly associated with royalty. 'Where religion is concerned she accepts the traditional simplicities of the church rather than its more colourful ceremonies as a basis for her own devotion. I would think that she was more comfortable with the simple rituals of the Church of Scotland than with the more flamboyant Anglo-Catholic worship in London. On the other hand she has her own mind about what is appropriate. She once told me that she had been invited to a festival by a charismatic but extraordinarily unconventional High Churchman who was a vicar in Deptford in London. Every ethnic group was represented, Pearly Kings and Queens attended along with local MPs and media celebrities. Afterwards she said to me: "It's not my sort of religion, but my goodness he's in touch with the people and I felt we ought to support it." So she was obviously impressed even if it wasn't exactly to her own taste. She is a devout Christian and a regular worshipper who is also very private and reticent about the practice of personal religion. But I have been sitting alongside her when she is praying and you can feel her true sense of devotion. She also remembers sermons and can pick up a point after a year's interval. No mean achievement considering how many she must hear.'

While one cannot state positively that all the royal family are religious, church is certainly an integral part of their lives. They all attend regularly, with the Queen Mother and Princess Margaret joining the Queen for communion most Sundays, while Prince Philip, who has been known to glare at preachers if he thinks their sermons are too long, is perhaps not always regarded as the most devout of men. His practical interest in religious affairs can be dated to 1966 when he helped establish St George's College at Windsor as a forum for serious religious discussion. He has also conducted lengthy correspondence with two Deans of Windsor: the Right Rev. Robin Woods in the sixties and the Right Rev. Michael Mann twenty years later, and he has published his own thoughts and their opinions about Christianity in relation to science and morality.

Prince Charles is arguably the most deeply committed of them all. He insists on being able to worship wherever he is and never goes to bed without first saying his prayers. Charles also has a strong conviction that a life without God is a life wasted; and even though he is a staunch supporter of the established Church of England, he has, many times, expressed views giving sympathy to other religions, including Roman Catholicism, Buddhism and the Jewish faith. His personal beliefs mean that the taking of communion is a truly holy sacrament, and while he has suffered hours of indecision about many things, his religion is not one of them. He has never wavered in his belief in a life after death and has spent long evenings discussing this with members of the clergy. The idea of Heaven and Hell doesn't frighten him at all; in fact a number of his closest friends say he has an insatiable curiosity about what comes next. Speaking at a Macmillan Fund anniversary, he said, 'death can be seen as a doorway to renewed life'.

Prince Charles's strong religious certainties are mirrored by his fascination for old churches – of any denomination. Near his Gloucestershire home, Highgrove, he divides his Sunday mornings between several parish churches – except the main one nearest to him at Tetbury, which he has refused to enter after the vicar, the Rev. John Hawthorne, was quoted in the national press condemning the prince for his relationship with Camilla Parker Bowles. Royalty does not forgive easily.

In the second half of the twentieth century church attendances fell to their lowest ever level with membership of non-Christian faiths challenging the established Church. At the same time, respect for the monarchy as an institution fell to an alarming level. 'I think they both – the Church and the Monarchy – suffer from a diminution of the sense of the sacred, and I believe that sense is part of our humanity and we are impoverished without it,' explains Lord Runcie. 'Many people claim that what you need to get through life today is a sense of humour and I wouldn't argue with that, it gives you a sense of proportion. But a sense of humour without a sense of the sacred trivializes life; just in the way that a sense of the sacred without a sense of humour can become leaden. We need to retain a sense of reverence for some of the mysteries of life which have appertained to religious practice and also to the hereditary principle of a monarchy. What we have to distinguish is the difference between deference and reverence. Reverence has a wholesome effect on your humility while deference has an unwholesome effect on your independence as a human being.'

The Queen has often been accused – mostly by people who have never met her – of not having much of a sense of humour. Lord Runcie disagreed. 'For instance, I recently told her that Peter Carrington was saying to me that he found Woodrow Wyatt difficult to take and was certainly not going to buy his book [Volume I of *The Journals of Woodrow Wyatt*, published posthumously in 1998]. However, on finding himself in a bookshop he couldn't resist looking in the index for his own name. Finding the page, which described how Wyatt had been at a party and "Peter Carrington was there looking grey and wizened and much older – I don't think he will last very long," Peter said, "I felt a curious sense of triumph about this." The story delighted her because it was about someone whom she regarded as an amusing friend; but if you tried pushing a joke too far, that would be very unpopular. However highly placed you were you wouldn't get away with it.'

After half a century on the throne, what did Lord Runcie consider to be the Queen's greatest strength? 'I think consistency and stability. It is remarkable that she has given to her people a sense of consistency and stability when there has been such constitutional turmoil and such turbulence in people's behaviour patterns. We have become such a consumer-oriented society, where words like "duty", "loyalty" and "public service" have been relegated to school speech days and things like that. She is able to make the commonplace true, because those words have a true meaning for her and she has lived by them so consistently and as such has commanded such deep respect from people from all walks of life and across the generations.'

CHAPTER THIRTEEN

Hostess to the World

'The State Visit to Britain is the highlight of
any Presidential term of office.'
RONALD REAGAN, US PRESIDENT 1980–1988

On a chilly February evening, a cavalcade of cars is converging on Buckingham Palace. It is directed towards the inner quadrangle where a squad of police officers, equipped with long-handled mirrors, search beneath the vehicles to make sure no explosive devices have been attached. The occupants then cross the gravelled courtyard to the Grand Entrance where, after showing their invitations – for these are guests of the Queen – they are guided towards the Bow Room at the rear of the Marble Hall, which has been converted into a temporary cloakroom. Then Palace officials gently urge them up the Grand Staircase, where they congregate in the Picture Gallery. Strangely, they do not appear to be in the least bit interested in the pictures, preferring to look around to see who else is there.

There are three hundred of them altogether and they have been invited to this reception to meet the Queen and the Duke of Edinburgh because of their special achievements in

182

industry, exports and technology. All are successful business-men and women, who are, nevertheless, still slightly apprehensive about meeting their sovereign and her consort face to face. Meanwhile, in the Royal Closet – which isn't a cupboard, but a comfortable sitting room, rarely seen by visitors and containing the finest mantelpiece in the Palace and a small collection of paintings assembled by Prince Albert – a royal tableau is being set up. In this smallest State Room hidden just behind the White Drawing Room the family are having a private drinks party before the official part of the evening begins. The Queen has a gin and tonic, Prince Philip sticks to whisky. The drinks are not too large; just nice little 'stiffeners'.

Thirty seconds before six o'clock, the large ornate looking-glass in the upper left-hand corner of the White Drawing Room swings open to reveal the Queen, Prince Philip and the rest of the royal party standing there. She is wearing a knee-length print dress in muted tones of blue and white, he is in a single-breasted, dark grey suit. He dislikes double-breasted suits. They walk into the White Drawing Room and stand together in front of the fireplace. The supporting cast of the Duke of Kent, Princess Alexandra and her husband, Sir Angus Ogilvy, relying heavily on the aid of a walking stick, move quickly towards the other State Apartments. They are not in the official presentation party, but will be playing bit parts later on. The whole show is brilliantly choreographed; everyone knows what they have to do and their place on stage.

Standing alongside the Queen is the Master of the House-hold, Major General Sir Simon Cooper – he retired in August 2000 – whose staff have marshalled the guests into a long line. As each approaches, Sir Simon is handed a card bearing the name of the guest and the company he or she represents. He then tells Her Majesty the name of the person she is about to meet. So begins the ritual of the royal handshake.

Every guest receives the same smile and greeting as they give either a neck bow or a little bob. The Queen never stops smiling. Prince Philip has mastered the knack of shaking hands while at the same time gently manoeuvring the recipient out of the way – without in any way giving this impression or causing any offence. He has a friendly word with nearly all the guests, particularly the younger females. There are two men in kilts and they are given a few seconds longer as Prince Philip chats about the tartan. Anything out of the ordinary gives him an opportunity to vary the mind-boggling boredom of the occasion. Meanwhile members of the royal household are standing nearby to guide discreetly those who seem a little overawed towards the other rooms, where liveried footmen are waiting with silver trays of drinks and canapes. White wine, soft drinks and mineral water only. No spirits, beer or red wine.

Once the handshaking is over – and every one of the three hundred guests is presented – the Queen walks slowly – she never hurries – into the Music Room next door, where she and Prince Philip split up, each one taking a different side. It's obvious they have done this many times before as there is no hesitation. Sir Simon Cooper is always one step ahead of the Queen, quietly shepherding the waiting guests into groups of three or four, and finding out from them who they are and what they do. The Queen appears to have an uncanny instinct for knowing just how long to remain with each group, before catching, out of the corner of her eye, Sir Simon's glance, and moving on. The whole evening is very informal and a far cry from receptions held even ten years before, when the idea of the Queen mingling in this way would have been unthinkable. So too would have been an evening reception where hosts and guests wore simply daywear, not even black tie or cocktail dresses. A courtier remarks on the way Her Majesty chats so easily with her guests. The previous week, during a State Visit by Queen Margrethe of Denmark in February 2000, a similar function was held with some forty or so young Danish students as guests. Queen Margrethe had been plainly unused to such informality, which is ironic when the so-called 'bicycling Monarchy' of her country is so often used as an example of royal democracy. In fact, she found the evening a strain and was unable to sustain the conversations for more than a few minutes.

There is no security around the Queen; two ladies-in-waiting and an equerry are nearby talking among themselves, but no policemen. And although the cars were searched as they entered the Palace, none of the guests was subjected to the slightest scrutiny.

In the Blue Drawing Room next door to the Music Room, a lot of noisy laughter is coming from one corner. The Duke of York has suddenly appeared and is surrounded by a crowd of young people all apparently amused at something he's said. At the other end of the room the Duke of Kent is 'networking' in his own quiet way. He is a very popular member of the royal family and always ready to support the Queen at these functions when her own children are abroad or otherwise engaged.

In the Picture Gallery, the Duke of Edinburgh has commandeered the upper end to hold court and it is hard to believe that he is a man approaching eighty. Still pencil slim, if slightly stooped, but remaining elegant and tanned, and this evening in sparkling form, as is Princess Alexandra, who seems to captivate her audience standing near one of the fireplaces. Her husband, Sir Angus Ogilvy, declines to sit down, even though he is obviously in some discomfort and leaning on his stick for support.

The reception lasts for two hours and the Queen gives no sign of fatigue throughout the evening. Suddenly, all the royals disappear. There's no mass exodus; they're just not there any more. Some of the guests try to linger as long as they can, but the staff are used to this sort of thing and have a routine for getting the hangers-on to go home. They simply stop serving drinks and also disappear.

For most of the guests it has been a once in a lifetime

experience; something they will be able to dine out on for weeks; for the Queen it is a duty she has carried out for half a century. Only this same week she held a similar reception for six hundred at the Palace – but no handshaking on that occasion. 'The Firm' handle this little party with the practised ease of true professionals and their experience shows. The Queen manages to make it all seem as if she really is enjoying herself. As the last of the guests leave, one of them remarks, 'I make machines for a living, they shake hands. It's their job.' Not everyone can make their job seem such a genuine pleasure.

Since she came to the throne in 1952, Elizabeth II has offered hospitality to hundreds of thousands of men and women from all over the world. Princes and presidents, potentates and prime ministers have all been welcomed to her homes at Buckingham Palace, Windsor Castle, Balmoral and Sandringham in the last fifty years. A few, very few, are personal friends who are asked to strictly private affairs, while the vast majority come because they, and she, are acting in their official capacity as representatives of their country. In any one year over 40,000 men and women are guests of the Queen at Buckingham Palace, Windsor Castle and the Palace of Holyroodhouse.

As with many royal customs practised today, much of the entertaining goes back to previous reigns. Queen Victoria started a tradition by instituting 'Dine and Sleep'. In theory it was an excellent idea: a way in which the sovereign could meet people with whom she would not normally come in contact. In practice, it simply meant that 'suitable' men and women, all from the highest levels of society, and all of whom had been thoroughly vetted beforehand, were asked to spend an evening in the company of Her Majesty. These were stilted and uncomfortable occasions when nobody dared utter a word unless answering a question from the Queen, and from which she learned absolutely nothing. She would also refuse to have anyone sitting next to her who was not royal and she spoke mostly to fellow royalty during the evening.

Elizabeth II has continued the tradition but these days the guest list is a much more eclectic selection. Film producers, actors, writers, scholars, the occasional politician (but never a member of the Government), teachers, prison governors, university professors, ambassadors, bankers and shopkeepers (or at least the managing directors of some of the leading chains), rub shoulders with soldiers, ship's captains and distinguished journalists and television producers. It is all designed to enable the Queen and Prince Philip to meet informally people who have made a success of their chosen career in a variety of professions.

The invitations are sent out by the Master of the Household four weeks before the intended date. In this way, if someone finds they are unable to accept, a suitable replacement can be found. There is usually a mix of six married couples and four single men and women, and the invitations specify that 'dinner jackets will be worn'.

'Dine and Sleep' nights are held three or four times a year, usually during the period when the Court is sitting at Windsor during April. The Queen does not hold these affairs at Buckingham Palace. Guests are asked to arrive between 6.30 and 7 p.m., when they are met by a member of the household and conducted to their rooms. A valet and housemaid are assigned to help them unpack and to provide a clothes-pressing and shoe-cleaning service, for which a £20 note discreetly left on the dressing table the next morning is the usual thanks.

The first time guests meet their royal hostess is when they gather in the Green Drawing Room for drinks. Designed by Wyatville, the Green Drawing Room at Windsor is an ornate room with acres of gilt decorations which were brought from Carlton House by George IV. He also brought some of his favourite paintings. The main colour scheme is reflected by the east gardens of the castle, opening out on to the lawns. The Queen has been provided with a complete brief on each of her guests; and if other members of the royal family are present – there are usually two or three to help out – they mingle easily, chatting and putting everybody at their ease. Dinner is served at 8.30. Her Majesty leads the way and is always escorted by the senior male guest. His wife, if he has one, follows with the Duke of Edinburgh. The rest then troop in; there is no particular order of precedence. Windsor Castle is not the warmest house in the land and the dining room, in the north-east corner, is said to be its coldest spot. But, not surprisingly, no one has ever heard a word of complaint. Nor are many disparaging remarks made about the food. The guests are here, as the Queen herself was once reported to have said, not 'to taste the food, but to eat off gold plate'. They don't actually get gold plate at these parties. The meals are served on magnificent Sèvres porcelain, but the point is well made, and Her Majesty is well aware of the impression that dining in one of her palaces or castles can make.

The seating plan has been worked out by the Queen and the Master of the Household so that every guest is within talking distance of a member of the royal family or the house-hold, who make up the numbers. Nobody has to wait to be asked before offering an opinion or comment, for the Queen encourages free discussion. When King George VI held these evenings, he ordered a string quartet made up of musicians from the Household Brigade to play throughout the meal. The Queen felt this was a distraction and the music was can-celled.

It is when the meal is over that the really interesting part of the evening begins. The Queen takes all her guests on a personally conducted tour of some of the treasures stored in the Castle. She has talked with the Royal Librarian about the particular interests of her guests and each one is shown something unique. When the author and film director Bryan

Forbes and his wife, the actress Nanette Newman, were at Windsor for dinner, joining other guests including Dennis and Margaret Thatcher and the Bishop of London, they were shown some rare first editions and also some of the scripts from famous plays that had been retained from the days when the Lord Chamberlain was the official censor. The Queen had obviously done her homework and displayed an in-depth knowledge of a subject one would not immediately identify with her.

Bryan Forbes and Nanette Newman are not guests who are invited only once, however, as he explained: 'On other occasions, stemming from our long friendship with HRH the Princess Margaret, I have been allowed the freedom of the library, to browse at leisure, and on one notable occasion HM the Queen invited us to take dinner with the entire family at Windsor on Boxing Day. So, we have been very spoilt.'

The evening ends with a final drink in the drawing-room, and once Her Majesty and Prince Philip have retired – usually around midnight, with protocol demanding that no one leaves before they do – the guests can stay as long as they like. Members of the household remain to entertain them, showing no signs of tiredness or giving any hint that it is time to go to bed.

The guests will have made their farewells to their royal hostess as that is the last they will see of her. Breakfast is served in their rooms and they are encouraged to leave before lunch. For them, it has been a once in a lifetime experience; for the Queen, just another duty which she has made appear as spontaneous and enjoyable as if she were doing it for the first time – but which she will be repeating two or three times in the coming weeks.

When Neil Kinnock was Leader of the Opposition, he and his wife, at that time teaching in a London school, were invited. He recalls the occasion: 'I was coming from the Commons and Glenys was coming straight from school. So, as you would expect from somebody with her background, she insisted on going home first and having a bath – thereby turning up at Windsor in a great state of respectability – only to be asked minutes after we arrived, if she would like to have a bath. Glenys replied, "No thank you very much, you don't think I would come to Windsor Castle without having a bath first, do you?" We were given a wonderful suite of rooms and some very nice people to look after us. Nobody had given us any guidance about what to expect or what was expected of us, which would have been rather patronizing anyway, I suppose. The assumption was that you knew what you were supposed to do in any case. This could be a bit of a disadvantage in a sense, because there are some conventions with which a lot of people might be unfamiliar, and if you aren't informed about them you could drop a clanger. I was very fortunate, though, in having a friend in the House of Lords, Baroness Pat Llewellyn Davies, who in the Labour Government had been Chief Whip, which meant she was also a part-time member of the royal household as Captain of the Honourable Corps of Gentlemen at Arms. Anyway, Pat came to see me after I'd been Leader for a couple of weeks and said, "Listen, there are a few things it would be just as well for you and Glenys to know, so that you never embarrass yourselves or expose yourselves to the kind of sneer you might get from newspaper diaries and so on." One thing we remembered – and it was just as well – was that women never wear black at Court.'

The reason is that Queen Victoria always wore black after the death of Prince Albert, and subsequent sovereigns have preferred black not to be worn out of respect for her memory. 'Glenys was very glad to know that', Neil Kinnock continued, 'because automatically when you want to look smart and formal, the inclination is to put on the little black dress. It wouldn't matter a damn to the Queen if somebody turned up in a black dress, but that is the sort of story that would have done the rounds and eventually turned up in one of the gossip columns. So it was as well we had little safeguards like that, and never had any problems either on that occasion or at other times when we met the Queen. The other thing that was very enjoyable was that when the party split up into small groups to be shown around the Castle, I found the Queen had taken it upon herself to be my personal guide. Of course, it's a pretty distinguished museum in its own right and she knows a heck of a lot about it as you would expect.'

The Duke of Edinburgh is always on hand on these Dine and Sleep occasions, helping his wife with their guests and taking his share of the host's responsibilities. 'He was fine because I've always been able to get on with him even though I had told many jokes at his expense. He liked to chat about rugby and there was never any conversational problem with him. He has never struck me as being self-conscious about his position, and he loves an argument, as I do. We disagreed on a number of topics, but he never seemed to me to be put out by this.'

At Buckingham Palace alone the Queen holds more than eighty functions every year. Some are informal luncheons with just eight or nine specially selected guests; others range up to the three annual Garden Parties (plus another at the Palace of Holyroodhouse in Edinburgh) to which some 9,000 people from all walks of life and every level of society are asked. In between are occasions such as the annual Diplomatic Reception held at Buckingham Palace every November, when 1,200 members of the Diplomatic Corps in London join Her Majesty in the State Ballroom for cocktails at nine o'clock in the evening and depart promptly at midnight.

Then there is the yearly house party at Windsor every June during Royal Ascot Week, the Queen's Christmas party, also at Windsor, just for the family, when some forty-odd relatives gather for the festivities, and a whole series of official lunches and dinners throughout the year. Even on holiday in Scotland,

191

the entertaining does not let up. The Prime Minister is invited for a weekend, which includes a lot of constitutional discussions and also allows time for relaxing. And the Queen will give a Ghillies' Ball for all the staff who work on her Scottish estates. It is held with as much formality as any state function south of the border. It is in Scotland, though, that the royal family tends to let down its collective hair. A former Lord Chamberlain revealed to me that the first time he attended a dinner party at Balmoral, he suddenly felt a blow on his shoulder and to his amazement found he had been hit by a bread roll. Looking up he discovered that he was being watched by Princess Anne, with a twinkle in her eye. Next, Prince Charles joined in and soon bread rolls were being hurled at practically everyone – with one notable exception. The Queen, sitting at the head of the table, chatting to her nearest dining companion, appeared oblivious of the throwing match – and it was noticed that no bread roll ever went anywhere near her. Informality obviously goes only so far.

While Prince Philip can and does say outrageous things which are often quoted, the Queen must never be placed in a position where anything she has said could be quoted to her embarrassment. On one occasion, she was present at a private dinner party where the conversation was flowing a little more than usual and Her Majesty made a flippant but innocuous remark about someone well known. Nobody thought any more about it until the following morning, when a lady-in-waiting telephoned each of the guests to remind them of the discretion that was demanded and also, without coming out and actually saying it, letting them know that should the remark appear in a newspaper and the offender be identified, banishment from Court would immediately and irrevocably follow. Not a word emerged.

There is no doubt that the Queen is truly hostess to the world; a generous and enthusiastic participant in the never-ending round of diplomatic and political receptions, dinners, luncheons and cocktail parties. For her it's all part of being the centre of society, the focal point of the nation's hospitality. She considers her role as national hostess to be almost as important as any other of her functions as Head of State, and has developed an unequalled sense of social assurance over five decades of top level entertainment.

The main difference between the Queen's role in these matters and that of, say, her father, King George VI, is that a male sovereign would not need to involve himself in the day-to-day detail of social events. He would leave that to his consort. But Prince Philip is not the sort of man who would accept such delegation; neither would the Queen dream of asking him to do so. She does, however, consult him on practically every aspect. But because the monarch happens to be a woman she also has to assume the responsibilities of the 'lady of the house'. As it happens Her Majesty has never tried to shirk this side of her job, and indeed manages to make it appear to be something she thoroughly enjoys.

Every year since she came to the throne, the Queen has invited two heads of state to stay at either Buckingham Palace or Windsor Castle. The State Visits are an integral part of the royal year, and each visiting guest is treated in an identical fashion as to the protocol, length of stay and accommodation. It does not matter if the country of which the visitor is head of state is the most powerful in the world, or the tiniest and poorest, the treatment is exactly the same and the arrangements are worked out in precisely the same amount of detail, so there is no chance of any country taking offence at a possible slight.

At Buckingham Palace all heads of state are given the Belgian Suite, which is situated on the ground floor at the rear of the Palace and opens through French windows on to the south-west terrace of the Palace gardens. Named after King Leopold I of the Belgians, Queen Victoria's uncle, who would not stay anywhere else, the suite also has more recent connections with the present royal family. When the Queen first came to the throne in 1952, on the death of her father, she and the Duke of Edinburgh occupied it until arrangements had been completed for the Queen Mother to move into Clarence House. And both the Duke of York and his younger brother Prince Edward were born there.

The three principal rooms of the Belgian Suite are furnished in a style which gives the visiting heads of state an idea of how royalty lived in previous reigns and tells a little of the history of the British royal family over the past two hundred years. In the main room, the Eighteenth Century Room, the predominant colour is yellow. The furniture is a mixture of English and French with sofas and chairs upholstered in silk to match the yellow curtains. Among the royal portraits are three-quarter-length paintings of King George III and Queen Charlotte, while works by Canaletto stand alongside one of Gainsborough's most famous paintings, that of Diana and Actaeon.

Visiting heads of state sleep in the blue Orleans Bedroom where they are reminded of the ancestry of their hostess as the room contains no less than three pictures of Queen Victoria. There are two beds, each one canopied, and some of the furniture was designed by a refugee from the French revolution.

The third, and smallest, of the main rooms, is the Spanish Room, intended to be used as a dressing room but also occasionally brought into use if required as an extra bedroom. The two most fascinating pictures here are both of Napoleon Bonaparte: one showing him crossing the Alps, the other during his final years of captivity on the island of St Helena.

Although the Master of the Household makes all the arrangements when an important guest is expected, the Queen involves herself in the details. She finds out the likes and dislikes of her visitors and goes to considerable lengths to make sure they are made as comfortable as possible. As many come from countries with cultures vastly different from her own, she tries to anticipate their particular preferences, both in terms of diet and also the style in which they like to live. She always attaches her own personal equerry to the visiting suite to act as liaison between the two households and iron out any possible difficulties. Most visiting heads of state are experienced travellers and know what to expect, but some, particularly from the Middle or Far East, or certain parts of Africa, arrive with very large entourages who resist all efforts to separate them from their leader.

Generally speaking, there are few problems that cannot be solved with the famous Palace diplomacy and tact, but there have been occasions when the Master of the Household has had to put his foot down. One such was when a Middle Eastern potentate brought his own chef who insisted that all his master's food had to be cooked on an open fire – on the floor of the suite. Eventually a compromise was reached when a section of the stone-flagged kitchen was allocated to the visitor – with a fireman standing by.

Housemaids and footmen at the Palace have become used to the unusual, and don't even blink at the sight of a servant lying across the doorway of the Belgian Suite in the early hours of the morning. It's fairly commonplace for some foreign monarchs and princes to order such precautions and the Queen takes it all in her stride, behaving as if these customs are an everyday occurrence in her home.

The highlight of any state visit is the State Banquet, usually given in the Ballroom at Buckingham Palace, less often in St George's Hall at Windsor. It is without doubt a theatrical production with the Queen the star and the visiting head of state her leading man. Every one follows an identical pattern, refined into the smoothest operation over many years. Again it is the master of the Household who organizes the event, and even though he has performed the same task scores of times, great attention to detail is lavished on every one.

Planning starts up to a year before: who is to be invited, where they sit and what will they all eat.

Once the menu has been agreed a copy is sent to No. 10 Downing Street and the Lord Mayor of London's office, so that they will not duplicate the meal when it is their turn to entertain the visitor. A copy is also despatched to the head of state's ambassador, to make sure there have been no dietary errors.

Guests – a total of 170 at Buckingham Palace or 162 at Windsor Castle – are given the run of the State Apartments while they wait for their hostess to appear. Aperitifs are offered, gin and tonic and martini being the most popular. But the Palace wine steward is prepared for most unusual requests. He draws the line at the most complicated, exotic cocktails, explaining that time does not allow him to make these.

The Queen gets ready in her first floor bedroom helped by her dresser. She invariably wears any decoration that might have been given her by the visiting head of state. In his nearby dressing room, the Duke of Edinburgh is in full Court Dress: tail coat, knee breeches and black silk stockings, and wearing the Order of the Garter. Once ready, he goes to the Belgian Suite to collect the guest of honour, and the party moves into the Royal Closet, with its crimson damask walls and ornate, but non-working, fireplace. There they have their own pre-dinner drinks, gin and tonic for the Queen, dry sherry for the Duke and a glass of vintage champagne for Queen Elizabeth the Queen Mother.

Meanwhile, in the White Drawing Room, many of the most important guests are waiting. At a signal from the Queen, a footman presses a button and a complete section of the mirrored wall swings back. Several unwary guests, inspecting themselves in the looking glass, have found themselves suddenly confronted by almost the entire royal family and their distinguished guests – to their secret amusement, and their own acute embarrassment.

While the official photographs are taken the guests move into the Ballroom where dinner will be served. Then a Royal Procession is formed, usually restricted to twenty-eight. It is preceded by the two most senior members of the royal household, the Lord Steward and the Lord Chamberlain, who have the tricky task of walking backwards, for tradition has it that they never turn their backs on the sovereign. They follow the pattern of the carpet to make sure they don't veer away from a straight line. It usually works but on occasion they have been brought back into line by a gentle motion of the Queen's eyes or whispered enjoinder to 'slow down; this isn't a race'. It all adds to the sense of occasion and first-time guests are fascinated by the majesty of the ceremonial.

On an evening such as this extra staff are recruited to supplement the Palace's permanent crew. Footmen have to be five feet nine inches tall with a thirty-six inch chest (because they have to fit the existing livery, some of which dates back to the reign of Edward VII), while members of the Fulham Road branch of the British Legion help out with the washing up. All the dishes are washed by hand in wooden sinks to prevent any breakages. Automatic dishwashers were tried out but discarded as 'unreliable'.

It is a well known and often repeated fact that at State Banquets a set of 'traffic lights' is used to control the service of the meal. However, it is not true that the Queen herself operates these lights. The Palace Steward, the senior domestic servant, stands immediately behind Her Majesty's chair and signals for the lights to be worked. There are two sets, each concealed within elaborate flower arrangements in corners of the Ballroom. One is amber, which means the servers – seventy-six of them at each meal – should take their places; then, when the green light shows, they start serving the food or clearing the plates after each course.

It sounds rather complicated but actually works very well and rarely are any mistakes made. More than 800 English cut crystal glasses grace the horseshoe-shaped table: five for each person: sherry, white wine, red wine, champagne and water, with port and liqueur glasses added at the end of the meal. And guests do not have to ask anyone to pass the salt either; there is a cruet set at every place. The distance between each place setting is measured with a ruler and each guest is given a booklet measuring 4 × 6 inches containing everything about the banquet: who is in the Royal Procession, details of the menu and wine list, the complete programme of music played in the minstrels gallery, plus the name of every guest and the seating plan. Throughout the evening there will be many surreptitious glances to see who is sitting where and next to whom. The household also have the plans but they have memorized them, so they can answer any question about the company without checking.

Members of the royal household are placed at strategic points to make sure conversation flows easily. When the late Lord 'Chips' Maclean was Lord Chamberlain he revealed that the ladies-in-waiting used to beg him not to seat them next to a former Prime Minister, who was said to be lacking in basic conversation skills. But another former Prime Minister, James Callaghan (now Lord Callaghan of Cardiff), is highly sought after as one of the most congenial dinner companions.

Speeches at these functions are restricted to the Queen and her chief guest and never last longer than nine minutes. Her Majesty knows better than most how fidgety people can get if an after-dinner speech goes on too long, and Prince Philip has been known to make his feelings all too clear if there is too much talk.

State visits vary greatly in both popularity at home and usefulness. The visit by President Heuss of Germany early in the Queen's reign, in October 1958, was the first by a German head of state since before the war. It was considered successful in helping to heal old wounds – in which Philip's German affiliations and command of the language helped. The most disastrous was probably that of Emperor Hirohito of Japan in October 1969. Many former prisoners of war lined the processional routes and turned their backs as the royal carriage passed. Earl Mountbatten – who had accepted the surrender of the Japanese at Singapore in 1945 – refused to attend official functions. The visit of Ceauçescu of Romania in June 1978 was also a mistake, for both Britain and the Queen. Nowadays when enquiries are made as to why he was invited nobody can give a satisfactory explanation. By contrast, Kenneth Kaunda of Zambia said after his visit in March 1983 that it had been the most delightful time of his life, and that he had 'fallen in love' with the Queen.

Harold Wilson, said to be one of the Queen's favourite Prime Ministers, once showed his displeasure in the choice of visitor. It was in 1963 when a state visit to Britain was undertaken by King Paul and Queen Frederika of Greece. (Greece became a republic in 1974.) The visit was unpopular because of Greece's poor record on civil rights, and also because Queen Frederika had shown sympathy with the Nazis before the Second World War. Wilson, as Leader of the Labour Party, in opposition, had received the customary invitation to a state banquet at Buckingham Palace, which he declined. If the Queen took offence at his gesture, she never made it known and their relationship blossomed once he became the occupant of 10 Downing Street. Anyway, Wilson's refusal was not a deliberate snub to the Queen, but to the State Visit, which he and his party opposed.

It is sometimes thought that the Queen herself invites a particular head of state to visit Buckingham Palace. But actually the Government asks her to issue the invitation and as the head of state of a democratic country, she has to obey their wishes, even if privately she may have little in common with her visitor or does not approve of his or her regime. The Foreign Office is the conduit through which such business is conducted and it is on their advice that Her Majesty will invite a particular head of state. That is why the occasion is called a State Visit. She could not invite a head of state on a private visit while he is in office; that would seem to be a political move. But there is nothing to prevent her inviting him or her once they are no longer head of state. This has happened many times, including an occasion when former President George Bush of the United States was in London on a private visit with his wife. The Queen heard that they were in town and she invited them to tea at the Palace. It had nothing to do with the Government and she was not required to ask or inform the Prime Minister of the invitation.

The private luncheons she gives are seen as an ideal way for the Queen to meet socially a cross-section of men and women from different walks of life. They are all organized with a special theme in mind even if it appears that the guest list has been randomly selected. And while guests are made most welcome, they soon find that certain standards of behaviour are expected. Nor is it possible to ingratiate oneself with this hostess simply by trying to show interest in subjects or people of which she might approve.

Jocelyn Barrow, a former governor of the BBC, was invited to lunch at Buckingham Palace and, together with her fellow guests, she waited in the Bow Room for the Queen to join them. 'We were going to have lunch in the 1844 Room and a lady-in-waiting explained the seating plan, with the Queen sitting in the centre of the table, not at the head. This was so she could talk to everyone. The first we knew of her approach was when several corgi dogs suddenly scampered through the doorway, shortly followed by their mistress. One of the other guests, no doubt hoping to find favour with the Queen, bent down to pat one of the dogs on the head, only to be sharply told by Her Majesty that "they don't take to strangers; it might be advisable not to get too close". It wasn't an auspicious start to what turned out to be a thoroughly enjoyable and convivial occasion. I noticed that the Queen regards her dogs as very much her own personal property; she liked to feed them biscuits which she kept in her pocket and didn't encourage anyone else to do so.'

Most of the household regard the corgis as absolute pests – but they make sure their feelings, and any comments they might make, are kept strictly to themselves and never uttered in the presence of their employer. Neither is it advisable to voice even the mildest criticism in the hearing of any other member of the royal family. The Princess Royal has been known to reply waspishly when someone has said something even jokingly that might imply criticism of her mother's dogs.

Royal hospitality is legendary throughout the world. When the Queen had the use of the Royal Yacht *Britannia*, she entertained former President Ronald Reagan and his wife, Nancy, on board in San Diego to celebrate their 31st wedding anniversary. After a reception and banquet, the Reagans were escorted on deck where they watched the band of the Royal Marines Beat Retreat under floodlights. Turning to the Queen, President Reagan said, 'I've spent much of my life in Hollywood, the entertainment capital of the world, but we couldn't beat this.'

Other countries may mount more lavish banquets or more spectacular amusements but it is generally agreed that the Queen has few equals when it comes to staging a State Visit. Years of practice have refined the occasions into an art form and several countries have sent officials to study the way Buckingham Palace manages to produce such faultless events year after year.

CHAPTER FOURTEEN

With Her Ministers – at Home and Abroad

'We all go that little extra mile for her.'
LORD OWEN, FOREIGN SECRETARY 1977–1979

Every Tuesday evening at 6.30 a car arrives in the inner quad-rangle of Buckingham Palace and stops at the King's Door. It is still called the King's Door on the insistence of the Queen, in deference to her late father. Out of the car steps the Prime Minister to be greeted by the Queen's private secretary. They chat for a few minutes and then the equerry on duty escorts the Prime Minister upstairs to the first floor, where he knocks discreetly on the door of Her Majesty's Audience Room. Without waiting to be called, he and the PM enter, stop just inside the door and bow from the neck. The equerry announces, 'Your Majesty, the Prime Minister.' The Prime Minister then advances across the carpet to where the Queen is waiting. She offers her hand, he bows once more and the equerry withdraws.

For the next hour, whatever transpires inside that room remains a secret known only to the two people concerned. The Tuesday meeting is for the Prime Minister to update the Queen on her government's progress in legislative matters and also to acquaint her with any international problems involving the United Kingdom. This is not a social occasion, so the Prime Minister is not offered any refreshment, alcoholic or otherwise. There may be a few minutes of general conversation when the Queen may ask after the health of someone in the Prime Minister's family, but the purpose of the meeting is business, political and constitutional. A new Prime Minister may well seek the advice of Her Majesty; after all she has been there longer than any of her ministers, and her experience has been invaluable to practically all of them. The late Lord Home of the Hirsel (Prime Minister 1963 to 1964) recalled one occasion which illustrated perfectly the Queen's vast – and lengthy – experience. They had been discussing a problem which he had not encountered before when the Queen commented that she had come up against an identical situation 'two Prime Ministers before'.

The Prime Minister is accompanied to Buckingham Palace by his private secretary, who waits with his opposite number. So while the PM and the Queen are talking privately, their two most senior aides have their own meeting down on the ground floor, over a generous whisky and soda.

None of the ten Prime Ministers who have served the Queen has ever revealed the details of their private weekly meetings, apart from James Callaghan, who indicated that on one occasion, when government business was rather slow, he and the Queen spent the entire time discussing their respective gardens. 'The weather was so nice, we left the sitting room and walked around the gardens of Buckingham Palace talking about the flowers and various shrubs and trees.'

Nearly all the Queen's Prime Ministers have regarded the Tuesday meetings as sacrosanct, only postponing them in the event of a national or international crisis. However, during Tony Blair's first term of office, he sometimes cancelled the meetings, due to what was described by Downing Street as 'pressing matters elsewhere'. The press were quick to seize on these alleged 'insults' to the Queen but Buckingham Palace did not comment.

Another fixture in the royal calendar is the summer invitation to Balmoral which the Queen extends to her Prime Minister. A weekend is set aside so that the PM and the Queen can discuss various matters in an informal setting, usually when walking in the Castle grounds.

The Queen meets all her ministers when they 'kiss hands' on taking up their appointment, but the most frequent meetings occur during gatherings of the Privy Council. This is the oldest part of Her Majesty's government whose origins can be traced back to Norman times. There are nearly four hundred Privy Counsellors, as members are appointed for life and, as governments come and go, and reshuffles take place, the working membership changes fairly frequently. But attendance at the regular monthly meetings, in the 1844 Room at Buckingham Palace, is usually limited to four.

An unusual aspect of Privy Council meetings is that all the business is conducted with everyone standing, including the Queen. This custom dates back to the reign of Queen Victoria and the death of Prince Albert in 1861. Out of respect for the Queen's wishes, the members stood in memory of her late consort and since that time all meetings have been held this way. It is a custom that has recently been adopted by high-flying business entrepreneurs and has the advantage of making sure the meetings do not last too long.

Before each meeting of the Privy Council the Queen is briefed by the Clerk to the Council. The business can vary from international matters such as diplomatic immunity and overseas taxation to the fundamental task of prorogation of Parliament or dissolving it. When a member of the royal family is to be married the sovereign's approval is required, and usually on these occasions a large number of Counsellors are summoned to witness the formal consent. There are only two occasions when the entire Privy Council is summoned: the first is on the accession of a new sovereign, when the Council meets at St James's Palace, not Buckingham Palace; and the other is if an unmarried sovereign announces his or her intention to marry. The last time this happened was in October 1839 when Queen Victoria announced her betrothal to Prince Albert. The Queen appoints the members of the Privy Council; they include all cabinet ministers, the Leader of the Opposition, and normally a number of other government ministers. High dignitaries of the Church of England, such as the Archbishops of Canterbury and York and the Bishop of London, are Privy Counsellors as are judges when they become Lords Justice of Appeal. There are also Royal Counsellors of State, two of whom must act for the Queen in her absence. Queen Elizabeth the Queen Mother, the Prince of Wales, the Princess Royal and the Duke of York are all Privy Counsellors and have stood in for the Queen as Royal Counsellors of State on several occasions.

When Neil Kinnock became Leader of the Opposition in 1983 he 'became a Privy Counsellor against the background of having a fair bit of fun at the royal family's expense – notably the Duke of Edinburgh. And while I've never had strong republican learnings, nobody could ever describe me as a devout monarchist. As far as I'm concerned the royal family is a fixture. It's there and I suspect it will be for some time to come. Anyway, when I was invited to become a Privy Counsellor, I went to the Admiralty for a rehearsal which was organized by two retired officers who obviously had done this many times before and who, equally obviously, absolutely loved the theatricality of it all. They made it into a real pantomime. They had a mock-up of the stool we had to kneel on to take the oath of allegiance and then we were told how to stand in line, which was composed on that occasion almost entirely of current Conservative Cabinet members, who had, of course, just won the 1983 General Election. We were advised that you then kiss the Queen's hand, although you don't actually do it, there's no touching, take the oath and retire back into line.' (The late Alan Clark, who loved to shock, once advised a colleague about to become a Privy Counsellor, about the kissing of hands, 'Keep your lips closed, don't press the flesh and definitely – no tongue!')

After several rehearsals the new members arrived at Buckingham Palace for the real thing. 'We had two slight complications. There was another new Privy Counsellor from a Commonwealth country and he was in a state of almost complete collapse from nervousness. In real life he was a brain surgeon – I was glad he didn't have to operate that day. The Privy Council had its attendance rather swollen that day because of a government reshuffle due to the departure from the Cabinet in unusual circumstances of Cecil Parkinson. [Parkinson resigned after the birth of a child to his mistress, Sarah Keays, was disclosed.] So it meant that while some people, such as Norman Tebbit, were getting their first Seals of Office, others were moving from one Cabinet post to another. Willie Whitelaw, as Lord President of the Council, had to read out the list of accomplished legislation since the last meeting, and one was a statutory instrument on "Absent Fathers' Charges Bill". The Queen looked up and we happened to catch each other's eye; I knew exactly the same thought was going through both our heads at precisely the same time.'

Neil Kinnock has been able to observe the Queen at various functions, social and political, and it is clear that he admires her professionalism. 'The great skill that the Queen has acquired over the years is to use the word "fascinating" in about five different tones. A couple of those tones really do denote genuine fascination. The other two or three are by way of saying "Right, I've listened to you long enough, now please go away." It's the same word, but what she's developed over the years is the technique of giving evidence of really rapt interest and attention whilst at the same time being able to slip her mind into neutral; which, given the number of

The traditional way in which members of the family greet the Queen is to kiss her hand and then her cheek. Here, Earl Mountbatten of Burma welcomes his niece to the Imperial War Museum for a special showing of a film of his life.

Two old friends meet during the Second World War. The American film star, Douglas Fairbanks Jnr, is greeted by King George VI in Scotland. The King later awarded Fairbanks an Honorary KBE, though, as an American, he did not use the title that accompanied the knighthood.

An historic meeting as the Queen and the Duke of Edinburgh are welcomed by Pope John Paul II at the Vatican in October 1980.

Exactly twenty years later, Her Majesty and His Royal Highness again meet the Pope. On this visit the Queen had to speak a little louder than usual because of the failing hearing of His Holiness.

people she meets, and the number of situations in which she meets them, is a necessary and rare skill. The other thing I've noticed about her is you can tell when she is really enjoying herself, because she does appreciate the company of a particular visitor. This was the case in 1998 when Nelson Mandela came to London. Things generally were not going too well for the Queen, but she had a certain vivaciousness on that occasion because it was a joyous event. There have been some more mundane official guests, and one has been able to observe that the Queen is very professionally going through the motions – but without the slightest hint of detachment or boredom. It's simply when you've seen her being animated, then you know what she looks like when she is not.'

Lord (David) Owen, former Foreign Secretary, has known the Queen over many years and first met her when he was Under-Secretary of the Navy in 1969 and had responsibility for the Royal Yacht. He says, 'She was always in a relaxed mood on the yacht, and anyway she had a special affection for the Royal Navy; she was always at ease with them. It was interesting to see her on *Britannia* when the doors were shut, as it were, and the last guests had left. I suppose I saw her in ideal circumstances.' David Owen has also had the opportunity of assessing the Queen's role as constitutional monarch. 'She has the courage to be boring and I believe that is one of her great features. Which is not to say she is a boring person, because she certainly is not, but there isn't a great deal of scope for extravagant or quotable statements when she is making a State Visit overseas. She is not usually the conveyor of new information and she doesn't feel at all unhappy in that role – she accepts it. She doesn't need to make headlines. She understands that being unquotable risks being boring – unlike certain other members of the royal family, who have come unstuck because they want to be newsworthy. That's not her style at all. Even when one meets her in informal surroundings she just steers clear of stating her own opinions on politically controversial issues. She doesn't think, "I'm in private now, I can speak freely." She never loses sight of the fact of her unique position. It's a considerable skill and one which she has learnt over many years.'

When David Owen accompanied the Queen abroad he always saw her speeches in advance. 'I certainly vetted all her speeches personally and I don't think she ever made a speech on policy that I wouldn't have given myself. She accepted this, and should any mistakes occur, then the buck stops with the Foreign Secretary, it is his responsibility.'

In 1978, Lord Owen accompanied the Queen on a State Visit to Germany, which, he says, has a special place in her heart. 'The Queen's visit to Berlin was very important to Berliners. We were a former occupying power; we had our own sector and we mattered. The Queen was very well briefed, which did not surprise me in the least as by then I had come to expect nothing less. She is also very well read and informs herself brilliantly about places she is visiting. What was particularly helpful was the manner in which the Queen oils the wheels of diplomacy without any apparent effort. She really does have an extraordinary talent for getting on with people of very different opinions and views.'

I asked Lord Owen if he actually liked the Queen. His reply showed an interesting perception of her personality and also revealed something of his own attitudes. 'It's difficult to use the word like when you speak of your relationship with the Queen. Admiration, respect certainly. I'm not normally a person of great deference, but I do want the monarch to be someone who doesn't feel they have to come down to my level. I think a certain amount of distance is very necessary. Having said that, I enjoy her company very much and I feel quite relaxed about eating at the same table. Perhaps if I said I liked her it might seem too familiar.'

Lord Owen was the youngest Foreign Secretary of the twentieth century and he held the office during some of the world's

– and Britain's – most crucial times. There was, for example, unrest in Rhodesia (now Zambia) and an oil crisis in the Middle East. Some of these difficulties did not, of course, concern royalty in any way. But Owen was involved in the Queen's proposed State Visit to Iran at a time when the Shah was about to be overthrown. 'The Queen was determined the visit should not be cancelled early, and we should wait until it was obvious to all that it could not go ahead, and I agreed with her, even though there were domestic political reasons why the Prime Minister [James Callaghan] felt it should be cancelled earlier. I think part of the Queen's reason was to show that she was not a "fair-weather friend" – also it was a sort of "monarchs trade union", I suppose.

'A similar problem occurred with Margaret Thatcher. President Kenneth Kaunda, Zambia's leader, was due to host a Commonwealth conference in Lusaka, soon after the General Election in 1979. Rhodesia's Ian Smith had earlier attacked Joshua Nkomo's camp on the outskirts of Lusaka. Margaret Thatcher wanted the conference postponed, because of a possible threat to the Queen's life. Eventually the Queen's visit went ahead. The Queen would never have allowed her personal safety to be a factor. She had been personally involved in planning the conference in Lusaka for a year before, as a way of helping to bring about a settlement. She knew the risks and the reasons for choosing that location at that time.'

Lord Carrington is another who has had a rare opportunity of getting to know the Queen over a number of years. As First Lord of the Admiralty, he was responsible for the maintenance and running costs of the Royal Yacht, which meant he frequently came into contact with her and other members of the royal family; and as Foreign Secretary, he accompanied Her Majesty to various countries both inside and outside the former British Empire.

A further connection with royalty was through his Great-uncle Charles, Lord Carrington, an intimate friend of King

Edward VII, and previously Lord Chamberlain to Queen Victoria, in the days when such appointments were not made solely by the sovereign, but by Parliament. Charles was Lord Chamberlain from 1892 to 1895. He was unpopular with Victoria because she wanted to choose her own household and Carrington was a political appointee, but also because he was a close friend of her son 'Eddie' Prince of Wales, whom she regarded as useless and frivolous. She accepted Carrington only after Disraeli promised her he would not get up to 'any larks'.

When Great-uncle Charles left royal service he received a singularly cold and unappreciative letter from Queen Victoria which even included unfavourable comments about his clothes. A member of the Privy Council since 1959, Peter Carrington was made a Companion of Honour in 1983 and a Knight of the Garter in 1985. He won a Military Cross for bravery in 1945, during his war service with the Grenadier Guards. His international network of friends includes such diverse characters as Henry Kissinger, the late Robert Runcie and Robert Mugabe. As Foreign Secretary from 1979 to 1982 Peter Carrington was required to attend the Queen when she made State Visits overseas. Among the countries they visited together were Tunisia, Germany and Italy, where, in the Vatican, the Queen and the Pope found they had much in common, including a mutual interest in ancient sacred documents, which they discussed in private. At the most recent meeting between the Supreme Governor of the Church of England and the Head of the Roman Catholic Church, in October 2000, when the Queen paid a state visit to the Vatican, the Pope gave her a 13th-century Bible for the library at Windsor. She showed her concern for the ailing Pontiff by speaking a little more loudly than usual and walking at his pace. There was obviously a great mutual regard between the heads of what have been described as the two most stable states in the world.

These trips meant that Lord Carrington was able to see at first hand the effect Her Majesty had on people abroad. 'She has an aura about her, a glamour that republics and even some kingdoms don't have. Her demeanour has an extraordinary effect when she is abroad that is reflected in people's perception of Britain as whole. I was with her in Italy – where they are all republicans – and the turnout was fantastic. I've rarely seen such a welcome. So obviously they regard the monarchy as glamorous. Added to which we had the Royal Yacht with us and when you saw *Britannia* entering Naples harbour dressed overall, flags flying and the Royal Marines Band playing, the effect was quite brilliant.'

The mention of *Britannia* reminds Lord Carrington of his period as First Lord of the Admiralty, a post which meant responsibility for the Yacht. And when, for once, he was on the receiving end of the Queen's displeasure. 'She really did give me the most fearful rocket over a refit which cost some £2 million, a lot of money in the sixties, which resulted in a great deal of criticism in the press. Anyway, I was sitting in my office when the telephone rang. It was Michael Adeane [the Queen's private secretary from 1953 to 1972]. He said, quite abruptly, "The Queen wants to see you at 6.30." I could tell by the tone of his voice, I wasn't going to get the Garter or anything like that. I presented myself at the Palace at the right time and marched in. I wasn't asked to sit down. The Queen said, "I see the Yacht's being refitted. Why?" I replied, "She is in urgent need of repairs, Ma'am, and we can't have her breaking down with you on board." I went on a bit and she said, icily, "I see." Then she added, "Who's paying?" Feeling on stronger ground, I said – I thought, rather reassuringly – "It's all in the Admiralty Vote." There was an even longer pause and then she said, again, "I see. You pay and I get the blame." Not another word. I was dismissed and marched out. The funny thing was, even though I had been given an extremely uncomfortable few minutes, it

211

was exactly the right thing for her to do. She was marvellous and I respected her even more after that.'

There was an occasion though when it was Buckingham Palace who were at fault, when an omission on the part of the household might have led to an international incident. 'On a visit to Saudi I had been given a personal letter from the Queen to hand to King Faisal. I suspected that the letter was not signed and that this would have been terribly impolite. I held the envelope up to the light and indeed, I could see there was no signature. After some deliberation I decided to open the envelope to check and my doubts were confirmed. I telephoned Buckingham Palace and spoke to Philip Moore [private secretary from 1977 to 1986]. He was a bit huffy and barked, "Not meant to be signed." I had my doubts about that. They had simply forgotten to place it before the Queen but wouldn't admit it. Anyway, we resolved the problem by saying the letter was in its formal state because it was necessary to have it translated. But one doesn't easily open the Queen's private correspondence.'

After knowing the Queen for so many years – and becoming an even closer friend of Queen Elizabeth the Queen Mother – Peter Carrington has been them both at close quarters, in public and private moments. His admiration for them is unashamed and perhaps unexpectedly so, coming from a man who has spent a lifetime in politics, where scepticism and cynicism are the norm.

David Owen's feelings for the Queen perhaps reflect those of many when he says, 'The enduring thing about the monarchy is that they take a little bit more from you than you would normally give. There's a certain gut loyalty that's difficult to explain. The Queen calls on reserves within all of us. We all go that little extra mile for her.'

Lee Kwan Yew, Senior Minister of Singapore – and its first Prime Minister – is one of the few political leaders who has actually heard the Queen express an opinion on government policy. 'When I saw her in London in January 1969, she said she was sorry the British had decided to withdraw from Singapore. She looked sad to see an important chapter in Britain's history come to an end.'

Harry Lee – as he is known to other Commonwealth leaders – had become, and remains, one of the Queen's most ardent supporters who recalls their first meeting more than thirty years ago: 'I first called on her in September 1966. She was amazingly good at putting her guests at ease without seeming to do so. It was a social skill perfected by training and years of experience. She was genuinely interested in Singapore because her uncle, Lord Louis Mountbatten, had told her of his time here as Allied Commander-in-Chief, South East Asia Command.' The Queen had also been due to visit Singapore for the Commonwealth Conference of 1971 but the British Conservative government, under Edward Heath, decided that she should not attend. There was unrest at the time among several African members of the Commonwealth because of the attitude of other member states towards the supply of arms to South Africa during the apartheid period. Heath felt the meeting might prove uncomfortable for the Queen.

However, the following year she did make an official visit, where her reception in this former outpost of Empire was not what was expected. 'Surprisingly huge crowds gathered on the roadsides waiting to see her pass by,' Lee said. They surged forward to surround her whenever she got out of her car. Her assistant private secretary, Philip Moore [now Lord Moore of Wolvercote], formerly deputy UK High Commissioner to Singapore in the 1960s, asked me not to have the security officer hold the crowds back as they were friendly. The Queen was completely at ease, happy and relaxed.'

On such occasions the Queen often confers an honour on her host. 'To commemorate her visit,' Lee continued, 'the Queen made me a Knight Grand Cross of the Order of St Michael and St George (GCMG). I had already been made a Companion of Honour (CH) in the 1970 New Year's Honours List, so before I was fifty I had received two British honours, much coveted by those brought up in Britain's former empire.' Lee Kwan Yew was actually forty-seven when he received his CH, which was considered to be unusually young. He had also received honours from many other countries including Japan, Egypt, Indonesia and Korea, 'But they did not have the same sentimental significance.' He did not use the title 'Sir' that went with the GCMG. 'I did not think it appropriate . . . but I was pleased and proud to have received two coveted British trophies, although they no longer opened doors with the British like they used to in the days of Empire.'

During Commonwealth conferences every head of government is granted an audience with the Queen as Head of the Commonwealth. She also invites all delegates to an official banquet on the opening day where one's place at table depends on how long one has been in office. 'With the passage of time, I became one of the longer serving prime ministers and was often seated at the Queen's table,' Lee recalled. 'She would reminisce about her prime ministers. I remember her comment that her prime ministers were "getting old so quickly" . . . I told her the world she had been brought up to rule had changed, and Britain's role was much reduced.'

The Commonwealth is a voluntary organization made up of independent sovereign states which were once part of the British Empire. There is one exception: Mozambique, a former Portuguese colony, which voluntarily joined in 1995. Although most of the present members joined after the Second World War, particularly after India gained her independence in 1947, the origins of the Commonwealth go back to the last century.

It was in 1839 that murmurs of discontent were first heard in Canada. There were real fears that if the country was not granted some modicum of self-government, the Canadians might follow the example of their nearest neighbours in North

America and opt for total independence from the mother country. To forestall any such move, Britain decided in 1847 to grant a system of 'responsible government' to Canada, which was shortly extended to the Dominions of Australia, New Zealand and South Africa, the former 'white' countries of the Empire. This then was the beginning of what is now known as the Commonwealth. Those four countries, while electing their own governments, still retained the British sovereign as head of state.

When the Commonwealth was expanded after the Second World War certain countries also decided to keep the King or Queen as head of state while the majority, which were republics, have an elected President as head of state. Four more: Lesotho, Malaysia, Swaziland and Tonga, have their own monarchies, while Western Samoa has a Paramount Chief as its head of state. But each country has agreed that the Queen should be Head of the Commonwealth. It is the only title she holds by acclamation. She was not subjected to the indignity of an election, but even if she had been, she would probably have been returned unopposed. The Queen regards her position within the Commonwealth just as important as her role as sovereign of the United Kingdom, and Commonwealth High Commissioners in London enjoy a unique relationship with her. They do not have to go through British government channels on matters concerning their own countries in relation to the monarchy; they have direct access to the Queen. It is a situation jealously guarded by both parties. There is no compulsion for any of the former colonies to join the Commonwealth, and neither do they have to stay in once they join. Eire was once a member but left in 1949 on becoming the Irish Republic. South Africa, one of the original members, left in 1961 following criticism of its then racial policies, and then rejoined in 1994, after Nelson Mandela was elected President and apartheid ended. During South Africa's exile from the Commonwealth, the association intensified its opposition to the regime. There was a ban on the sale of arms and all sporting links were severed in addition to further extensive economic sanctions.

Five former colonies decided not to join the Commonwealth when they became independent: Burma, British Somaliland, Cameroon, the Republic of the Maldives and Aden (now the Yemen).

Many Commonwealth leaders have become personal friends of the Queen. Kenneth Kaunda, President of Zambia from 1964 to 1991, is quite open in his admiration for her, saying, 'She is the cement that holds the organization together. Without her as mother, this family of nations would have divided years ago. And remember, we are not members just by accident of colonial history but by conviction.'

As previously mentioned, two of the Queen's former Foreign and Commonwealth Secretaries are Lord Owen, who held the post in a Labour Government from 1977 to 1979, and Lord Carrington, who was appointed in 1979 by Margaret Thatcher when the Conservatives came to power. David Owen recalls the Queen's skill when dealing with the leaders of certain African nations at her Silver Jubilee Heads of Government Commonwealth Meeting in London in 1977. 'She showed her true worth with some of the longer-serving African leaders who had experienced quite prickly problems with the mother country, but whom she had known for ages. I saw that she could and did say things which would have been impossible for me as Foreign Secretary to say. I would soon have been told it was none of my business, but she could get away with it without anyone taking umbrage. They had a respect for her judgement and also for her as a person. It was fascinating to see the Queen's relationship with some of these leaders – she gave the completely correct impression that the Commonwealth matters to her personally. She treats Commonwealth countries differently, as if she wants to be involved in their own domestic situation, which, of course, she would never do with any other foreign country. She talks to Commonwealth leaders quite openly and freely and never in a grand manner, whereas when she is visiting a country for the first time, outside the Commonwealth, it is very much as Queen of the United Kingdom and operating in a tight political framework of control.'

When Lord Carrington was offered the post of Foreign and Commonwealth Secretary after the 1979 election, his closest professional association with the Queen began: 'The Commonwealth is this rather agreeable club, and I think she feels there is a particular role for her because this is a family of what was once the British Empire, though, of course, she was never Empress.'

Many of the members of the Commonwealth are suspicious of Britain, feeling that it regards itself as the fulcrum of the organization and its most important member. 'There was a bad patch over South Africa and again over Rhodesia, when things became decidedly rocky. But it survived, due to a large extent to her influence. At the Lusaka Conference, all the African countries were hostile to Margaret Thatcher, thinking she didn't believe in black majority rule. It was a great eye-opener to see the way the Queen dealt with this. She saw each one of the Heads of Government individually, for exactly the same amount of time – and they all melted. From that moment on the whole atmosphere of the conference changed. It was very interesting to see the effect her efforts had. Her secret was – and remains – that she treats everybody the same. There's no preference for Britain, and that came as a very pleasant surprise to some of the other members.'

The Queen never reveals what goes on between her and her ministers – either those in Britain or in any of the Commonwealth countries. But whatever it is, it seems to work without exception. 'She's enormously respected, not just as Queen, but as a person. There's a huge affection for her which is not the sort of emotion there was for Princess Diana, but

217

genuine affection nonetheless, coupled with respect and admiration. She never puts a foot wrong. She's never been connected with anything dishonest, sordid or dishonourable in all her years on the throne, so people can look up to her. She's managed to become the reliable guide to how people should behave.' The principal task of the Queen at Commonwealth conferences is to make herself available to discuss matters any of the countries' leaders might want to talk over in confidence.

'She is the one who binds it all together', says Lord Carrington. 'It wouldn't be the same if she were not there. She gives the Commonwealth a dignity and status it would be hard to sustain without her presence. It's absurd to think that the rest of the Commonwealth would simply accept Britain as its head, without the Queen – they wouldn't. I believe the role of Head of the Commonwealth is as important to her as being Queen of the United Kingdom.'

A reminder of the world she once ruled is contained in the magnificent Commonwealth Vase which was presented to her at the time of her Coronation in 1953. Standing twenty-four inches high and weighing twenty-nine pounds, the ten-sided vase is surmounted with a crown, while its centre panel is made up of the Royal Coat of Arms. In the panels on either side are the symbols of the United Kingdom: the Rose of England; the Thistle of Scotland; the Leek of Wales and the Irish Shamrock. Other panels contain emblems of those countries which were members of the Commonwealth at the time. It is presently kept at Holyroodhouse in Edinburgh.

It was in February 1959 that the Queen made a decision that not only endeared her to the former British Empire, but ensured that Britain would become, and remain, the centre of the Commonwealth. The organization was looking for an administrative headquarters that would be suitable for all its members and grand enough to reflect the importance of this family of nations. The Queen placed Marlborough House, a royal palace and formerly the home of Queen Mary, at their disposal. The offer was immediately accepted and since that date it has remained as the headquarters of the Commonwealth.

The chief executive, or secretary general, is appointed by the members, with the United Kingdom having no more say or influence than any of the others. The location of the headquarters does not give Britain any advantages over its colleagues in the group. At the time of writing, an Australian, Don McKinnon, has taken over these responsibilities. His immediate predecessor was an African, Chief Emeka Anayoko, from 1990 to 2000, while the most successful and longest-serving holder of the office was Sir Shridath Ramphal, known as 'Sonny' to one and all, who held the office from 1975 to 1990. A Guyanese, he exercised his right to have regular audiences with the Queen and she welcomed his informal but correct approach. He said, when speaking of her regard for the Commonwealth: 'She did care and she did convey that caring. And I believe that this is the key to her unquestioned success in the Commonwealth . . . It mattered to her . . . this was an important side of her life . . .' Just how important was exemplified in her Christmas broadcast of 1972, when she said, referring to the concerns of many of her people about Britain's entry into the EEC: 'The new links with Europe will not replace those with the Commonwealth . . . Old friends will not be lost: Britain will take her Commonwealth links into Europe with her.' And this was not a speech written for her by Downing Street. The Christmas broadcast is the one speech of the year which is not limited by ministerial 'advice', although, as a courtesy, the text is shown to the Prime Minister in advance.

As Head of the Commonwealth, the Queen attends all its Conferences, but does not take part in any of its plenary sessions. Neither does she formally open the proceedings – unless Britain is the host, or she is invited to do so by another host nation. Her role is to be available for advice if required. Because she is by far the longest-serving head of state and completely apolitical, every Prime Minister or President in the Commonwealth knows he can talk things over with her in complete confidence and receive impartial counsel from an unimpeachable source. And when, as often happens, serious rivalries emerge between member states, even between neighbouring African or Asian countries, who might be expected to 'gang-up' on others, the Queen is sometimes able to help resolve these difficulties through her personal and long-standing friendship with the principal figures involved. But being in the Commonwealth is no guarantee against hostilities between members; India and Pakistan have fought a war against each other while both were members, and the troops of several African nations have often been sighted fighting on the wrong side of their own borders.

From time to time, former colonies have expressed their distaste – even hatred – for the mother country, blaming Britain for most of the ills that have befallen them. When this happens, they always seem specifically to exclude the Queen from their attacks. As the symbol of the former power that ruled them, she might have been expected to be the target of their abuse, but it rarely happens. When during the summer of 2000 President Mugabe of Zimbabwe was at his most vitriolic, attacking Britain and inciting his supporters to perform acts of violence against the white citizens of his country, he made no mention ever of wanting to leave the Commonwealth. And he was delighted when Her Majesty, in a rather ill-timed and ill-advised gesture, sent him her personal congratulations on the occasion of the 20th anniversary of his ascent to power.

But at the time of writing there is a growing feeling among the 'white' members of the Commonwealth that the organization benefits mainly the 'black' states and they doubt that Charles will be able to hold it all together – or even if there will still be a Commonwealth by the time he comes to the throne. The original aim of the Commonwealth was, in the Queen's words, 'to make an effective contribution towards redressing the economic balance between nations'. It hasn't happened. Australia, New Zealand and Canada have become wealthier and more isolated, while the poorer nations, in spite of their independence, have often seen their standards of living drastically reduced.

To many people in Britain's former Colonies and Dominions, as in the Mother Country, the Commonwealth is an irrelevance, its benefits obscure. But, as the Queen has claimed, 'Notwithstanding the strains and stresses of nationalism, different cultures and religions, and its growing membership, the Commonwealth family has still managed to hold together.' Perhaps that is the Commonwealth's greatest achievement, simply that this entirely voluntary organization has survived.

CHAPTER FIFTEEN

Royal Money

*'The image of the monarchy will be gravely
damaged unless the nation realizes the truth
of that fortune.'*
EARL MOUNTBATTEN OF BURMA, IN A LETTER
TO THE QUEEN

In August 1992, the Prime Minister, John Major, together
with his wife, Norma, was paying his annual weekend visit to
Balmoral as a guest of the Queen. As they walked alone in
the gardens on the Saturday afternoon, Her Majesty confided
to her Prime Minister that she had decided to pay income tax
for the first time. Mr Major wasn't surprised. After all, his
Treasury ministers had been in touch with the Keeper of the
Privy Purse at Buckingham Palace for some time, discussing
the issue. It wasn't a question of if the Queen should pay but
when. The announcement actually came some six months
later, in February 1993.

The Prime Minister told a packed House of Commons,
'The Queen had approached me in July 1992 to ask for a
change in the current arrangements to be considered. She
asked me then to consider the basis on which she might volun-

tarily pay tax and further suggested that she might take responsibility for certain payments under the current Civil List arrangements.' It was widely reported in the media that this was one of the most momentous constitutional decisions of her reign and that Her Majesty was to be applauded for her generosity and realistic approach to life in the final decade of the century. The *Sunday Times* commented: 'By joining the ranks of sovereigns who pay income tax, the Queen has seized the opportunity to sweep away some of the cobwebs that have surrounded the royal finances for centuries.'

In reality, what the move meant was that the Queen had agreed to what was seen by many people as merely a cosmetic exercise in royal public relations. There had been calls for many years for the sovereign to be taxed, and indeed, in earlier reigns, several of Britain's monarchs had paid a nominal amount. Queen Victoria, Edward VII and George V all paid some form of income tax when the rate was measured in pence in the pound rather than the punitive amounts in the second half of the twentieth century, But, in this instance, the spin that was put on the announcement indicated that Her Majesty was to be treated just like any other British taxpayer. It was yet another brilliant move by the palace to forestall further attacks prescribed by the extravagant lifestyle enjoyed by some members of the royal family. Princess Margaret, the Duchess of York and the Princess of Wales had all attracted wide criticism for the large sums of money they spent on their privileged lifestyles, while at the same time behaving so badly. The dual announcement that the Queen would not only pay tax but also accept financial responsibility for certain of her relations was intended, and succeeded for a time, in silencing this particular source of irritation.

When the Earl of Airlie, the Lord Chamberlain, spoke to journalists at St James's Palace informing them of the Queen's decision, he began by saying, 'Paying tax and meeting the costs of other members of the royal family will place a considerable burden on the Queen's finances . . . The recent emphasis on royal wealth has tended to obscure the Queen's contribution to national life, and this – not the embarrassing publicity surrounding her children – had prompted the change.' The denial itself was a tacit acknowledgement of the Queen's awareness of the public's attitude.

What we have never seen, of course, nor are we ever likely to see, is one of Her Majesty's tax returns, or to see published the amount she pays, although she is believed to be a higher-rate taxpayer. It might be argued that nobody else has to disclose such information either. The official palace line is that, like any other person, the Queen's finances are a private matter. But nobody else is in her unique position. She is not a private person with the right to confidentiality the rest of us enjoy. As the most public of figures, the Queen's expenses are paid by the taxpayer, some of whom demand, always without success, the right to examine our Head of State's balance sheet.

If the Queen had listened to her Uncle Dickie, Earl Mountbatten of Burma, she might have avoided much of the criticism many years earlier. Mountbatten had a keen eye for public relations, and he certainly knew how to anticipate what reaction there might be to a controversial issue. Nobody knew better than he how to woo the people, and in the early 1970s he brought up the matter of the Queen's personal fortune. He knew that many people believed she owned the Crown Jewels, Buckingham Palace, Windsor Castle and the entire royal art collection. He also realized it was vitally important that she clear up these misunderstandings and issue some sort of statement of her real worth, if only to stem the tide of newspaper articles that periodically trumpeted stories about how wealthy she really was. Mountbatten, who was probably the only person in the world who could have raised the subject and got away with it, wrote to the Queen on 5 June 1971, saying, 'The image of the Monarchy will be gravely damaged unless the nation realizes the truth of that fortune . . . please believe a loving old uncle and not your constitutional advisers.'

But the situation in the seventies was far removed from that of 1992–93, when Britain suffered a record number of bankruptcies. The palace 'old guard', who resisted practically all change, had been replaced by professionals who reacted positively to the call for the royal finances to be streamlined. Major Sir Rennie Mawdsley, one of a long line of former army officers, had retired as Keeper of the Privy Purse. A number of others had also come and gone, and by 1992 Sir Robert Fellowes, who had a business background in the City – to which he was since returned – before arriving at the palace, in the Private Office, had a more realistic approach to the question of the Queen's money.

The whole question of the Queen's wealth has been a matter of debate ever since she came to the throne in 1952. How much is she actually worth? What does she own? How is the wealth divided between public and private income? Does she own shares? Is she a speculator on the stock market? Who pays for her travelling expenses? Who foots the bill for her clothes? Is she the richest woman in the world? What is the difference between what she owns personally and what belongs to 'the Crown'?

The Queen and Prince Philip like the 'divide and rule' principle, putting their advisers into separate compartments so that hardly anyone knows the full story. The 'need to know' basis is another rule they follow and it has proved to be remarkably successful for over fifty years. All the same one fact is acknowledged, even if grudgingly. The Windsor-Mountbattens are a very rich family, although the extent of that wealth is known to only a very few. However in 1993, the Earl of Airlie, at that time Lord Chamberlain, declared that estimates of the Queen's personal fortune being £100 million and upwards were 'grossly overstated', repeating an earlier Lord Chamberlain's comment over twenty years before.

It is perfectly true that estimates of the Queen's wealth have mistakenly included items which do not belong to her personally; she holds them on behalf of the nation. The royal palaces, art treasures in the Royal Collection and the Crown Jewels are not her private property. They are considered 'inalienable' and must be passed to her successor. Though who would sue her if she did decide to sell a few baubles is never made clear. Nevertheless, financial experts believe her Lord Chamberlain's 1993 claim that the Queen's wealth was nowhere near £100 million must be seen as a loyal servant's attempt to play down his sovereign's fortune to a more modest and acceptable level, rather than a realistic assessment.

For a woman who carries no money at all in her handbag – her equerry passes her a brand new five-pound note for the collection plate in church – the Queen has a very down-to-earth approach to her wealth. She regularly inspects her port-folio, knows exactly the value of the property she owns and expects market-rate rents for the houses and flats administered by the Duchy of Lancaster, her main source of private income. The Duchy has also always paid tax in the normal way, so the claim that the Queen has paid tax only since 1993 is inaccurate.

Of all the royal residences used by the Queen and her family, Buckingham Palace, Windsor Castle and the Palace of Holyroodhouse are owned by the State and are made available to the sovereign rent free for her lifetime. The upkeep is also funded from the public purse, so if it is true that Her Majesty likes to go around her palaces at night switching off the lights in unused rooms, then she is doing it to save us money not herself.

But the two most valuable private royal homes the Queen owns personally. Sandringham in Norfolk and Balmoral in Scotland were both left to her by her father, who bought them from his brother, David, when he abdicated as King Edward VIII in 1936. The details of this sale have never been released, but the value of these two properties today must be immense. The Sandringham Estate, which now extends to over 20,000 acres, was bought in 1862 as a twenty-first birthday present for Prince Albert Edward, later King Edward VII. It cost £220,000. Successive sovereigns have enjoyed its seclusion and Victorian comfort; the Queen's grandfather, King George V, said, 'In London I have a house; at Sandringham I have a home.' Still a huge pile of a place, in 1973 some ninety rooms were demolished in an attempt to make the house more manageable. A hundred full-time staff are employed in the house and grounds with 12,000 of its acres being rented out to farm tenants. If the estate were to be put on the market today, property experts estimate it would fetch in excess of £70 million.

Balmoral Castle and the surrounding estate of 11,000 acres were bought by Queen Victoria and Prince Albert in 1852 for £31,000. They immediately demolished the existing castle because it was too small for their needs, and built a new one, moving in in 1856. Various adjoining parcels of land, some with large houses, have been added in the last hundred years, including Birkhall, with its 5,400 acres, where Queen Elizabeth the Queen Mother stays during the royal family's long summer holiday. Another elegant property on the Balmoral Estate is Craigowan House which the Prince of Wales likes to use – and where Princess Anne and Mark Phillips became engaged in 1973. Today Balmoral is surrounded by over 50,000 acres of woodland, some of which is let to Forest Enterprise, tenanted farms and hills where the Duke of Edinburgh takes his guests on shooting parties.

The controversial sport of stag-hunting accounts for the bulk of the Balmoral estate's enormous value. There is an often repeated story that on one occasion Prince Philip had spent an uncomfortable day in freezing, wet conditions stalking a stag. The chase had been long and hard and finally he was about to shoot his victim when a couple of youngsters suddenly appeared in his sights, ruining his aim. Prince Philip, not known for his patience, shouted at them angrily, asking them what they thought they were up to. The reply stunned even him. 'We are doing our Duke of Edinburgh's Award Scheme,' they shouted back. For once a royal temper was silenced.

Each red deer stag is reckoned to be worth around £20,000, while the total value of the grouse moors is said to be over £10 million alone. Fishing rights on the River Dee are calculated to be at least another £1 million and altogether the 50,000 acres – some of them of much higher quality than others – are estimated to be worth, on average, around £800 an acre. It would be difficult to sell the estate as a single property, but its overall value is said to be well in excess of £50 million. The Queen uses Balmoral for between eight and ten weeks a year.

She also owns Sunninghill House, built for £5 million as a wedding present for the Duke and Duchess of York, but not registered in their names. And Gatcombe Park, the Gloucestershire country home, bought for Prince Anne and Mark Phillips for £500,000, and today worth well over £3 million, is also retained within the royal property portfolio. It was the purchase of Gatcombe that provoked the future Labour leader, Neil Kinnock, to utter a stinging rebuke when he said, 'I don't know which is worse – the Queen for being wealthy enough to give it to them, or them for having the neck to take it.'

The Queen provided £70,000 for the purchase of a house in Launceston Place in Kensington, London, as a home for the Earl of Snowdon, when he and Princess Margaret divorced. However, the house was never registered in his name; it became the property of a trust that was set up to benefit the two children of the marriage, Viscount Linley and Lady Sarah Chatto. The house is today worth in excess of £2 million.

The Queen's finances are so impenetrable because she receives money from several different sources. So while it is possible to be accurate about the amounts she gets from the public purse and how they are spent, that doesn't tell us much about her personal holdings.

The Civil List is intended to meet all official expenditure relating to her duties as Head of State and Head of the Commonwealth. This amount is set by Parliament for ten years and at the time of writing it remains at £7.9 million a year, set in 1990 and renewed in 2000. In addition Queen Elizabeth the Queen Mother receives £643,000 a year and the Duke of Edinburgh, £359,000.

But since 1993, the Queen has repaid to the Treasury the annual allowances received by her other relatives. They include: £249,000 to the Duke of York; £96,000 to the Earl of Wessex; £228,000 to the Princess Royal; £219,000 to the Princess Margaret; £87,000 to Princess Alice, Duchess of Gloucester; £236,000 to the Duke and Duchess of Gloucester; £225,000 to the Duke and Duchess of Kent and £225,000 to Princess Alexandra.

Buckingham Palace say that some 70 per cent of the Civil List goes to pay the salaries of those staff who work directly for the Queen. The actual salaries are not disclosed, but it is said that more people are employed in the White House press office than in all branches of the royal household. In addition, the Civil List pays for the eighty-odd public functions held every year, such as the royal garden parties at Buckingham Palace and the Palace of Holyroodhouse, state banquets and diplomatic receptions.

Next comes the Grant-in-Aid which pays for the upkeep of the royal palaces and for the travel of the Queen and certain members of her family. Although known as the Occupied Royal Palaces, some of the properties maintained by the Government through Grants-in-Aid are not. Buckingham Palace, Windsor Castle, St James's Palace and Kensington

Palace are clearly royal buildings, but the scheme also pays for the upkeep of Clarence House, Marlborough House Mews, Hampton Court Mews and 285 'Grace and Favour' houses and apartments rented out to staff and pensioners, plus a further nine properties used as communal residential accommodation for staff.

The Queen's official residence in Scotland, the Palace of Holyroodhouse in Edinburgh, is funded directly by the Scottish Executive.

The royal household is very proud of the fact that by good housekeeping they have been able to hand back to the Government substantial sums in recent years. In 1997 the Grant-in-Aid was £19,609,000, which was reduced to £16,409,000 the following year and further reduced to £15.8 million in 1998–99. It came down to £15 million in 1999–2000. Back in 1991–92 the costs amounted to £23.9 million.

Until 1997 the costs of transporting the Queen and her family around the world were divided between the Ministry of Defence, the Department of Transport and the Foreign and Commonwealth Office. Then, in April of that year, it was decided to allow the royal household to look after the financing through another scheme, the Royal Travel Grant-in-Aid. When the Queen travels by air, she uses aircraft of 32 (the Royal) Squadron as there is no longer a Queen's Flight. Alternatively, for long-haul journeys, she will charter a commercial aircraft. In 1997–98, 32 Squadron cost £14,441,000 for royal flights while a total of £1,471,000 was spent on chartering aircraft. The following year there was a reduction to £12.8 million and in the year ended 31 March 2000, the amount was £8.6 million. By contrast the cost of maintaining and running Air Force One and Two for the US President and Vice-president is more than $20 million a year.

The Royal Train is another major source of expenditure, costing around £1 million a year to run. The royal family are charged for every journey. Economy measures are also being introduced here. The operational fleet is being reduced from fourteen coaches to eight and, with far more air travel, the train was used less than twenty times in 1999.

In the garages of the Royal Mews at Buckingham Palace are eight limousines: five Rolls Royces and three Daimlers. These are used for official duties, so none of the cost comes out of the Queen's private pocket. But the Jaguar and Vauxhall Estate car which she drives herself are paid for out of her own income, as is the Range Rover the Duke of Edinburgh prefers for private use. Both Prince Charles and the Princess Royal have Bentleys which they lease for around £2,000 a month.

The third source of income for Her Majesty is the Privy Purse, whose principal responsibility is to manage her private income. This derives mainly from the Duchy of Lancaster, the landed estate which, since 1399, has passed from monarch to monarch. The administration of the estate is the responsibility of a government minister, the Chancellor of the Duchy of Lancaster, who is appointed by the Prime Minister. He receives just over £1,000 a year for his duties and has a full-time professional team of twenty-nine to handle the legal and administrative affairs of the 33,000-acre estate which ranges from Yorkshire in the north to Lincolnshire in the east and down as far as the South Wales valleys. One peculiarity of the Duchy is that the property and assets of anyone who dies intestate passes to the Duke of Lancaster, who happens to be the Queen. During 1999, the Duchy received £1,394,030 from this source, which, after administration costs were deducted, was transferred to the Duchy of Lancaster Benevolent Fund, a separate charity.

The investments of the Duchy of Lancaster include government securities, fixed interest stocks, equities and cash totalling in the financial year ending 31 March 2000, £79,566,528, an increase in value over the previous year of £8,448,598. The balance sheet for the same period reveals that the total assets of the Duchy – property, fixed assets and investments – were £195,809,696.

Arguably the most valuable properties the Duchy owns are the Queen's Chapel of the Savoy, the chapel of the Royal Victorian Order, and the land on which the Savoy Hotel stands. A number of freeholds are held by the Duchy in other parts of central London, including Lancaster Place, off the Strand, where the Duchy has its headquarters. The capital remains within the Duchy, but every year a sum of money is paid 'to the Keeper of the Privy Purse, for Her Majesty's use'. In the financial year ending in March 2000, this amounted to £5,777,767 before tax.

Is the Queen the wealthiest woman in the world? According to Buckingham Palace the answer is a resounding 'No.' They go to great lengths to emphasize that all estimates of Her Majesty's fortune are greatly exaggerated, without giving any indication of the real figures.

She also deals in stocks and shares and, with the sort of advice she is able to command, it would be difficult to believe that she has not made considerable profits on the Stock Market over the years. Her stockbrokers are Rowe and Pitman, known throughout the City for their financial acumen and their utmost discretion in dealing with a client's affairs. The profits from these dealings are funnelled through a private account at the Bank of England.

More than twenty years ago, the Queen was described by the left-wing politician Archie Hamilton as having the machinations of a 'shrewd and calculating businesswoman'. Archie Hamilton was a member of the All-Party Commons Select Committee formed in 1971 to examine the Civil List. It was under the chairmanship of Antony Barber, the Conservative Chancellor, and it was at a meeting of this committee that Lord Cobbold, a former Governor of the Bank of England, then Lord Chamberlain, made his famous remark that 'estimates of the Queen's wealth being £100 million are wildly exaggerated'. Hamilton made his comment then and repeated it in his book, *My Queen and I.*

The Windsors have always been the recipients of valuable gifts, especially at royal weddings. When Princess Elizabeth and Lieutenant Philip Mountbatten married in 1947 they received wedding presents from all over the world worth, even in those days, over £2 million. And none of those was 'inalienable' – every one became their personal property.

When King George VI died in 1952, leaving a sum believed to be over £20 million – though few outside the royal family know the exact figure as royal wills are private – the entire amount was handed over intact. The sovereign did not, and still does not, pay inheritance tax – or death duties as they were called then. It is this immunity from a tax to which everyone else, including the richest people in the country, is subject that has consolidated and increased the vast fortune of the royal family.

Whether or not the Queen is the wealthiest woman in the world, she certainly does not flaunt her wealth. Ostentation is anathema to her. She prefers an old tweed suit, a twin-set and headscarf to the latest designer outfits and the idea of spending thousands of pounds on a dress simply would not occur to her. Although she has scores of tiaras, millions of pounds' worth of jewels and diamonds and furs by the dozen, she is rarely seen other than simply dressed. Similarly, her tastes in other areas, while reflecting her upper-class background, are not those normally associated with the super rich. The Queen dislikes hot weather so a holiday lying on a beach in the Bahamas, sipping exotic cocktails, would have little appeal. Skiing is a sport she has never tried, so the fashionable winter resorts of Gstaad and St Moritz can never expect to see her. She has often said that her idea of a perfect vacation is 'a couple of weeks in the rain at Balmoral'.

This is not to say that the Queen does not enjoy the best of everything. She does. Nothing she wears, eats, drinks or uses is anything other than the very finest money can buy. Even her corgi dogs are fed from silver bowls. When she travels, either in Britain or abroad, she does not have to lift a finger for herself. Everything is done for her. She has never packed a suitcase in her life, ironed a dress or washed her own underwear. Even when she was serving in the Auxiliary Territorial Service during the Second World War, she lived at Windsor Castle, where servants attended to her laundry and cleaned her shoes. It is not surprising that a woman who has been used to such treatment all her life should take it for granted. What does illustrate the very human face of the Queen, however, is the way she hates waste in any form. Which is why stories have emerged of her parsimony: how she saves pieces of cotton and wool, and insists that her grandchildren make use of the toys her own children enjoyed in the nursery when they were young. The royal family has a reputation, if not for meanness, then for what the household describes as 'an acute feeling for conservation of income'.

A story about the Queen's thrift is told by George Wiltshire, who used to own a leather goods shop in Rose Street, the home of master craftsmen in Edinburgh. He once received a telephone call from the Palace of Holyroodhouse when the Queen was in residence. He was told that 'Her Majesty has a bag that needs repairing ... She knows you will think it isn't worth repairing, but would deem it a great favour if you could take a look at it. It has been around the world with her four times.'

Mr Wiltshire, now retired and a sprightly seventy-five, told me the rest of the story: 'An equerry delivered the bag, and it was, as the caller had indicated, in a pretty poor condition, with battered corners and broken zip. The only thing that distinguished it from any other old leather handbag was a discreet tag attached to one of the handles bearing the legend 'The Queen' in gold letters. It was very old-fashioned. The sort that women used to carry during the war, and I think it might have been with the Queen since she was in the ATS. It was certainly not the sort of bag you would have seen Her Majesty carrying in public, but I guess it was a favourite and she obviously wanted to hang on to it. I was pleased to do what I could and it didn't take too long to fix. Anyway, some time later, I received another call from the Palace of Holyroodhouse asking if it was ready. The next thing was that a motorcycle despatch rider turned up to collect it.

'About a month afterwards someone rang up to ask why I hadn't sent an invoice. I replied that I didn't know the address to send it to. So they gave it to me and I wrote it down but lost the piece of paper. So I never did get paid for my only royal repair job – but it was my own fault so I didn't list the Queen as a bad payer, and didn't put her name in the window which is what we always used to do when people failed to pay up.'

This anecdote is not intended to show that the Queen is mean. What some people call meanness is in fact economic prudence. In this case, though, it was pure nostalgia for a much-loved item that had been around for many years and which she didn't want to throw away. If she was really as miserly as has been rumoured, would she have continued to support her extended family: the Gloucesters, Kents and, in the early days of her reign, the Duke of Edinburgh's mother?

The Queen's personal bill for maintaining her mother's lifestyle is said to be around £2 million a year, but Queen Elizabeth and her grandson, Prince Charles, are the only members of the royal family who can honestly be said to live at an extravagant level. At least that was the case until the establishment of the Earl and Countess of Wessex came about. Their £10 million house, Bagshot Park, is set in eighty-eight acres of parkland and is also used as an office for Argent, Edward's television production company. So part of the running costs comes from his allowance from the Queen and part is defrayed as business expenses. Exact staff numbers are difficult to come by, but it is a massive house, worth millions of pounds, and the upkeep must be very costly.

Princess Anne shares with her mother a dislike for spending. As she once told me, 'I have my clothes made with extra long hems so that they can be taken up or let down according to fashion. In that way a good suit can go on for years.' And she has the wardrobe to prove it. Her Christmas present to her private secretary never varies; it is always a bottle of whisky.

At Buckingham Palace, staff have long become accustomed to such money-saving devices as re-using old dusters until they fall apart and saving all the newspapers so they can be shredded and used in the royal stables as bedding for the horses.

Every member of the royal family, from the Queen down, is expected to keep an eye on expenses and save wherever they can. So it is not surprising that at Buckingham Palace and the Queen's other homes every advantage is taken of the grants that are available – to protect the fabric of the buildings, help irrigate the gardens and, in Norfolk and Scotland, to assist in farming the land as productively as possible. Prince Charles and the Princess Royal also make sure their properties receive everything they are legally entitled to, in much the same way as any other landowner does. They are really in a no-win situation. If they are seen to be getting grants, they are accused of 'milking' the country. On the other hand, if they did not they would be charged by some people with not acting like the rest of us.

It was the Duke of Edinburgh who brought the whole question of royal finances into the open when he commented on the royal family's money in 1969. He was in the United States taking part in a television programme entitled *Meet the Press* when he spoke about what was arguably the most sensitive issue facing the Queen at the time. Among his other comments, Prince Philip said: 'We go into the red next year . . . if nothing happens . . . we may have to move into smaller premises, who knows? . . . For instance we had a small yacht which we had to sell, and I shall have to give up polo fairly soon.'

It wasn't a statement guaranteed to garner much public sympathy back home, where the average British family were more concerned with heating their homes and coping with the household bills rather than having to sell a yacht or give up polo. But Prince Philip had brought the previously unmentionable subject of the Queen's money into the public debate. Neither the Government nor Buckingham Palace welcomed his intervention, but while the manner in which he spoke, flippant and apparently patronizing, was embarrassing to both parties, his actual words rang true. The allowance the Queen received had not kept up with increasing costs over the years, and unless something drastic was done quickly the monarchy would indeed be overdrawn. It wouldn't have had much effect on the Queen's private lifestyle, of course; her financial advisers were far too shrewd to allow that. But the result of Prince Philip's public pronouncement was that Parliament agreed to a more realistic approach to funding the Queen and her family – and they have never looked back. The yearly amount was £475,000 in 1952, on her accession, which rose to £980,000 in 1971 and has stood at £7.9 million since 1990.

The Queen's Civil List allowance is the largest of any European monarchy. Belgium is second in the money league, with a total Civil List of £6,111,535. The King and Queen receive £4,033,613 and five of their family divide up the remainder. Next comes Spain, where King Carlos's State allowance is £4,500,000, out of which he pays for all family and royal household expenses, but the costs of royal travel are met by the Government. Queen Beatrix of the Netherlands is said to have a personal fortune approaching £3 billion. Her official allowances are £3,764,705 a year, which also covers seven members of the royal family, and in addition a sum of just over £7 million is allocated for staff and expenses. No part of these allowances is taxable. In Denmark, Queen Margrethe, who acceded to the throne in 1972, has a Civil List of £3,670,568, with five of her immediate family also receiving allowances amounting to £1,588,627 a year. She has the use of a royal yacht which is maintained by the Danish Royal Navy.

In Sweden, King Carl XVI Gustaf is the only person to receive money under the Civil List. The total amount is £2,667,627, of which part is paid as salaries. Ten royal palaces are maintained by the State, and His Majesty has always paid tax on his personal wealth. The Royal Train is a modest affair consisting of just one coach, which is normally attached to one of the State services. Norway appears to have the cheapest monarchy to maintain. King Harald V's Civil List is set at £1,680,672, but he does have a royal yacht operated and manned by the Royal Norwegian Navy. There is a Royal Train but no official King's Flight aircraft. The Norwegian royal family use commercial airlines.

Every one of the royal houses of Europe is required to balance the books and their accounts are open to public scrutiny at any time. However, although nearly all of them live modestly compared with their predecessors, and they do appear to appreciate the need to give value for money, each of them enjoys a lifestyle almost any of their subjects would love to be able to afford.

In Britain, the reforms of recent years have been intended to convey a feeling of a more open and accountable monarchy, but no government, Labour or Conservative, has ever managed to obtain accurate figures for the extent of the Queen's fortune. And no government has ever really tried. It suits all parties to maintain the secrecy that surrounds royal wealth. So long as the mystery remains, the public can be expected to go on funding the monarchy in the way it has for generations. Once too much daylight is admitted, more searching questions would need to be answered, almost inevitably to the detriment of the sovereign and her family.

No modern Prime Minister would jeopardize his popularity by suggesting a cut-down, economy version of the monarchy, riding on public transport or giving up their palaces and castles. If Britain wants to maintain the Crown in its present form – and every poll comes out overwhelmingly in favour of doing so – then its dignity and style must be preserved. The royal show must continue to be seen in all its glittering spectacle. What does irritate a large number of people is the secrecy surrounding the Queen's private wealth. If she really is worth less than £100 million, then why not reveal her assets and still the criticism once and for all? Her decision to pay income tax was seen by some merely as appeasement of the anti-monarchist section of the people. Others claim she did it at the urging of those ardent monarchists who felt that a dramatic gesture was needed to still the wave of criticism directed at the royal family. Either way, the debate over her wealth continues and will do so for years to come – unless a balance sheet and bank statement is produced, and that is not going to happen.

Parliamentary rules forbid MPs from asking direct questions about the Queen and her wealth; her name must not be mentioned. So the Labour member, Paul Flynn, has got around this by asking hypothetical questions such as: 'How much should a person pay in tax if they earned £5 a week, £50 a week, £500, £5,000 and £50,000?' As he says, 'One of those figures was supposed to be the Queen's income and the question had to be answered. The press, quite rightly, interpreted it to mean that the Queen had to pay a very large tax bill. But even now we don't know how much. I'm sure we would all like to know how much she pays and under what circumstances. She is a servant of the people – as I am. My tax bill is available for everyone to see. My income is a matter of public knowledge, so should hers be. There was a perceivable public reaction when the Queen paid no income tax and that was seen as an injustice, but they very cleverly got around it by giving the idea that they are paying their whack. Maybe they are – maybe not. Who knows? It's all packaging to present them as being the same as us, which of course they are not.'

Unlike his colleague Paul Flynn, another Labour MP, Alan Williams, who had vastly more experience, not only as a back-bencher, but also as a former government minister and Privy Counsellor, does not believe the Queen's private fortune is a matter for public concern. 'Her personal wealth is none of my business, and not a matter of great interest to me. One needs to know that the same rules apply to her as to everyone else. In a private capacity, what she pays the tax man is between her and him. I would no more expect to see the Queen's tax return than I would expect her to see mine. That's always going to be one of the great secrets, and so it should be.'

But Alan Williams has been a thorn in the side of royalty over the cost of the monarchy since the day of the great fire at Windsor Castle in 1992. 'I was driving down the M4 on my way back to my constituency when I saw the clouds of smoke away to my left as I passed near Windsor. That evening on the radio I heard a Palace spokesman saying, "But of course the Castle is not the property of the monarch, it is the property of the State." In other words, what he meant was that the tax-payer has got to pick up the bill for repairing the Castle – and that got me rather cross. I issued a statement saying that the fire would be a catalyst as far as the relationship between the royal family and the public was concerned, and it was. The media turned against the meanmindedness of the royal household – and I'm emphasizing it was the household, not the Queen herself.'

Alan Williams then began a campaign to bring about what he calls 'accountability for the spending of public money'. He still insists that this has nothing to do with any animosity towards the Queen herself, or even the monarchy as an institution. 'I'm not anti-monarchy, because I can't think of any practical alternative that would really work . . . and I've actually made the point several times that the Queen does a good job. The problem with the royal family is that the younger royals have not been benevolent in their impact on the reputation of royalty. I've never gone for the royals as royals, or even royalty as an institution; all I've attacked has been wastefulness or unaccountability surrounding the wider institution.'

Alan Williams supported a Bill to give Prince Charles an increase in his allowance when he married Princess Diana in 1981. 'I actually led for the Opposition in support of the Bill to give him more money after his marriage, and I have a letter of personal thanks from him for the role I played in that. The rules governing the Duchy of Cornwall [which provides Prince Charles with his income] were very tight, and in order to give him more money they needed to be loosened. I would add that since then they have been loosened very considerably, so that in nine years his income has increased from £2.9 million to £6.4 million – an enormous pay rise.'

As a member of the House of Commons Public Accounts Committee, Alan Williams has concerned himself with the very large sums of public money being spent without anyone knowing where it all goes. For example, the cost of the Occupied Royal Palaces and the lifestyles of those who live in them. 'We're not talking about just the royals but a much wider network of very cosseted royal servants in the household who live, in certain cases, in very lavish accommodation. I found there is enormous secrecy about the lifestyle of this group and how much they pay in rent, if anything at all.'

It was revealed some years ago by the Keeper of the Privy Purse that members of the royal household who occupy 'Grace and Favour' homes are required to pay up to 17½ per cent of their salaries as rent. When Alan Williams tried to get detailed information about these houses and apartments in 1992, he came up against a brick wall. 'They didn't even know how many of these "Grace and Favour" homes there were and so answers varied by as much as a hundred. When I tried to find out how much they were worth and how much rent the tenants paid, it was the same story. It was the biggest load of Palace misinformation I've ever heard. One thing I was sure of was that there were lots of hangers-on living at our expense. We eventually summoned Sir Michael Peat [Keeper of the Privy Purse] to a Public Accounts Committee and asked him to give us the value of these properties for rental purposes. His reply was typical Householdspeak: "There's no point in valuing them for rental purposes, because if we did then no one could afford the rent."'

In fairness, Sir Michael acquitted himself with credit on other matters pertaining to royal finances. 'He was much more understanding of the possible public reaction of what might appear to be misuse, or questionable or challengeable use of public assets, such as the use of royal aircraft. I happen to believe that flying is the most sensible way for them to travel because it is a way in which we can be most sure of their security at probable minimum cost. Until questions were asked, the royals were not charged for private flights. Eventually charges were levelled. I came across a case where Prince Charles used an RAF executive jet to take his two children and a couple of friends over to Zurich and then on skiing. I asked how much of that Prince Charles had paid himself. I was told that all he was responsible for was the marginal cost of running it – in other words the fuel they used. Then the Metropolitan Police were charged for the two bodyguards who accompanied them.' (The rule is that the police authority pays for all travel expenses incurred by members of the Royalty Protection Department in the course of their duties with the royal family.)

By the year 2000, the royal family was advised to use commercial aircraft where possible, and where it was more economical. In April of that year, Prince Charles again took a party to Switzerland, this time flying on a commercial airline for the first time ever. The savings amounted to thousands of pounds.

Alan Williams also chose to look closely at the running costs of the Royal Yacht. After several years of probing its high cost and little use, *Britannia* was decommissioned in 1997.

It was when he began investigating the allowances paid to those members of the royal family who did not undertake frequent and regular public duties, that Williams's arithmetic made him see red: 'As an example of the lesser royals I looked at several years' engagements for Princess Margaret and found that fairly consistently over the years she had been doing just two engagements a week for about £4,200 a week. I challenged the value of that and fortunately, some time later, it was decided to take these lesser royals off the Civil List.'

Understandably, Alan Williams is not Buckingham Palace's favourite Member of Parliament. But there have been occasions when his persistence has paid off, such as when he uncovered an unusual item in the accounts of the Duchy of Cornwall. 'Buried under the improbable heading of "Non-Distributable Reserves" was a little note saying that – despite the heading – £830,000 was dispersed to His Royal Highness in the period after the end of the financial year. Which meant that this sum went to him before it became taxable. Strangely enough, the Lord Chamberlain delivered his account of royal finances a month later, which went into great detail, but nowhere did it refer to this £830,000 which had disappeared into the mists. I pointed it out to the *Guardian*, who ran the story, and I then received a letter from Commander Richard Aylard, at that time Prince Charles's private secretary. He said that this was not an attempt to conceal anything. I replied that I accepted this but it was a remarkable coincidence that such a sum should appear as a footnote on page 14 and that the Lord Chamberlain also happened to forget to mention it in his presentation on Royal Finances.'

Nothing more happened for a week or so and then Alan Williams was invited to St James's Palace to meet the Duchy of Cornwall's accountant. 'I thought, why not? Here's a chance to see where some of my constituents' money goes. When I got there it was all very pleasant and civilized and my first question was "Where did the £830,000 come from in the first place?" The accountant said he didn't know. I asked him, "Why don't you know?" And he said, "Well, it all goes back so far. It's been there a long time, since before the Prince was married." I then said, "That makes it twice as bad. In those days, he was paying a voluntary contribution of 50 per cent, when normal tax rates were as high as 60 per cent or 70 per cent. But on marriage his contribution was to drop to 25 per cent. Which means that they put the money away then and now he was taking it out when about to start paying tax at the higher band of 40 per cent." We didn't get very far and there was no further explanation and, in fact, that has been the only direct response I have had from the Palace.'

As a Privy Counsellor, Alan Williams has had the opportunity to meet the Queen on a few occasions, including at least once in a social capacity. 'I went to a cocktail party at the Palace and the Queen was extremely pleasant, very friendly and very susceptible to a joke. I've found her easy to talk to. That was before I started asking parliamentary questions. My quarrel is with the lack of accountability of the monarchy and that has nothing whatsoever to do with the Queen personally. If the institution wants to survive it has to come into the present world and has to recognize that if it wants the public to pay to sustain it it has to make sure we understand why. We have as much right to know about royal finances as we do about the support costs of any department of State. And it wouldn't do them any harm for a little light to be shed. If anything it would make people feel they are more accessible.

After all it's our money. In Parliament at the moment we are restricted from asking direct questions about Civil List money. They refused to give job descriptions for the royal courtiers living at taxpayers' expense in Grace and Favour accommodation – and would not even say whether they were full-time or part-time. If they have nothing to hide, what's the problem?'

Many people, in Britain and throughout the Commonwealth, believe the Queen is a billionaire. It is certainly true that, because of her special taxation advantages, she has immense capital resources which will not be diminished when she dies. So Prince Charles, as her son and heir, will inherit a substantial fortune to add to his already considerable holdings. It is highly unlikely that ever again will a Prince of the House of Windsor-Mountbatten have to plead poverty and talk about 'going into the red' or being forced 'to sell a small yacht and move to smaller accommodation'.

The main criticism aimed at the wealth of the Windsors is not so much the amount they have – nearly everyone accepts that they are very rich indeed – and few would realistically expect them to give up their lifestyle and live in suburbia. It is the secrecy with which they guard their money that irritates many people, and the complete lack of accountability. Why should such obfuscation be necessary if there truly is so little to hide?

The Queen is the most popular member of the royal family and the majority of her subjects believe she is worth every penny of the £7.9 million a year she receives to finance her public duties. It's the private wealth: the homes, jewellery, wardrobe, investments and personal money that remains so mysterious, particularly in the way so many items of personal possessions and public property appear to overlap. While the Palace argues that Her Majesty has the same rights as any other individual to protect her privacy, wouldn't it be in her own interests, as well as satisfying the understandable curiosity of Members of Parliament and the general public, if the books were open to inspection? It would put an end to all the criticism, once and for all.

As Alan Williams has said, 'If there is nothing to hide, what's the problem?'

CHAPTER SIXTEEN

The Sport of Queens

'The aim of all of us is to breed a Derby
winner for the Queen.'
THE EARL OF CARNARVON

'There's only one person who can get through to my mother
at any time and that's Henry Carnarvon.' The speaker is the
Princess Royal and she is referring to the Earl of Carnarvon,
the Queen's racing manager, though to the Queen he is
known as 'Porchy', from the days before he inherited the
earldom and he was Lord Porchester.

Tall, urbane, with perfect manners and charm in abundance,
Lord Carnarvon – or to give him his full names and style,
Henry George Reginald Molyneux Herbert, 7th Earl of Carnarvon – looks every inch the ideal courtier he is. He has been
associated with the Queen's racing interests for over thirty
years, but he has known Her Majesty for far longer. 'When I
came back from the war I was transferred to the Mounted
Squadron based in Knightsbridge Barracks. I was on guard
duty for two and a half years altogether, and as I had always
been involved in racing and also being approximately the same
age as Princess Elizabeth, as she then was, I was asked to go

to Buckingham Palace quite often to escort the Princess to the races. We went to Epsom, Newmarket and Ascot and, in addition, the King was very keen on shooting. Even in those days I had had a fair amount of experience, so I used to go shooting with them to Sandringham and Balmoral. That's how it all started.'

The royal family has always been keen on racing. The Queen's first win came when she was still Princess Elizabeth, and Astrakhan, the filly that two years earlier had been a wedding gift from the Aga Khan, won at Hurst Park in 1949. When she came to the throne three years later, racing was still very much a hobby. But today her racing interests are run on a business footing, and she pays corporate taxes just like everyone else in the sport. 'The Queen asked me to chair a committee to look at the whole of her bloodstock involvement,' Lord Carnarvon recalls. His report to the Queen was delivered in 1968 and he took over as her racing manager the following year. 'It's been a wonderful experience,' he says.

The main difficulty was that all the best stallions in the world were based in Ireland, which was strictly 'off-limits' for the royal stud. 'The political situation made it impossible for us to go there, not because of any personal threat to the Queen, but because we felt the studs involved might attract some sort of trouble.' The alternative for an owner who wanted her mares to be bred with world-class stallions was to travel to the United States. 'It has proved to be well worth while. The Queen has benefited enormously from going to America. She won the big race at Arlington with a horse trained in England and she has also won with horses she has trained there. The difficulty with racing in America now compared with when we first started going there is the money involved. So many Americans are making fantastic sums of money these days and lots of them want to get into racing; it's the thing to do. The result is that prices have gone through the roof. They'll pay anything to get into racing.'

When the Queen goes to America in a private capacity to see her horses, she is usually accompanied by Lord and Lady Carnarvon, and they stay as guests of Sarah and Will Farish (the newly appointed US Ambassador to Britain) in Kentucky. 'It's very relaxed,' Lord Carnarvon says, 'just like staying in any other private house, with the exception of the security. The Americans have such an incredible amount; they take no chances at all, which is very laudable and, of course, the Queen accepts it. She goes to the sales; she has visited the racecourse where the Kentucky Derby is run – though not when the race is on – and talked to all the experts, and she really does have a very good knowledge of all the better American stallions.'

The Queen's mares are stabled on the Sandringham Estate where her stud manager is Joe Grimwade, who took over from Sir Michael Oswald, while the bloodstock director is John Warren who is based at Newmarket. Lord Carnarvon is in constant communication with these two from his home at Highclere Castle in Berkshire.

The subject of who pays for the Queen's racing has provoked controversial argument for many years. Lord Carnarvon is in a position to know the truth. 'Every penny the Queen spends on her racing activities comes from her private pocket. Nothing comes from the Civil List.' The only horses which have public money spent on them are those kept in the Royal Mews and are used for state occasions such as the State Opening of Parliament.'

The Queen has twenty to thirty horses in training at any one time, and as the cost of each one is approximately £15,000 plus a year, it is not too difficult to work out the overall bill. This is clearly the sport of kings – and queens – and not for those with slim wallets. 'Very few people make money out of racing. You've got to hit the jackpot to do it – win a classic, or have just one horse in training. Otherwise it's like fitting a drain to your pocket, so a strict budget is adhered to. There's no bottomless pit of money to call on. Regular financial meetings are held attended by the Keeper of the Privy Purse, Sir Michael Peat, so there's no question of overspending.'

As the Queen has been passionate about racing practically all her life, how knowledgeable is she about the sport? 'She's a very good judge of what a horse should look like. She knows the correct shape and pedigree. After all she's been steeped in it for most of her life. You never have to explain anything to her – she gets the picture straight away. And she is arguably the best judge of a photo-finish I've ever seen. She sits in the same seat in the royal box at Ascot every time. She watches every race and it is right on the finish line. I can honestly say I have never known her to be wrong about a photo-finish.' Bookmakers would pay a fortune to have someone with her eye, sitting where she does at every race.

Lord Carnarvon is in constant contact with the Queen during the Flat racing season. 'I will telephone several times a week from April to October, before a race and afterwards, to discuss the horse's performance, and again earlier in the week to decide whether or not to enter a horse in a particular race.' But who is the final arbiter? 'As the owner it is always the Queen who makes the final decision, though if, for example, she was abroad on an official visit and I couldn't get hold of her then I would take the decision, but otherwise it is a recommendation.' Do they ever disagree? 'There's been no direct disagreement, but I'm quite sure she has been furious at some of the things that have happened. The Queen will sometimes query something I or one of her trainers may have suggested. After all, I wouldn't be doing my job properly if I didn't base my conclusions on what I considered to be my experience and my best judgement of a situation. And in everything I do, it's the Queen's interests I have at heart. But racing is a pretty democratic sport in many ways and all of us involved in the Queen's racing activities voice our opinions, even if occasionally they may not find favour.'

It is often said that the Queen races only on the Flat to

avoid being in competition with her mother, whose horses race mainly 'over the sticks'. However, this is not strictly true as the Queen Mother has, on occasion, had horses running on the Flat.

One of the less well known and rather endearing traits of the Queen as a race horse owner is that she insists on naming all the horses herself. As Lord Carnarvon explains: 'What happens is that the Queen takes suggestions from all sorts of people, mainly family and friends, and asks them to come up with suggestions. She then sorts through them; sometimes she accepts a name, at other times she might take part of it and add something of her own. The names then all come to me and my job is to see that nothing unsuitable gets through. You have to remember that the horse is going to run in the Queen's colours [purple body with gold braid, scarlet sleeves and black velvet cap with gold fringe] so *double entendres* have to be avoided. What might sound all right when it's suggested, can look rather different when it's written down.'

The Queen herself never had any ambition to ride in races, and certainly it was not possible for someone in her position to take part in a race with other jockeys even before she came to the throne. But she was thrilled when one of her horses was ridden by her daughter Anne first past the winning post, placing her daughter in the company of such racing heroes as Sir Gordon Richards and Lester Piggott, both of whom have also ridden winners for Her Majesty. But, as Lord Carnarvon recalls, the Queen is no slouch even today when it comes to riding: 'Her Majesty used to ride down the course in the early morning before Royal Ascot, sometimes at a real gallop.'

Every owner in the world has one ambition: to win the Derby, and the Queen is no exception. 'The aim and objective of everyone who has anything to do with the Queen's racing is to breed a Derby winner,' Lord Carnarvon says.

What about celebrating a big win? How does the woman who reigns over 900 million people let her hair down when one of her horses wins a classic? 'I remember when the Queen won the Prix de Diane (French Oaks) at Chantilly with High-clere. It was a wonderful moment, and in the aircraft coming back from Paris the Queen suddenly told Martin Charteris [later Lord Charteris of Amisfield, at that time her private secretary] to get hold of her trainer and jockey – Dick Herne and Joe Mercer – who were flying back to Heathrow on a separate aircraft and to invite them to Windsor Castle for dinner that evening. Then she made the arrangements from the plane for all the evening's entertainment so that when we landed we went straight to Windsor. Everything was ready and brilliantly organized and we had a fantastic time.'

As well as enjoying over forty years of royal friendship, Lord Carnarvon has also been honoured publicly by the Queen. In 1982 he was invited to join Her Majesty's personal Order of Chivalry, the Royal Victorian Order, when she made him a Knight Commander (KCVO). Nothing could illustrate more clearly the esteem in which he is held by his royal patron. Previously he had also received the award of KBE – Knight Commander of the British Empire – for his services to Local Government.

As he looks back on three decades of association with the Queen, what are his thoughts? 'Well, it's been a wonderful honour to help give her pleasure in an area in which she is so passionately interested. We've had ups and downs, of course, great highs and some sadness as well, particularly when a horse she was very fond of died. But in racing you've got to be an optimist and the Queen is exactly that.'

Horses have taken precedence over all the Queen's other sporting interests, and inevitably through increasing age and affairs of state she has found it necessary to become little more than an interested spectator in recent years. But when she was a young girl she hunted regularly with the Pytchley in Northamptonshire, at a time when such sports did not attract the anger and adverse publicity they do today, and hunting was considered a normal – even essential – part of the upbringing of any well-to-do young lady. But the young Elizabeth was never among the sport's most enthusiastic supporters and in her adult life she abandoned it altogether.

One sporting pastime more usually associated with working-class areas of the north of England has long had the Queen as a keen participant. Her Majesty inherited from her father the Royal Pigeon Loft at Sandringham and is one of Britain's most successful pigeon fanciers. Her birds have competed with great success in competitions at home and abroad and the Queen is always kept fully informed of their progress when they are racing.

Whenever the Queen is seen walking in the grounds at Windsor, Sandringham or Balmoral, she is invariably accompanied by a couple of her dogs. Indeed, she has said many times that one of her greatest pleasures is to walk alone in the hills above Balmoral with just one or two dogs for company. Dogs feature strongly in the lifestyle of all the royal family and even though corgis are the breed usually associated with the Queen, her own preference is for working gun dogs. She breeds black labradors at Sandringham, from where they are sold – at prices up to several hundred pounds – to enthusiasts all over the world.

Her Majesty is a highly skilled handler in gun-dog events, although in her case these have to be restricted to private trials on her own land. If she entered public gun-dog events, the security problems would be a policeman's nightmare. All the same her expertise as a handler places her in the ranks of the professionals, and she has on a number of occasions acted as judge at one of the Kennel Club's Retriever Trials.

As an owner, breeder, trainer and handler of horses, pigeons and dogs, the Queen has achieved great success and suffered disappointments. The fact that she has been able to accept each with equal grace and dignity proves what a true sportswoman she is. Although, like any other competitor, she loves to win, for her the taking part is all important. But that elusive Derby winner would be a fitting climax to a long and distinguished sporting career.

CHAPTER SEVENTEEN

The Case Against the Monarchy

'The Queen has perfected the art of using one
of the most effective weapons in her formidable
arsenal — that of selective hearing.'
NEIL KINNOCK, LABOUR LEADER 1983–1992

In his book *Commons Knowledge: How To Be a Backbencher*, the MP Paul Flynn devotes an entire chapter to the subject of 'How to Avoid Royalty'. He states: 'Members of the Windsor family are of no advantage to an MP. They are a major potential cause of embarrassment and a waste of precious hours of time.' He goes on to elaborate on royal functions: 'Royal occasions are a sinful waste of time and incite emotions of tedium and fury. The sad "subjects" assemble hours beforehand and wait. Cattle waiting to be slaughtered are treated more kindly. The sole purpose for the event is to reinforce royalty's delusion of omnipotence by abasing the peasantry before them.'

A Labour MP who perhaps would be more accurately described as an Independent, such is his irreverent attitude to even his own party's authority, Paul Flynn has openly criticized the monarchy for many years. His weapons have been wit and humour, which he uses with devastating accuracy. Among his more reasonable sayings have been: 'In the twilight days of royalty they are feverishly thrashing about to find a role. No longer the blue-blooded super beings that stepped out of a fairy tale, not the ideal of family life after a triple stain of divorces. All that's left is good causes ... It is not the royals who are selflessly shoring up the charities, it is the charities who are shoring up a dying institution.'

On a more serious note, in 1996 Flynn introduced a Bill to the House of Commons which aimed 'To make provision for referendums to be held on the future constitutional status of the Sovereign as Head of State and on the means of electing any future elected Head of State.'

The questions included in the Schedule of the Bill were:

1. DO YOU AGREE THAT ON THE DEATH OR ABDICATION OF HER MAJESTY QUEEN ELIZABETH NO ONE SHOULD SUCCEED HER AS SOVEREIGN AND HEAD OF STATE, AND THAT FUTURE HEADS OF STATE OF THE UNITED KINGDOM SHOULD BE ELECTED?

        YES ☐   NO ☐

2. IF FUTURE HEADS OF STATE OF THIS COUNTRY WERE TO BE ELECTED, DO YOU THINK THAT THEY SHOULD BE ELECTED BY –

    A. MEMBERS OF BOTH HOUSES OF PARLIAMENT?
     OR
    B. POPULAR VOTE?

The Bill didn't get anywhere as the Government killed the second reading. As Flynn says, 'The Queen could have stopped the Bill in its tracks. I had to submit copies of the Bill to the Palace in order for it to proceed, and I received a letter saying that "Her Majesty was prepared to put her prerogative at the disposal of Parliament for the purposes of the Bill."'

All this was in fact normal practice. The Queen has never been known to stop a bill, and clearly she knew the action the Government would take to support her. To use her right to refuse the Royal Assent would have attracted a massive amount of adverse publicity. By allowing the Bill to proceed, she was putting the onus on Parliament, knowing full well that there was virtually no chance of it becoming law. The Queen has not dealt with Parliament for half a century without learning a thing or two. Both she and they are well aware that calls for the country to be a republic have always been – and continue to be – a 'non-vote-getting' issue for the British electorate.

Flynn questions the validity of confining the choice of head of state to one family: 'The Queen's unhappy father judged himself to be unsuitable to be king. Her uncle would have served happily under Adolf Hitler. There are grave doubts about Charles. One out of four is not good enough . . . Choosing a head of state on the hereditary principle is as sensible as choosing a football team on the same basis.'

He insists that his criticism of the royal family contains no personal animosity. 'I am quite fond of them as individuals, in fact, I'm rather sorry for them . . . it's the institution I find so objectionable. The most outrageous example of an unequal, unfair, privileged society is the institution of royalty. It doesn't make any sense keeping one family in a billionaire lifestyle when they don't achieve any objective that is worthwhile. On the other hand, if we had an election, either by a college of MPs or a popular vote, to elect a head of state, I'm convinced that either the Queen or the Princess Royal would make excellent candidates. They have both shown how tough they can be and we do need someone who serves the interests of the country and is above the political system. But I don't believe that Charles necessarily has the tough personality to take on a Blair or a Thatcher. I once went to Buckingham Palace with my wife, who was involved with a charity event, where I met the Princess Royal and had a chat. She's obviously a highly intelligent, hardworking woman. It's impossible not to feel respect for her.'

Paul Flynn gives an example of how the Queen's power could have been used to prevent a serving Prime Minister from acting in her own interests. 'The late Robert Rhodes James, a distinguished historian and long-serving Conservative Member of Parliament, delivered a speech to a Cambridge college in which he argued that the Queen was the only person who could have prevented Margaret Thatcher from calling a general election in 1990, when she was under great pressure. [The 'Poll Tax' she introduced was universally unpopular; her Foreign Secretary, Geoffrey Howe, had resigned and her treatment of members of the Cabinet had made her a feared and disliked leader.] It was a crisis period for her; her own party wanted her to go; the Cabinet had lost faith and they all thought the only way she could survive was by calling an election. Parliament itself had no power to stop her and neither did her own party. The only person with the power to prevent it was the Queen, if she had felt it to be "not in the best interests of the country". This was a case of the sovereign using not only her power but her personality. I somehow doubt that either her late father – a decent, but weak man, or her eldest son, who I'm sure is an equally decent man – would have been strong enough to do the same. They might well have been a push-over for the Prime Minister.' In the end Mrs Thatcher stood down, and in the ensuing leadership battle John Major emerged as the winner and became Prime Minister on 28 November 1990.

But doesn't the fact that Flynn believes that the Queen or the Princess Royal would be good candidates for the elected office of President rather defeat his argument? 'Not at all. There's a vast difference between choosing someone, even a member of the royal family, as a head of state, to serve for a prescribed term of office – say five years – and having, through the hereditary principle, someone totally unsuitable there for life. It would be most unfair to prevent anyone standing for office simply because they happen to be born royal. But if they were elected it would be because they were the people's choice – now there is no choice.' Flynn goes further in saying that he would campaign for the Princess Royal to be the first President of the United Kingdom for a five-year stint, 'but not for her children or grandchildren to inherit'.

Monarchy is a family profession. The Mountbatten-Windsors are related to every other European royal family, with most of whom they can trace their joint lineage back several centuries. So they are able to prove family ties with ease. For example, the Queen is related to King Harald of Norway, whose grandmother, Princess Maud, was a daughter of Edward VII (the Queen's great-grandfather), while another cousin is Carl Gustaf XVI, King of Sweden, whose great-grandfather, Prince Arthur, Duke of Connaught, was the third son of Queen Victoria. Queen Margrethe II of Denmark is a great-great-granddaughter of Victoria, with King Juan Carlos of Spain being the great-grandson of Princess Beatrice, Queen Victoria's youngest daughter. Queen Beatrix of the Netherlands, King Baudouin of the Belgians, Prince Rainier III of Monaco and the Queen share a joint ancestor in Willem IV, Prince of Orange, who married Anne, the Princess Royal (1709–59), a daughter of George II.

Looking back even further, to the reign of James I, who died in 1625, the Queen is also related to Umberto, the last King of Italy, Otto, Archduke of Austria, Albrecht, Duke of Bavaria and Simeon II, the last King of the Bulgarians.

The Queen can also claim a relationship with many other historical figures, including Rurik (862–79), founder of the

Russian monarchy, Philip I of France, Mohammet II, the King of Seville and Pedro the Cruel of Castile. So if a sovereign of another country is deposed or abdicates, a slight quiver of apprehension runs through the British monarchy.

A prime example of the royal family's instinct for self-preservation came in 1917 at the time of the Russian revolution. At first the provisional Russian government simply wanted the Czar and his family to be expelled, never to return. Their murder in 1918 came only after it was too late for them to leave and the difficulties of finding a country that would accept them had become insurmountable. The first overtures for asylum came to King George V, who was already concerned about his own position. In the penultimate year of the First World War there was unanimous anti-German feeling throughout Britain and the Empire; which is why the King changed all royal names – including his own – from German to English and founded the House of Windsor. He expressed deep personal sympathy for his cousin the Czar but raised a number of objections, the first being where the Imperial family were to live. Balmoral was suggested but the King rejected this saying it was most unsuitable in the winter. Then the cost of maintaining the exiles was mentioned as an obstacle. The King was not prepared to foot the bill; the Russian Government wouldn't pay and the British Government were not anxious to take on the responsibility either. But these problems could have been easily overcome if the will had been there. The real reason the King did not want the Russian royal family in Britain was because of the less than secure position of his monarchy at that time and his belief that his own popularity might suffer; indeed, his throne could be in danger. The British people had suffered nearly three years of terrible warfare and deprivation and the sight of foreign royals being welcomed – and paid for – would not have been well received. So, while feeling real sorrow for a fellow sovereign – and, like George himself, a grandson of Queen Victoria – the future of the monarchy was the most important issue and the King turned his back.

Even after Australia voted to keep Elizabeth II as its head of state in 1999, the former Premier Bob Hawke said he still believed that the first decade of the twenty-first century would see his country a republic. As far back as 1970, Palace officials were admitting that they would not be surprised if Australia left the Commonwealth within ten years. Prince Philip, in a televised press conference even earlier, said the same. Both Philip and the Palace were wrong at the time, but the portents were there.

Canada has long been ambivalent towards the monarchy. More than thirty per cent of Canadians are of French descent, and there are other ethnic groups: Chinese, German, Dutch and a large contingent from eastern Europe, so it is hardly surprising that a large section of the population regards the British sovereign as having nothing to do with them. The idea of being ruled by a queen who lives three thousand miles away and to whom few feel they owe the slightest allegiance, seems ridiculously outdated, though there is still a strong monarchist league in Canada, supported mainly by those of British descent. And the former Prime Minister, Pierre Trudeau, was proved to be many years premature when he said, in 1967: 'The values of the new generation ... may lead Canada to give up its connections with the royal family in the coming decade.'

In Britain itself, the monarchy is seen as an irrelevance by many under thirty. It is generally only the diehard older generations who loyally support the status quo.

The argument of would-be republicans is often based on the cost of the monarchy as opposed to a presidency, and the lifestyle enjoyed, not only by the sovereign, but also by so many of her relatives. Paul Flynn is one of these who objects to the money spent to provide the royal family with luxurious places to live. 'I refuse to believe that a president would need to be housed in eight palaces, some with over a hundred rooms – one with over three hundred. And you certainly would not be expected to house the President's extended family – first and second cousins and so on. The houses they occupy and the land they own is obscene for one family. A huge amount of money goes out from the state to the Queen. She receives large sums to fund her lifestyle and that of her husband, her children and to keep her ex-servants in Grace and Favour houses. No president would ever expect that sort of privileged treatment.'

No politician has ever been successful in obtaining support to dislodge the monarchy. Is this discouraging to Paul Flynn? 'Not in the least. I think things will change; they have changed in my lifetime. When I was a child in South Wales, people would queue for hours waiting to see the Queen pass by and the crowds would be twenty deep in the streets. During the last visit the Queen made to Cardiff, for the opening of the National Assembly in 1999, the lack of interest was embarrassing. The only ones waving flags were either schoolchildren who were allowed out for the day or people who had been bussed in from old folk's homes. The magic has gone and the fairy tale is over. They have been proved to be people just like ourselves: ordinary, foolish and vain. They want to be treated in a special way, yet they are trying to become like the next-door neighbour – and let's face it, we don't all like our next-door neighbour.'

Flynn may be among the more vociferous voices raised in criticism of the monarchy, but he is not alone in Parliament. A number of MPs show their dislike of the system when they take the oath of allegiance to the Queen. One, Tony Banks, a former New Labour Sports Minister, was among several who have crossed their fingers when speaking the words of the oath. Others insert a preamble; there is nothing in parliamentary rules to forbid them from doing so. One said, 'In as much as I believe this to be a load of mumbo-jumbo, I swear . . . etc.'

In 1992, Dennis Skinner declared his loyalty to an 'income tax paying monarch' while the Member for Chesterfield, Tony Benn, included the words, 'As a convinced republican . . .' all of which makes a nonsense of the oath. But if they do not affirm or swear allegiance, MPs are not allowed to claim their substantial salary and allowances. As Paul Flynn says, 'The rule is: No oath: No pay,' so perhaps practicality overcomes principle on these occasions.

In July 1998, Mr Kevin McNamara, the Labour Member for Hull (North), introduced a Bill to enable a person to take his seat in the House of Commons without either affirming or swearing the present oath. The Bill was seriously debated and eventually defeated, but not before 137 MPs voted for it.

The whole question of opposition to the monarchy has been a subject of debate throughout much of the Queen's reign. Two very public figures of the fifties and sixties, Lord Altrincham – who renounced his peerage and became plain John Grigg – and Malcolm Muggeridge, wrote essays criticizing the institution in previously unheard-of tones, and suffered for their pains. Both had been frequent broadcasters on BBC current affairs programmes and contributors to serious newspapers. When their offending articles were published, they suddenly found their services were not required, such was the deferential attitude of the establishment in those days. Of course the real reason was never given; the BBC dropped Muggeridge saying he was 'overused'. Eventually, both were reinstated. Commissioning editors realized they were losing two of their brightest – and most controversial – stars.

Muggeridge's article appeared in the New York *Saturday Evening Post* in October 1957, right in the middle of a visit to the United States by the Queen, and it could not have had a greater impact. He described the snobbery that, in his view, extended from the Queen down, and concluded, 'such a social set-up is obsolete and disadvantageous in the contemporary world . . . the monarchy is to that extent undesirable.' The attacks were not limited to the institution either. Referring to the Queen herself, he wrote, 'Duchesses find the Queen dowdy, frumpish and banal.' Obviously Muggeridge had abandoned all hopes of a knighthood.

These days it is highly unusual to find opponents of the monarchy mounting personal attacks on the Queen. It is also fairly pointless, as most people in Britain regard her with respect, if not always open affection, believing that she is an honest woman who performs her role as best she can, and not for her own aggrandizement. In any case, to all practical purposes, the United Kingdom is already a republic if you accept the dictionary definition as being a State in which the government is carried on nominally and usually in fact also by the people or their elected representatives. The fact that we have an hereditary sovereign acting as head of state does not mean that she governs us. And there are benefits. As Prince Philip has said, 'The advantage of a monarchy is that it doesn't enter into the political arguments of the day. It makes for a very good division of responsibilities; the Prime Minister does all the political business and this means that those who oppose him politically don't have to oppose him as head of state. The monarchy is above politics.' He might have added that, in the fifty years she has been on the throne, Elizabeth II has given her people more than enough proof that, for Britain at least, monarchy is the most acceptable system for providing a head of state.

The arguments for and against the monarchy have raged for centuries and will, in all probability, continue for many years to come. Supporters of the present system will always be willing to lay down their lives for 'Queen and Country' – in that order – while the cry of 'Up the Revolution' is not likely to be heard as the hordes rush down the Mall. Those who argue for abolition are not all revolutionaries who simply want to see the privileged lifestyle of the House of Windsor ended. They include genuine reformers who believe in a more modern, democratic way of choosing a head of state. But they will never convince the 'true-blue' royalists, faithful to the principle of hereditary monarchy.

One of the more realistic parliamentary voices on the subject is that of Austin Mitchell, a long-serving Labour Member of Parliament for a Grimsby constituency. As he told me: 'We've got it, it works and there is no argument for getting rid of it. The continuity is a great thing, in that if we had an elected president it always becomes the subject of party politics and therefore less attractive and popular. But the danger is that monarchy becomes an escapism factor with the people. On the whole I think the continuity of the monarchy is one of its most important characteristics because the whole position of head of state is important. The main function of the monarchy is as a symbol of unity . . . There is a tremendous feeling throughout the country for the Queen, and politicians of every party, with very few exceptions, would support the continuance of the monarchy – even if privately they belong to the anti-royalist lobby.'

We live in an age of sceptical uncertainty, when perhaps not even royalty any longer believes in its 'divine right' to rule. When pro-royalists point to the unblemished public service record of the Queen as an argument for preserving the monarchy one wonders what their reaction would be if she were suddenly revealed to be a secret drinker and drug-taker with a string of lovers. Would that mean she has been any less successful as sovereign? And would it also mean that, as an institution, monarchy itself has been a failure? The arguments for and against an hereditary monarchy cannot depend on the personal qualities and character of the incumbent. Edward VII was a gambler and womanizer throughout his life, yet he made an excellent King. His son, George V, is considered to be the dullest man ever to occupy the throne, whose main, indeed only, passion was stamp collecting, but his people revered him and mourned his passing. George VI, the Queen's father, the 'reluctant monarch', possessed none of the qualities expected in a sovereign. He lacked self-confidence, had a serious speech defect and hated public appearances. Yet, when the time came, he grew into the job and, with the support of a tough wife – and Winston Churchill – he too became a successful King, unifying the country and Empire throughout the Second World War.

Republicans claim they want to be citizens, not subjects. One only has to look at the fortunate 'citizens' of such 'enlightened' countries as China, Burma, and any number of East European or South American states, to see the 'advantages' they enjoy. And what if the British nation was allowed to choose a head of state? The big guns of the major political parties would throw their considerable weight behind a presidential candidate, the winner being the one on whom the most money was spent. It's happened so often in almost every republic in the world. Why should things be different here? As one United States President famously remarked: 'If it ain't broke, don't fix it.'

CHAPTER EIGHTEEN

Royal Protection

'I put my hand up and he shot me again
... there was no great pain or
excruciating agony.'
CHIEF SUPERINTENDENT JAMES BEATON GC,
ROYAL PROTECTION DEPARTMENT,
SPEAKING IN 1974

'Perhaps the main difference between British and American attitudes to security is that in Britain it is regarded as essential that those responsible for the safety of the head of state and political leaders remain as unobtrusive as possible; in the States the very opposite applies. The secret service like to be seen. They regard it as a deterrent to any would-be assassin.' The speaker is ex-Chief Superintendent James Beaton GC, who was for nine years the Queen's personal bodyguard.

The Queen is probably the least protected head of state in the world. When she goes out in public she is accompanied only by her senior personal bodyguard, a chief superintendent of the Metropolitan Police force, whose main task appears to be to ensure a rug is placed over the royal knees and hold aloft an umbrella when it rains. Obviously there are other police officers around: the motorcycle outriders who clear the path of the Queen's car and a following vehicle containing emergency medical equipment and a supply of blood of the same type as hers. But this is no more than many leading political figures enjoy. By contrast when the President of the United States ventures out of the White House, at least fifty armed security officers are in attendance, with ambulances and helicopters all within a few minutes' call.

Royal protection has always been low-key. King George VI hated being surrounded by armed guards even during the Second World War, when he was known to be a target for both the IRA and other German sympathizers. Similarly, his own father, George V, only agreed to a police presence as long as he did not have to see them.

These days the security of the royal family is the responsibility of the Royal and Diplomatic Security Department, who also look after all the foreign embassies and High Commissions in London. The total cost is over £30 million a year all told, and one of the most delicate problems they have to face is the burgeoning family of the Queen. Protection for the 'minor' royals places a great strain on police resources; it's a question of striking a balance. Some police officers believe the extended family is over-protected, considering their relative unimportance. None is thought to be in any real danger, and the police object to acting as extra pairs of hands to carry parcels or clear traffic for a visit to a restaurant or theatre.

Nevertheless, it is remarkable that even in this day and age, when the Queen retires for the night, her only protection is a lone, uniformed sergeant who sits outside her bedroom door all night, wearing slippers instead of his regulation boots, so that when he walks around checking the corridor – or answering nature's calls – his tread will not disturb the royal slumbers.

Inside the Queen's bedroom there is a 'panic button' which used to have a tendency to go off at regular intervals; so much so that when an intruder broke into the Palace and ended up sitting on Her Majesty's bed, the police office at the other end of the Palace ignored the Queen's frantic pressing of the button, believing it to be yet another case of electronic malfunction. This was early on the morning of 9 July 1982, when the Queen suffered what must be every woman's nightmare – to awaken in her own bedroom, to find an unknown man sitting on her bed. If a novelist made up such a story, it would never be believed. That an incident like this should happen in what was reasonably expected to be the most secure room in the safest building in Britain, Buckingham Palace, was so unlikely it was almost laughable.

Michael Fagan, a thirty-one-year-old schizophrenic, had entered the Palace at around seven o'clock in the morning by the simple expedient of climbing through an open, first-floor window in the Master of the Household's office. He wandered through the corridors and was seen by at least one housemaid who assumed he was a workman on duty, even though he was barefoot.

It is several hundred yards from the Master of the Household's office to the Queen's bedroom on the opposite side of the Palace and, apparently, Fagan made little effort to hurry or to hide himself. It was easy to identify Her Majesty's room as every door is labelled, the name of the occupant slotted into a brass holder on the door. And by this time, the police sergeant, Cyril Hunt, had gone off duty; his shift ending at six-thirty.

It is almost impossible to imagine the Queen's feelings when she found this stranger sitting on the end of her bed. He was dishevelled, barefoot and bleeding from a cut to his hand from a broken ashtray. He later claimed he had intended to cut his wrists in front of the Queen.

When she failed to get a response from the panic button beside her bed, Her Majesty quietly spoke to the intruder asking him what he wanted. He requested a cigarette and she then persuaded him to move outside the bedroom with her in order to find some. In the corridor they met a maid who was even more surprised than the Queen, exclaiming, 'Bloody Hell, Ma'am, what's he doing here?' It was probably the first and last time a royal servant had sworn in front of Her Majesty.

Just then, a footman, Paul Whybrew, who later became the Queen's Page, returned from the gardens where he had been exercising the royal corgis, and together with the maid he managed to get Fagan into a pantry, ostensibly to look for cigarettes.

By this time one of the Palace police force had arrived – not apparently in any great hurry – to investigate the ringing of the emergency button. When he saw the Queen standing there, not in the finest of tempers, he quickly moved to make amends and, with a colleague who had just arrived, arrested Michael Fagan, who later claimed he had been 'roughed up' in the process. Fagan also later said that throughout the incident, which lasted for about seven minutes, the Queen was calm and collected and not the slightest bit frightened or nervous. At least, that was the impression she gave.

Prince Philip was in his bedroom a few doors down from the Queen, and when he found out what had happened he naturally hit the roof, demanding the heads of everyone supposed to be protecting his wife. However, neither he nor the Queen wanted any publicity, so no statement was issued by the Palace. But inevitably the story was leaked and by Monday morning it was front-page news.

At first no one could believe that such a thing could happen, but it was later revealed that this was not the first time Fagan had been inside Buckingham Palace. On a previous occasion he had climbed over the railings, found the kitchens and drunk a bottle of wine before leaving without anyone being any the wiser.

In practically any other country in the world, an intruder into the head of state's private quarters would surely have been locked away for a long time. In Britain, Fagan was found to be mentally unstable, committed to an institution for a while and then released. He took to loitering outside the gates of Buckingham Palace, enjoying his celebrity status, talking to tourists and having his photograph taken with them.

After the incident a complete review of royal security took place. Details were not revealed (except that the police officer who sits outside the Queen's bedroom now carries a gun). Meanwhile newspaper columnists reminded their readers that in earlier centuries the Home Secretary, as the man ultimately responsible for the sovereign's security, as well as all the senior police officers involved – and possibly their families too – would have ended up in the Tower of London. As it was, nobody even lost his job, although the police sergeant in charge of the station where the panic button sounded was reprimanded. The Palace later described their emotions over the affair as being 'embarrassment and relief'.

It was the second time the Queen had shown her courage in the face of possible injury or worse. A year earlier, in June 1981, she had been riding her horse, Burmese, to the Sovereign's Birthday Parade on Horseguards when a young man stepped out of the crowd at the corner of the Mall and fired six shots at her before he was overpowered. As it happened, they were blanks, but nobody realized that at the time, certainly not the Queen. But she merely controlled Burmese, who had been frightened by the noise, patted him on the neck and rode on as if nothing had happened. Prince Philip and Prince Charles, riding immediately behind, closed up to shield her, as did Silver Stick in Waiting, the Sovereign's nearest escort, but the parade continued with none of the onlookers having any idea of the dramatic event that had just taken place.

The men who are selected to act as personal bodyguards to the Queen are all highly skilled, dedicated policemen who come from the uniformed branch. They are not detectives as

271

is commonly supposed; neither are they 'James Bond' types. But there is obviously a certain amount of glamour attached to guarding the most famous woman in the world.

Of all the many police officers who have worked for the Queen, three stand out. Her Majesty's first bodyguard, in the days when the word 'security' wasn't even mentioned in polite society, was Commander Albert Perkins. He was a formidable figure who used his furled umbrella – nobody ever saw it open – to keep at bay any reporter or photographer who had the temerity to get too close to his royal boss. The Queen had inherited Perkins from her father, for whom the Commander (then a Chief Superintendent) had been bodyguard for several months in 1951 and early 1952. The Worcestershire man had joined the police force in 1927, after working with a fishing-rod manufacturer when he left grammar school, and risen through the ranks.

Dressed usually in his daytime 'Court uniform' of blue, double-breasted pin-striped suit, white shirt and dark tie, Perkins never quite looked the part in the formal morning coat or black dinner jacket he was required to wear on occasion. He did, however, appear comfortable in jodhpurs and hacking jacket when he rode with the Queen at Windsor or Sandring-ham. Already an expert shot when he was appointed, Perkins, who had never ridden before, quickly enrolled for lessons at the Metropolitan Police Riding Academy in order to be able to accompany Her Majesty when she rode. None of his successors ever acquired this particular skill.

Commander Perkins, who had achieved considerable suc-cess in his police career before going to Buckingham Palace and was held in high regard by his colleagues, saw no humili-ation in being seen carrying royal handbags, fur stoles, umbrellas and bunches of flowers which the Queen would hand to him once they had been presented to her. He became so identified as the perfect companion to the Queen that he earned the nickname of the 'Admirable Perkins'. He also carried discretion to the nth degree, speaking only once about his job: 'I have an honourable and onerous task. I realize the responsibility of it, and dislike reading about myself. I cannot, and will not, say anything about my job. And never will.' And he never did.

In Perkins's day, there were rarely any serious incidents involving the Queen's security, and certainly no threats against her life. The most difficult task he had in his years at the Palace was during a State Visit to Austria, when the enthusiasm of the welcoming crowds was so overwhelming that they broke ranks and almost engulfed the Queen. Perkins nearly had apoplexy, but he managed to protect his royal charge and kept most of the wellwishers at arm's length. He later wrote a scathing report to the head of security at the British Embassy to make sure that nothing of the kind ever occurred again. His letter also became the blueprint for all subsequent visits overseas.

One of Perkins's two assistants at the Palace was Chief Inspector Michael Trestrail who took over the top job in 1973 and served in that position for nine years, becoming one of the closest servants the Queen has ever had. The Queen rarely becomes friendly with any of her staff – her old dresser, Bobo McDonald, being the exception – but she was extremely fond of Michael Trestrail, as were many of the royal household. So it came, not only as a shock, but also a personal loss when, just two weeks after the Fagan incident, a newspaper reported that Trestrail had had a homosexual relationship. He resigned immediately, not because there was any danger that his private life would affect the way he carried out his police duties, but for fear that the publicity would be embarrassing to the royal family. Michael Trestrail has remained on good terms with the Queen and is frequently seen at Buckingham Palace Garden Parties chatting with his former colleagues.

The third high-profile bodyguard of the Queen was Chief Superintendent James Beaton, the man who had once saved the life of the Princess Royal. He is also the only royal body-guard ever to fire his gun in anger.

It was on Wednesday, 20 March 1974 that the Queen could have lost her only daughter. Princess Anne and her first husband, Mark Phillips, had been married for only four months, and were living at the Royal Military College, Sandhurst. They had been invited to a special showing in London of a film, *Riding for Freedom*, which told the story of the charity Riding for the Disabled. On the way back to Buckingham Palace, where they were to collect their own cars and drive back to Sandhurst, they were ambushed in the Mall, less than two hundred yards from the Palace.

An armed madman intended to carry out one of the most audacious crimes of the century. His aim was to kidnap Princess Anne and hold her to ransom for £3 million. And although the gunman – his name was Ian Ball – was later proved to be mentally and criminally unstable, his plan had taken three years to prepare and had been designed with meticulous attention to detail. False identities had been established, including driving licences in several names; a number of addresses were used, making Ball virtually impossible to trace; and he had hired a car for the kidnap attempt using one of his aliases.

As the royal limousine (registration number NGN1) passed the turning for St James's Palace, Ball struck. He drove his Ford Escort in front of the Princess's car, forcing it to stop. He jumped out of his car and ran backwards shooting as he ran. Apart from the chauffeur, Alexander Callendar, Rowena Brassey, the Princess's lady-in-waiting, and Jim Beaton were in the car with the Phillipses.

Jim Beaton jumped out of his seat, ran around to the Princess's door and was shot in the chest, causing his right lung to collapse. 'When I first heard the crack of the gun I knew something serious was happening, but I didn't feel a thing when he shot me. I just felt a bit hazy and I couldn't raise my arm so I used both hands to shoot back.'

In spite of his wounds, Jim Beaton placed himself in front of the Princess, 'I could see he was pointing the gun right at her through the window, so I put my hand up and he shot me again . . . again there was no great pain . . . no excruciating agony or loud bangs.' But worse was to come. Ball calmly shot Beaton for a third time, the bullet passing into his stomach, through the intestines and pelvis. It was a miracle that he wasn't hit in the spine, which could have paralysed him for life.

The incident took less than seven minutes, and several other people, including Callendar, the Princess's chauffeur, a passing journalist who tried to help and a young police constable who also joined in, were all shot before Ball was overpowered.

Jim Beaton spent weeks in hospital, but five months after the incident he returned to royal duty as Princess Anne's body-guard and remained with her until 1979.

All those who had helped to foil the kidnap attempt were rewarded by the Queen. Jim Beaton received the George Cross, the highest award for bravery it is possible to win in civilian life. After the ceremony in Buckingham Palace, Jim, his wife Anne, and Linda and Shona, his two daughters, were invited to a reception by the royal family. Shona was then just five years old and she had been fascinated by the appearance of two priests in their clerical gowns. When the Queen asked the youngster how she had enjoyed the Investiture Shona replied: 'It was fine, but why were those two men wearing their pyjamas and dressing gowns?' The Queen thought it was marvellous to hear such honest remarks and rocked with laughter. This happened after the official photographs had been taken, but by lucky coincidence one photographer had remained behind. He took the final picture and got the scoop all press photographers are hoping for. And his was the one that appeared on all the front pages the next morning. The Queen also made a point of saying to Jim, 'Thank you for what you did.'

When Jim Beaton left the Royal and Diplomatic Protection Department he returned to normal police duties. But on Michael Trestrail's departure in 1982 it was felt that someone not already on the Palace's strength should be brought in. Beaton was an obvious choice. He was totally reliable, and he knew the ropes. As he said, 'I wasn't interviewed by the Queen but I was asked to go to Sandringham for a week to see if I was suitable. Nobody ever told me the result but I stayed on so it must have been all right.'

It was like old times when Jim Beaton moved back into the Palace, but with one exception. He was now the number one man in an organization where everyone's sole concern is the welfare of the Queen. As her bodyguard, 'I had a large office which was also a bed-sitting room on the ground floor. I spent most of my time there as on my desk I had the latest equipment to give me instant contact with everyone and everywhere I might need: Scotland Yard, our own police headquarters in another part of the Palace, the Queen's Page, who could summon me at a moment's notice, and also all the other various department heads in the royal household.'

Over the years two significant moments have affected royal security: the first was the incident in the Mall, in which Jim Beaton was so actively involved, and after which one of the Queen's private secretaries said to him, 'At least now we know what you are there for. Before this we used to wonder.' The other occasion was, of course, the Fagan break-in. As Jim Beaton recalls: 'After that there was a major reassessment of our security – more money, more personnel and more vigilance. The whole thing moved up a notch. Though I believe Fagan was a very lucky man. Everything went in his favour. It was a one in a million chance.'

As the Queen spends much of her time inside Buckingham Palace during the working week, how onerous is the work of her personal bodyguard? 'We used to have long periods with little or nothing to do but then everything would come at

once. A lot of my time was spent in long-term planning. You
have to remember that every visit that the Queen makes means
at least two for her police officer. He makes the 'recce' trip
to check all the security problems both in Britain and overseas,
liaises with his opposite number in the police and security
services abroad and also makes sure that any house the Queen
might be staying at is fully protected. Sometimes I would
know two years in advance if we were planning a major State
Visit. On other occasions it might be two minutes if Her
Majesty was making a quick trip to the dentist. If that was
happening her Page would ring down so I could get around
to the Garden Entrance with the car and make sure I had the
door open when she came out. The Queen was never kept
waiting so the door was always open. The footman on duty
would place a rug over the Queen's knees – I would do the
same on the return journey – and then I would jump into the
front seat and off we'd go.'

Unlike the 'Admirable Perkins', Jim Beaton was not
required to ride with the Queen when they were at Sandringham or Windsor. 'I always kept her in sight, but I didn't go
on horseback for a very good reason. When you ride you have
to contend with the horse as well as concentrating on your
royal charge. So instead I used to take a Land-Rover, with a
back-up protection officer, and keep my distance, trying all
the time not to be too intrusive. That was the secret: to be
able to get to her side in an instant but to remain out of her
eyeline. The Queen knew we were there, of course, but she
preferred to ignore us – and rightly so. She realized we had
to be there and treated her personal protection officer with
resigned tolerance. In fact the only occasion when she actually
ordered all police officers not to be present was when the
young Princes, William and Harry, were playing in the garden
at Buckingham Palace. This was regarded as a "safe area" so
she would not have any policemen around.'

In Britain, Beaton recalls, there was an established routine which the Palace followed whenever the Queen travelled and there were rarely any problems. Abroad was a different matter. 'The royal family does not like change. They like to see familiar faces around them, so when I first joined the Queen I was told to go on every important visit, at home and abroad, so she would get used to having me around. The difference between British security and that in other countries took some getting used to. My first "recce" visit was to the United States, and when I arrived I was asked the size of my "team". When I told them I was it, they couldn't believe it at first. We travelled around the States on the President's official aircraft, Air Force One, and I was the only British security man on board – there were fifty-five American secret service agents. When we returned for the State Visit, the Queen and President Reagan were in the first limousine and there were fifty-seven other vehicles in the convoy. In fact it was on this visit that the only incident occurred when I had to physically handle the Queen. Someone – I didn't know if he was an agent or not – got too close, so to make sure, I hustled her away. You never know in circumstances like that.'

As Jim Beaton explains, the different regulations governing the security of a head of state can also be something of a nuisance to the very person they are trying to protect. 'American secret service rules clearly state that the nearest agents are never to be more than three feet away from the person they are assigned to. Which means they are virtually on their shoulder at all times. I knew the Queen would be unhappy with this arrangement and tried to persuade them to leave a little space. On the official part of the visit they stuck to their regulations, but when we went to Yosemite Park, which was supposed to be for a three-day break, I knew it would ruin the holiday if they insisted on sticking rigidly to the rules. Eventually, they agreed, but only because it was made clear how unhappy the Queen – and the President – would be if they didn't relax the rules a little. The secret service were –

and are – a law unto themselves. They were very off-hand with the royal household, and with the White House staff. In fact they believed that no one – president or monarch – could go against them in security matters.'

All of which did not prevent a gunman from shooting President Reagan as he stepped into his car in Washington DC on 30 March 1981. In fairness, though, it was accepted that they did an excellent job in getting him away afterwards.

When the Queen visits the United States to pursue her racing interests in a private capacity the destination is always Will Farish's Kentucky home. And of course nothing is entirely private for a reigning sovereign, so during Jim Beaton's nine years as the Queen's personal protection officer he accompanied her there a number of times. 'The secret service used to provide their normal safeguards: bullet-proof cars, medical back-up and sophisticated communications. At first we had a few problems, mainly because they wanted to take over the whole thing. Whereas Mr Farish has his own chauffeur, whom he wanted to drive the Queen, the service wanted their own man to sit behind the wheel. We won. There was a single agent based in the area who became familiar with our requirements, so on subsequent visits I used to ask if he could be assigned to us. Reluctantly – because they always rotate their officers and find it difficult to cope with any change in their routine – they finally agreed and we got along fine.'

During the years from 1983 to 1992 when Jim Beaton was with the Queen, he became privy to many royal secrets, for the glass partition that divided the front of the car from the seats occupied by the Queen and Prince Philip was not always fully closed. There was one occasion when the Queen had been to visit her old nanny 'Bobo' McDonald in hospital in the last days of her life. 'As Her Majesty got back into the car, after having long overrun the allotted time, she said, very quietly, "She's been with me since I was six weeks old." So of course there was a very special relationship.'

Working so closely for the Queen it was inevitable that Jim Beaton came into contact with other members of the royal family. So what was his reaction to them? 'When I first started at the Palace, I did two trips with Princess Margaret. I had heard all the tales of how difficult she could be. However, she was fine. She told me what she wanted done, where things should be placed, and then left me completely alone. There were no tantrums. I knew nothing about the system – I'd only been there a week – but she was decisive, knew exactly what she wanted. I provided the service she demanded and it seemed to work OK.'

What about the man who has been described as the rudest, most aggressive member of the family? 'Prince Philip was full of surprises. At one time he even apologized to me. His own policeman was amazed. He said to me, "I can't believe it. That's the first time I've ever seen him do that." I found him one of the easiest to get along with. Now Prince Philip never liked policemen and he made no secret of the fact. But he was fair and if you were accepted as part of his "group" he would look after you.'

Within Palace circles it is well known that there has always been a certain coolness between the household and the police officers, mainly because the police are paid much more than their colleagues on the royal staff. In 1992 a Chief Superintendent such as Jim Beaton would have earned over £40,000 a year, more than even the Queen's senior aide. In addition, members of the royal household have tended in the past to give themselves certain 'airs and graces' because of their close proximity to the sovereign, regarding others, including the protection officers, as mere 'hired help'.

Jim Beaton had a little experience of this. 'Wherever the Queen goes the "brown bag" always goes with her. This contains her essentials; things like an extra pair of shoes, stockings, gloves and all the other items a woman might need. On one of our American trips, the bag was left on the aircraft, so an airman brought it and gave it to me to pass to the Queen. A member of the Household took it from me saying he would hand it to Her Majesty. It was as if it was important that nobody else should do it. The same thing often happened when an umbrella had to be given to the Queen, not that it made the slightest bit of difference to her of course.'

Jim Beaton has an apt phrase to describe Robert Fellowes's difficult stint as private secretary, a time that covered the last turbulent years of Diana, Princess of Wales: 'He walked through a minefield and I doubt if anyone could have negotiated it better.'

Since he has left the Palace in 1992, Jim Beaton has remained in contact with the royal family more than most former police officers. 'I'm still on the Christmas card list, but so are plenty of others. The main reason I stay in touch is that I get invited to stalk at Balmoral.'

Some of his former colleagues have said that working for the royal family is just like being 'part of the furniture'. Jim disagreed. 'You're more than a bit of furniture – but only just!' So did he relish being with the Queen for nine years? The reply is typically discreet, 'I enjoyed the work.'

CHAPTER NINETEEN

The First Eleven

*Within the Royal Household, there are some
servants who are positively terrified at the
prospect of coming face to face with the Queen.
Old Palace hands refer to it as
'Reginaphobia'.*

'The royal family are not always right, but they are never
wrong.' This was the view of a man in the know, who occupied
the most senior position in the royal household for thirteen
years, from 1971 until 1984. His name was Lord [Charles]
Maclean, known as 'Chips' to everyone, including the Queen.
A former Major in the Scots Guards, Chief of his clan and a
one-time Chief Scout, Chips Maclean had all the attributes
needed to be the perfect courtier. He was gregarious, loved
the parties he was required to attend, and thoroughly enjoyed
the ceremonial aspects of the job, even taking pleasure in
learning the art of walking backwards, an essential skill for all
who would aspire to be Lord Chamberlain.

But even he, with a distinguished war record and a life of
public service behind him, knew that the one thing he dare
not do under any circumstances was to answer back. As he

once told me, 'The only rules that royalty obeys are the ones they make themselves. It's no good trying to judge them by ordinary standards because they simply don't apply. That is not to say they are not considerate because I've found them to be extremely thoughtful and kind: a marvellous family. At the same time, you can be made to stand and listen to an absolute tirade of abuse even if you are not the guilty party.' In the royal household you have to be able to take it without flinching. That and total discretion are two of the most valuable qualities any royal servant needs, from the Lord Chamberlain down to the humblest footman.

Lord Maclean also told me how mystified he was at getting the post. 'I knew no one in the royal household and there was no interview. I was simply told by Lord Cobbold, the retiring Lord Chamberlain, that the Queen would like me to be the new head of the household. That was it. The first time I met Her Majesty as Lord Chamberlain was on the day I started the job.'

There is a common misconception among many people, including some of those who have worked inside Buckingham Palace for years, that faithful old retainers become valued friends of the royal family. It is not always true. Once a servant – and that is all they are, no matter what grand-sounding titles they may hold – leaves royal service, he or she is virtually forgotten. They may be fortunate enough to remain on the Christmas card list, but that again is the responsibility of other servants, there's nothing personal about it. And other than that there is usually little contact between members of the royal family and former staff. There is a saying among old hands that 'once you have fallen off the log, you've had it,' meaning, no matter how high a position one has held, once one leaves it is all over, with little further contact. There are few things more 'ex' than an ex-Courtier. Unlike some other aristocratic families where loyal servants are regarded as life-long friends, even if not necessarily included in the same social circles, with royalty the cut-off point is final once the professional relationship has ended.

Former Lord Chamberlains and private secretaries may find themselves appointed as part-time extra equerries, to be called on when needed, such as representing members of the royal family at a funeral or memorial service, but they are rarely invited to a royal function in any personal capacity. This exclusion applies also to men of high rank who become used to being members of the 'inner circle', such as the former Archbishop of Canterbury, the late Lord Runcie. 'A common mistake among those who feel they have lived close to the royal family through their office is that the relationship will continue afterwards. Understandably it is part of the Queen's duty to build up her relationship with the person who succeeds you. Hence I have known it come as something of a shock to those who are suddenly struck off the invitation lists. How could it be otherwise? I still get a personal Christmas card and the occasional invitation to a retirement party; which probably comes from the household rather than the Queen herself. The Queen is very successful, it seems to me, in the discretion which she exercises over her feelings about people with whom she must necessarily do business and to whom she must give a degree of her time. This balance between personal friendship and dutiful relationships is part of her genius as a sovereign.'

The royal household is staffed by men and women who are supremely confident of their own abilities and use their charm and self-confidence to make guests feel at ease rather than intimidated. Good manners are taken for granted and the idea of any of them deliberately making anyone feel uncomfortable would be as unthinkable as drinking sherry out of a tankard. And although salaries remain low compared with market rates outside, the Palace is still able to attract plenty of upper–middle-class young men and women, so it is rare to hear Estuary English accents spoken. Among the middle-ranking clerical staff, however, regulations have been relaxed to the extent that a blind eye is turned to the odd young man sporting a single earring.

New members are quickly made aware of some of the Queen's likes and dislikes. For example, she hates moustaches and beards and won't allow any of the men in the household to wear them. She even ordered Prince Philip to shave off his beard in the early days of their marriage when he returned from his ship sporting a 'full set'. She also dislikes men wearing waistcoats, so three-piece suits are out, and her private secretaries know that whenever they are in her presence their jackets should be buttoned. At weekends and when they are in the country, sports clothes are permitted – but no jeans.

The Queen does not approve of the metric system. She still uses yards and inches, while weights such as kilos are completely foreign to her. Her staff have despaired of ever persuading her to fasten her safety belt when she drives her twenty-year-old, dark green Vauxhall shooting brake around the Sandringham estate, nor will she wear protective headgear when she is out riding, sticking to her favourite old silk headscarf.

The titular head of the royal household is the Lord Chamberlain – of which the Queen has been served by seven – but by far the most important and influential member is Her Majesty's Principal Private Secretary. He is the conduit through which all information to the Queen is channelled and no one – the Lord Chamberlain and the Prime Minister included – gets to see her without his knowledge and consent. The only exception was a former Crown equerry, Sir John Miller, late of the Welsh Guards, who was a law unto himself. As the man who had taught the Queen's children to ride, he had earned a special place in her affections and he used to infuriate his colleagues by popping in to see Her Majesty without first checking with the private secretary, who controls her diary.

To be the Queen's private secretary places a man – so far no woman has risen higher than assistant private secretary – in a unique position. He is privy to many secrets, royal and political, and his influence, if properly exercised, can affect government policy. An astute private secretary is able to anticipate problems that might emerge and in doing so he can then let Downing Street know in advance the possible reaction of the sovereign. As the Queen is the most experienced head of state in the world, it would be a foolish Prime Minister who ignored such advice,. The two Harolds, Macmillan and Wilson, both said that they had been helped by listening to the private secretary of the day before they approached the Queen. For example, in 1962 Harold Macmillan wanted the United States to support Britain's entry to the Common Market, and the Queen's private secretary, Sir Michael Adeane, advised him to mention the matter to Her Majesty. She then wrote a friendly letter to President John F. Kennedy which did not directly mention Europe but which praised Macmillan and spoke warmly of his high regard for the United States.

Among his many duties, the private secretary also sits on all the most important committees at the Palace. These can range from matters dealing with the honours system to the regular heads of department meetings, at which every aspect of Palace life is discussed.

Together with the Earl Marshall, who is in overall charge, the Lord Chamberlain and the Crown Equerry, the private secretary is also involved in the preparations necessary for burying the sovereign, where precedent is the all-important word. Almost every occasion that involves any member of the royal family is covered by a thick file in which is listed every detail required and what happened at previous similar events. 'Refer back' is one of the most common phrases used within the household. Nowhere is this more noticeable than when a royal funeral is being planned, which is why there was such initial confusion over the funeral of Diana, Princess of Wales.

There was no file, because there was no precedent for the burial of a divorced former member of the family who was not a Royal Highness. So they had to start from scratch and make all the necessary arrangements in days. The decision that the royal princes and Diana's brother, Earl Spencer, should walk in the procession was a first in royal procedure.

The question of what should cover the coffin was another problem. Diana had not had her own Royal Standard designed – which would have incorporated her own coat of arms – so we saw the unusual sight of a conventional Royal Standard edged with an ermine border – another first in modern times. Had she had her own coat of arms, the standard would not have been trimmed with the ermine border. The only other member of the royal family whose personal coat of arms has not yet been submitted to the College of Arms is the Duchess of Kent.

Macabre as it may sound, the preliminary preparations for the Queen's own funeral began even before her father was buried on 16 February 1952, and they were given the code-name 'London Bridge'. (Arrangements for the Duke of Edinburgh's funeral are listed under the codename 'Forth Bridge'.) There is a long-established blueprint for these preparations, dating back to 1901 and the reign of Queen Victoria, whose funeral was the first to be held in daytime. Prior to this all royal funerals were held at night.

Surprisingly, no ceremonial plan existed for Queen Victoria's funeral, even though she was eighty-one when she died and her death was not entirely unexpected. The household were taken completely by surprise as they had all assumed – without checking – that there would be a file to which they could refer back. They had also forgotten that the last funeral of a sovereign, William IV, had taken place some sixty-four years earlier, and it had been a private affair with no ceremonial involved.

Victoria's funeral was a truly international event. She was

Empress of India, ruling over a quarter of the world's people, so representatives of practically every country in the world attended. In addition to any other logistical problems there was the difficulty of managing three venues: she had died at Osborne on the Isle of Wight, the funeral service was to be held in Westminster Abbey and the interment at Frogmore in the grounds of Windsor Castle.

With remarkable speed for a royal event, particularly one for which there was no precedent, everything was arranged and the short voyage from the Isle of Wight to the mainland was arguably the most impressive part of the proceedings. Thirty-eight ships of the Royal Navy, at that time the greatest fleet in the world, formed up as a guard of honour through which passed the Royal Yacht *Alberta* carrying the Queen's coffin. Also present were five German battleships, one Portuguese, a French cruiser and a battleship of the Imperial Navy of Japan. That the ceremonial apparently passed off with the usual royal efficiency was a triumph of last-minute planning without any appearance of undue haste, and this is the blueprint from which the Palace still works today.

For an event such as the present Queen's funeral, no detail is overlooked, and every year since the accession the working-group of six people from the Lord Chamberlain's Office and the College of Arms has met to update the file under the chairmanship of the Earl Marshal. As Earl Marshal the Duke of Norfolk, the UK's premier duke, has total responsibility for the funeral of the sovereign. The committee takes account of any changes in personnel who have to be present and the requirements of the media. For example, during the early years of the Queen's reign it would not have been necessary to accommodate television cameras, which were considered too intrusive on such a sad occasion. Today, it would be unthinkable for the sovereign's funeral not to be televised live throughout the world, with cameras, microphones and commentators placed at strategic points along the route and inside

Westminster Abbey. In 1936, when George V was buried, the BBC were first allowed to broadcast the sounds of the marching men and the solemn beat of the drums along the route, but not the service itself inside the Abbey.

There is machinery in place for contacting all the Heads of State and other VIPs who have to be informed, plus the mechanics of transporting them to London and arranging suitable accommodation. Among the details to be organized are the order of service in the Abbey and the seating plan – where the remaining crowned heads sit, and in what order. The funeral of Edward VII in 1910 was attended by fifty-eight kings and princes, a number not expected in the twenty-first century. The security of the Heads of State attending is a priority and the dignity of Commonwealth leaders must also be ensured, so the representatives of the countries which joined the Commonwealth first take precedence over the more recent additions.

The number of troops taking part and their place in the funeral procession is decided, the regiments of which the Queen is Colonel-in-Chief coming first. However, the privilege of pulling the gun-carriage, on which the royal coffin is carried, rests with, and is jealously guarded by, the Royal Navy – the Senior Service. This is another tradition that dates from the funeral of Queen Victoria. The lead horses of the Royal Artillery, which were pulling the gun-carriage, suddenly kicked out and broke the traces, so the naval guard of honour stepped in to drag the gun-carriage to St George's Chapel in Windsor – and they have done so ever since. (In order to mollify the feelings of the Royal Artillery at Queen Victoria's funeral, they were later allowed to convey the coffin to Frogmore, its final resting place.)

On the death of the sovereign, the coffin is first taken to Westminster Hall for the Lying-in-State, where male members of the royal family will stand guard as the rest of the family, and then the household, are allowed to pay their respects before the general public is admitted. The Lying-in-State in Westminster Hall in the Palace of Westminster is the responsibility of the Lord Great Chamberlain, who is the Hereditary Keeper of the Palace of Westminster.

From here the Royal Navy becomes involved for the first time. The gun-carriage on which the coffin rests is pulled by 150 naval ratings as they transfer it to the Abbey. They also perform the same duty after the service, *en route* to Victoria Station where the royal train is waiting to convey the coffin and family mourners to Windsor Station; from here the gun-carriage is dragged up the steep hill into Windsor Castle and St George's Chapel. The type of coffin to be used – it will be lead-lined – has been decided many years ago and approved by Her Majesty, as have all the arrangements. She sees nothing melancholy in being made aware of such details; to her it is just another aspect of being head of state.

The Crown Equerry, who is responsible for all royal travel, checks the distance the cortège will have to travel, and times every yard of the route, stopwatch in hand. Then the journey from London to Windsor is rehearsed. The Royal Train will travel from Paddington Station to Windsor, the mourners hidden behind drawn blinds, while a separate train will follow, made up of vans containing the royal coffin and the bearer party.

At Windsor the chief mourner will travel to St George's Chapel in a horse-drawn carriage preceded by a procession of heralds, Yeomen of the Guard and members of the royal household, including all the chaplains and members of the ecclesiastical households in England and Scotland. The final resting place in the royal vault at Windsor Castle has been chosen. The dimensions of the tomb in St George's Chapel and the wording to be engraved have all been agreed.

Once the working-group have finalized their plans, they are submitted to a much larger committee. This includes representatives of the Prime Minister, the Ministry of Defence

(Army, Navy and Royal Air Force), the police, the Department of Culture and Environment and the local authorities in London and Windsor, all of whom are involved in some way.

But even the arrangements for the sovereign's final journey do not compare with those made by Earl Mountbatten. He supervised all the plans for his own funeral, carrying out the 'recce' visit himself, accompanied by the Lord Chamberlain and the Queen's Press Secretary. He decided it would require six velvet cushions to carry his medals, decorations and honours, and he set out the menu, and timed how long it would take to eat, for the lunch to be served on the Royal Train taking his body from London to his home in Hampshire, where it was to be buried. His legendary eye for detail was to be fully justified on the day, as the Queen was just finishing her coffee, minutes before the train pulled into Romsey station.

As a follow-up to his initial plan, Mountbatten forwarded an 'informal note' to the Lord Chamberlain with a 'few suggestions'. It ran to eleven pages. And whenever any of those involved raised the slightest objection to his elaborate plans, he quickly quashed them, saying: 'The Queen thinks this would be a good idea.' End of discussion.

Mountbatten said he thoroughly enjoyed himself organizing his own funeral and saw nothing morbid in doing so. He was proved right when his boat was blown up by an IRA bomb on a fishing trip in 1979. The funeral took place with great suddenness but the final result was a triumph of royal ceremonial combined with a stunning and moving display of naval and military pageantry.

Of all the men who have served the Queen as private secretary, the late Lord [Martin] Charteris had the highest profile, particularly so after he had left the Palace, when he spoke indiscreetly a number of times about members of the royal family. The most famous – or notorious – occasion was when he described the Duchess of York as 'Vulgar, vulgar, vulgar.'

But it was a remark he was quickly to regret and for which he tried to make amends at a private lunch with the Duchess.

That Martin Charteris was a successful private secretary has never been queried; after all he spent many years as assistant before succeeding to the top post, so he ought to have learned the ropes by the time he took over. But his period in office, from 1972 to 1977, was one of comparative peace. Charteris was a witty and charismatic figure with an exuberant style which often emerged in the speeches he wrote for the Queen. He also used to lead the laughter at jokes he had written himself. Nobody could ever have described Charteris as a cold, withdrawn figure. He was the exact opposite: flamboyant, enthusiastic and overflowing with *bonhomie*. He loved the theatre, fine wine and good company, with an instinctive feel for what was needed to project the image of the monarchy at any particular time. He also possessed the gift of being able to get on with anyone and was completely devoted to the Queen. His respectful love for her was well known in Palace circles. A former officer in the King's Royal Rifle Corps, he was one of the few survivors when the troopship *Yorkshire* was torpedoed in the Atlantic in 1940. For the period when he was private secretary, Martin Charteris was the ideal man.

Private secretaries are generally recruited through the 'old-boy' network. Most had been to Eton and it became standard practice for a prospective candidate to be 'sounded out' before being introduced into the royal presence. The Queen was never required to make a choice from several aspirants, she merely rubber-stamped the person selected by her Lord Chamberlain and the private secretary who was leaving. There is no record of her ever refusing to appoint someone whose name had been suggested.

By the time of the Waleses' crisis, it was Princess Diana's brother-in-law, the quiet, self-effacing and studious-looking Robert Fellowes, a former commodity broker in the City, who bore the brunt and successfully steered the royal family through their most dangerous period. In between had come two vastly differing characters: Sir Philip [now Lord] Moore, a former British Deputy High Commissioner in Singapore, followed by an Australian, Sir William Heseltine, so far the only Commonwealth citizen to hold the office, both of whom were considered successful without being outstanding.

Philip Moore was a former bomber pilot in the wartime RAF and had also played rugby for England, so his courage was never in doubt; yet he was considered to be the most cautious man ever to occupy an office renowned for its discretion. One of his colleagues once remarked, 'If you say "Good morning" to Philip, he will always consider his answer before replying.' Bill Heseltine was a more outgoing personality, who enjoyed Palace politics and also great popularity, not only with his own colleagues but also among the politicians and government officials with whom he came into daily contact. Robert Fellowes came from a much more traditional background than his two immediate predecessors. Educated at Eton, he was commissioned into the Scots Guards and his late father, Sir William (Billy) Fellowes, had been Land Agent to the Queen at Sandringham. So Robert was brought up knowing the royal family from birth. In 1978 he married Lady Jane Spencer, sister of Diana, at the Guards Chapel in Wellington Barracks.

When the true history of the private secretary to the sovereign comes to be written, it will be Fellowes who emerges as the strong man who did not allow family ties to blind him to where his duty lay. The royal family, and the Queen in particular, have much to thank him for. Without his strength and utter devotion and determination, the outcome of the crisis in the nineties could have been very different. The late Diana, Princess of Wales, expected him to take her side in the rows between her and the rest of the royal family. She was wrong. Fellowes was fair, but he believed his duty lay first and foremost to the sovereign, and it was her interests that he protected, even when, by doing so, it appeared that he was acting against his own wife's sister.

By the time of the Waleses' divorce, Diana was a very confused woman who imagined the whole of the royal household was plotting against her. And while it was quite true that there were elements at Buckingham Palace – and even more so at St James's – who would do anything to discredit her, Robert Fellowes was not one of them. The advice he gave the Queen in a difficult situation was sound and he was not afraid to say things which he knew she might not want to hear but which had to be said.

On one occasion he even offered to resign. In 1992 he had complained to the Press Complaints Commission about Andrew Morton's book, *Diana, Her True Story*, believing at the time that she had not cooperated with the author. When it was disclosed that she had, he was forced to apologize. He offered his resignation, which the Queen sensibly refused to accept.

In 1999 Fellowes decided to leave the Palace and return to the City, handing the reigns over to his deputy, Robin (now Sir Robin) Janvrin. Educated at Marlborough and Oxford, and with a spell in the Royal Navy, Janvrin is very much in the Tony Blair mould of senior courtiers, having an acute mind, good looks and a nice line in political philosophy. The phrase 'laid back' might have been coined for him. He rarely seems to hurry, always gives the appearance of being totally relaxed and, while his background is not aristocratic, he is completely at home in any company. He is sought after by bishops and barons, entrepreneurs and diplomats and deals with each one with equal facility and courtesy. Robin Janvrin is not a man with whom one would associate the word panic.

While the private secretary is the man all look to within the household, another key figure is the Keeper of the Privy Purse – who controls the money. Sir Michael Peat, who lives in one of the most glamorous Grace and Favour homes in Kensington Palace, has done more to modernize Palace finances than any of his predecessors and no important decision is taken without him being consulted.

The third person in the hierarchy is the Master of the Household. He runs the Palace and all the other royal residences and is responsible for the domestic arrangements of the Queen and her family and for every function that is held on their behalf. So far every holder of this position has been either a senior retired Army or Royal Navy officer, and the reputation for perfection and attention to detail that the Palace enjoys is evidence enough of the success of this method in selecting a royal 'hotel manager'.

If these days the senior male aides to the Queen can be said to be chosen more for their ability than their family pedigree, the same cannot be said for the women who occupy some of the positions closest to the sovereign. The Queen has fourteen ladies-in-waiting, all of whom are definitely 'top-drawer' with practically all being members of the aristocracy. Not that this singles them out to be lacking in ability, of course, it's just that when they were invited to become ladies-in-waiting, that wasn't the first consideration. 'Socially adept' is the phrase more usually associated with them.

They are headed by the formidable Duchess of Grafton, the Mistress of the Robes. Fortune Grafton is everyone's idea of a Duchess, grand, upright with just the right touch of arrogance to convey her awareness of her position and that others should not forget it. She and her husband live in Norfolk, at the stately Euston Hall. The Duchess is one of the longest serving companions of the Queen, having been appointed in 1967. Before that the post was held by the late Duchess of Devonshire, Mary Cavendish, who served from 1953 to 1967.

Immediately below the Duchess of Grafton in the ranking order are the two Ladies of the Bedchamber, who, in spite of their titles, have nothing to do with putting the Queen to bed – just as the only function regarding the Queen's clothes that involves the Mistress of the Robes is when Her Majesty is robed at the Palace of Westminster just before the State Opening of Parliament. The Ladies are usually the wives of peers: Ginnie Airlie is married to the Earl of Airlie, a former Lord Chamberlain to the Queen (and the elder brother of Sir Angus Olgilvy), and Diana Farnham's husband is (Lord Barry) Farnham. There is also an Extra Lady of the Bedchamber, the Marchioness of Abergavenny.

The only ladies-in-waiting who have anything like a full-time job are the five Women of the Bedchamber, who each attend the Queen for two weeks at a time. During their period on duty they spend all day – and most of their evenings – at the Palace, or wherever the Queen happens to be, making arrangements of a more personal nature, such as writing letters on behalf of Her Majesty to children (whom the Queen insists are answered promptly), or shopping for any small items she might need. Contrary to what one might expect, the ladies-in-waiting have slightly less to do for the Queen Regnant than would be the case if she were just Queen Consort. For a Queen Consort they would handle all her correspondence, official and private, whereas with a Queen Regnant anything official comes within the jurisdiction of the Private Secretary's Office.

Of the five Women of the Bedchamber, the two best known are undoubtedly Lady Susan Hussey – daughter of an earl and wife of Lord (Duke) Hussey, one-time Chairman of the BBC – and the Hon. Mary Morrison (Mossy to her friends). Both have been created Dames of the Royal Victorian Order and have attended the Queen for over thirty years, becoming not only loyal attendants but close friends. Sue Hussey is god-mother to Prince William.

Finally there are five Extra Women of the Bedchamber who are called on occasionally. One of these is Dame Anne Wall

DCVO. She was for many years assistant press secretary at Buckingham Palace and was asked to become an Extra as a reward for her long and distinguished service.

When the Queen is entertaining a male state visitor from abroad, she will normally attach one of her Women of the Bedchamber to her guest's suite in order to help his wife with the intricacies of Palace life. One of the Ladies told me of the State Visit of a certain ruler who brought with him more than one wife. It was left to her to persuade him that only one could be seated next to the Duke of Edinburgh at the welcoming banquet. She pointed out, no doubt with great tact and diplomacy, that the other wives would be placed in positions of great distinction and honour at various intervals around the table. After thirty years of dealing with almost every imaginable problem of etiquette, the ladies-in-waiting can cope with anything that's thrown at them. They have all developed an instinctive ability to mix with people of all races and from all walks of life. They may be aristocrats themselves, but there is never the slightest sign of condescension when they attend the Queen on walkabouts at home or abroad, or at any of the receptions which the Queen holds at Buckingham Palace where the guests can range from boy scouts and girl guides to trade union officials, leading politicians and High Church clerics. Their value to the Queen is immense and the rest of the Household know that no one can tell them the mood she is in better than the duty Lady.

One other member of the Household in close contact with the Queen is her Equerry-in-Waiting. This post is always held by an officer in one of the services who is seconded from his unit for three years, during which time he is in personal attendance on the sovereign. In conjunction with the Crown Equerry, he deals with her private travel arrangements, and also looks after all Her Majesty's private engagements. When visitors arrived at Buckingham Palace, for example, he will meet them at the King's Entrance, conduct them up to the

Queen's first-floor sitting room, and announce them. But he does not remain in the room.

Two of the most well known equerries were the late Group Captain Peter Townsend, whose ill-fated romance with Princess Margaret caused him to be removed with great haste and immediately posted abroad, and Commodore Tim Laurence, who was more fortunate and became the Princess Royal's second husband.

Some three-hundred-odd people work within the royal household, of whom only a handful come in contact with the Queen herself. But everyone involved knows they are essential to the way the palaces and other residences are run and each is dedicated to the service of Her Majesty. The pay is small, the perks are few but there is a great deal of satisfaction in knowing that by performing their tasks to the best of their ability, they might be making life a little easier for the Boss. After all, they say, 'She works harder than any of us.'

CHAPTER TWENTY

The Public Image

*'They may pretend to hate the media, but if
one of their visits isn't covered sufficiently they
always want to know why.'*
RONALD ALLISON, THE QUEEN'S PRESS
SECRETARY 1973–1978

In 1999, the Queen and Prince Philip undertook a State Visit
to South Africa. At the welcoming ceremony high on a hill
above Pretoria, all the usual dignitaries were lined up, waiting
for the national anthems to be played. The new President,
Thabo Mbeki, and his wife were standing alongside the Queen
and her husband. The Foreign Secretary, Robin Cook, and
his wife, Gaynor, were present along with top South African
Government representatives and officials. The accompanying
press party was also standing nearby. Suddenly, a 21-gun royal
salute was fired from a row of cannon with such a deafening
blast that everyone, even the President, nearly jumped out of
their skin. There was only one exception – the Queen – who
didn't move a muscle, apart from giving a slight smile at the
reaction of the newsmen, who all but disappeared in a cloud
a thick smoke.

Later, at a reception, an incident occurred that illustrated clearly the difference a few years have made in royal attitudes to the press. The Queen joined a small group of British reporters and photographers and explained how it was that she was not taken unawares: 'Last night I looked out of my hotel window and saw the guns being lined up, so I knew what to expect.' She then went on to make a joke of the episode, saying, 'I always find it incredible that a country welcomes one by shooting cannon at you.' The journalists present said it was extraordinary to see Her Majesty sufficiently relaxed to tell the story in such company. She would never have done so five years earlier, but it set the tone for the entire tour, which was one of the most successful ever.

It was on this visit that Her Majesty revealed her feelings about being always the focus of media attention. At the five-star Sheraton Towers Hotel, where the royal visitors were staying, the Queen met Nelson Mandela, one of her greatest admirers and an old friend. They had a private talk for twenty minutes or so in her suite, and when they walked back down the long corridor towards the room where a presentation to a small group of prizewinners in an essay competition was to be held, he whispered something in her ear that had her squealing with laughter. Neither would reveal what the joke was, but when the Queen organized the nine young prize-winners into a semi-circle for official photographs, she said: 'This is one of the worst parts of being Queen – having to pose for photographs.'

On an earlier occasion, when the Queen was visiting Germany in 1978, the pound was going through a difficult period and one of the journalists covering the tour found that no one was willing to change his British currency at any price. Once again, the Queen joined a group of mediamen, but this time there was one of those awkward pauses when everyone is waiting for someone else to speak. Eventually, Ashley Walton, then royal correspondent of the *Express*, broke the ice, mentioning that he had been unable to change a five-pound note 'with your face on it, Ma'am'. He said it jokingly but with respect, and handed Her Majesty the bank note for her inspection. He later said, 'She looked at it twice, almost as if it was the first time she had seen one.' Then she merely smiled but refused to be drawn into a possibly controversial discussion.

Ashley Walton is one of a group of royal reporters who have been on numerous tours with the Queen and Prince Philip. Whenever they met, in whichever country, they were always asked the same question: 'Are you based here?'

In the last couple of years, the royal family has gone out of its way to try and improve relations with the media. On public occasions, reporters and photographers are regularly invited to functions they would have been excluded from ten years ago. On overseas visits, they are even allowed, on occasion, to share the royal aircraft. But when they try to get behind the scenes and look in detail at the personal lifestyles and behaviour the trouble starts.

The private lives of the Queen and her family can be the subject of serious and legitimate public interest, but the press office tries to control the flow of information, which is why there is so much criticism from the media. The press office is mainly reactive rather than proactive, and by definition practically any information that's worth having is not available.

The Palace still insists the royal family are entitled to a private life away from media intrusion, while the press believes there are no areas that should not be subject to the glare of publicity. And royal stories still sell newspapers. The extraordinary behaviour of the Duchess of York, the startling revelations of the late Diana, Princess of Wales, Princess Margaret's unconventional lifestyle and the love-life of the Prince of Wales are all stories which the Palace would, naturally, prefer not to receive any exposure at all. The media believe otherwise and rightly so. The royal family are not any ordinary private clan whose behaviour does not affect the rest of us. They are the country's leading family and as such should expect their affairs to be subject to scrutiny. So the argument that certain aspects of their lives are 'private' and therefore should not be reported is one-sided and generally rejected by the press.

While it is true that the media's need for the monarchy is purely monetary – royal articles are excellent circulation boosters – the monarchy also has a need for the press. Without the constant reporting of royal events and personalities, public interest – and affection – for the royal family would quickly evaporate. The problem is that those who advise the Queen want total control of what is written and seen, while the media want to reveal everything. Neither side will ever be satisfied; an uneasy compromise is probably the best both can hope for.

The Queen's attitude to the media is ambivalent. She wants harmony, peace and a quiet life – the media demand headlines, soundbites and scandal. But she does not like it when her public appearances are not featured in the press and asks pointed questions of her press secretary. For generations, royalty has depended on the fact that their way of life has fascinated the nation. Prince Charles admitted as much when he once joked to a group of photographers, 'It's when you characters don't want to photograph me that I have to worry.'

Although the office of Press Secretary is a comparatively new one, there has been an official in the royal household called the Court Newsman since the days of King George III. Enraged at what he described as the inaccurate reporting of the movements of the royal family, Farmer George appointed a man whose sole duty was to distribute the Court Circular and to make sure that newspapers of the day printed it with not a single word changed or omitted.

The Buckingham Palace Press Office files show that in 1899 the Court Newsman's duties included personal attendance at the Palace every day, once in the afternoon and again in the evening, when Queen Victoria was in residence, and once a

The royal couple show their compassion when they visit the scene of the Aberfan disaster in South Wales in October 1966. A hundred and forty-four people, including a hundred and fifteen children, died when a disused coal tip collapsed and engulfed the village school.

The Queen once described Prince Philip as 'my rock' and it's easy to see the affection in which she holds him as they arrive for a State Banquet in Durban, South Africa in 1989.

day (including Sundays) when Her Majesty was away from London. He was also required to attend the Lord Chamberlain's office a few days before every official function and write out in his own hand a copy of the invitation lists which he then had to deliver himself to London's leading newspapers. His salary for these tasks amounted to £45 a year, but even then the Palace was looking for economies, and in 1909 the Court Newsman's annual salary was reduced to £20. Not surprisingly, the holder of the office made up for his poor recompense by selling royal stories to his favourite editors. So royal 'moles' are nothing new. Strangely enough, the sovereign did not frown on the practice, which was widely known, and the household thought it was a perfectly legitimate way for the Newsman to make up for his meagre earnings. Today if any of those employed in the current press office indulged in similar practices, the only sound they would hear would be that of the Palace's doors slamming behind them.

The only journalist who is regularly welcomed at Buckingham Palace is the Press Association Court Correspondent. He is issued with a green household pass that allows him to enter the palace or any royal residence at any time and without an appointment. Inside Buckingham Palace he has his own desk in the press office and any official press release is first given to him to distribute. He also attends most royal functions and to all intents and purposes he is a member of the household – with one exception. When it comes to Christmas he is not invited to the staff dance or other parties, and neither does he receive a present from the Queen like every other member of the household.

The job of the modern press secretary is not only far removed from that of the Court Newsman of a hundred years ago but also light years from that of the Queen's first press officer, the legendary Commander Richard Colville, who earned the soubriquet 'The Abominable No-Man' through his constant refusal to give out any information whatsoever.

Colville was a former Royal Navy officer with perfect manners when dealing with those he regarded as his equals, and absolutely no knowledge of what constituted news, royal or otherwise, and he made it clear to anyone who cared to listen that he didn't want to know. He considered his job was simply to report details of royal engagements, and any enquiry about any other issue was invariably met with the comment: 'That is a private matter, I'm sorry, I can't help at all.' He regarded journalists as mere tradesmen and as such none was ever invited to the Palace, with the exception of the Press Association representative, who arrived every morning to be given the following day's programme of royal events. He still does.

In Commander Colville's time there was still an air of deference by Fleet Street towards the Palace, which didn't really end until the late 1970s. As a result the press of the day, particularly the BBC, which has always prided itself on what it believes to be a privileged relationship with Buckingham Palace, allowed itself to be regularly humiliated by Colville, in order to obtain those few snippets of information he cared to distribute. Colville's main task in life, as he saw it, was to protect the Queen from newspaper reporters at all times and in this he became so successful that eventually they all but gave up telephoning the press office at Buckingham Palace and found other sources for their stories. If the present press secretary had the same attitude the royal family would soon be made aware of the media's displeasure and Her Majesty would be looking for a new man very quickly.

Nine press secretaries have served the Queen throughout her reign. Some have been both successful and popular while one or two have been neither. One of the most able in terms of getting the coverage he wanted was an Australian, Bill Heseltine, who later became private secretary to the Queen and was knighted as Sir William Heseltine before he retired back to his native country. The son of a schoolmaster, Heseltine was educated at Christchurch Grammar School, in Claremont, Western Australia and the University of Western Australia, where he took a first-class degree in history. Seconded to the Palace press office in 1965, he arrived dressed in a style completely different from what was usual at that time. But within a remarkably short time he found his niche and soon exchanged his blazer and flannels for the dress and manners of his colleagues.

The Queen liked Heseltine from the start. She once described him as 'a breath of fresh air', and after returning to Australia for a brief period to work in the private office of the Prime Minister, Sir Robert Menzies, he was brought back to Buckingham Palace as press secretary in 1968. It was Heseltine, together with Lord (John) Brabourne, the husband of Earl Mountbatten's elder daughter, Patricia, who originally thought up the idea for the royal family's first television documentary in 1969. Supported by the Duke of Edinburgh, he persuaded the Queen it could do nothing but good for the royal image, and he was proved right, even if today the programme looks contrived and sugary.

Heseltine was ambitious and made himself indispensable to the Queen; so much so that in 1972 he was promoted to her private office and eventually achieved the most influential position in the royal household as Her Majesty's private secretary. By that time all traces of any antipodean brashness had been eliminated and he adapted to the ways of the Court as if he had been born to them.

The man who succeeded Heseltine as press secretary was Robin Ludlow. He was the man who lasted the shortest time in the Press Office – a little over a year – and also the only press secretary to leave without being given an honour by the Queen. Invariably, Her Majesty gives a final audience to those members of her Household who are leaving and invests them with a rank in her personal Order of Chivalry, the Royal Victorian Order. Ludlow was the exception. Ludlow was working at the Palace at the time when Princess Anne first became involved with Mark Phillips. For months there had been speculation about the relationship and eventually the Palace issued a denial of an engagement between the couple. In January 1973, Ludlow told John Knight of the *Sunday Mirror* that 'an engagement is not expected at this time' – which was true as far as he knew. The trouble was he didn't know enough. The private secretary's office had deliberately kept the information from him so that he would not have to lie. This is quite common. The press office does not form policy and is only able to react when given the information it needs. Barely ten weeks later, by which time Ludlow had been replaced as press secretary, an official announcement of the engagement was made. The Queen's official spokesman had been placed in an impossible position. He had not been kept fully in the picture – and had suffered because of it.

His replacement was living proof of the change in attitude to the media. Ronald Allison had been the BBC's Court Correspondent for five years when he was approached to join the royal household in 1986. The appointment was greeted with pleasure by his former colleagues in the press as they knew he would recognize their problems and, hopefully, be sympathetic. They were right. Ron, as he quickly became known to everyone, including the Queen, rapidly established himself as the perfect conduit between royalty and the media. He was, without doubt, one of the most successful and popular occupants of the press office, liked by the royal family and respected and admired by those he had to deal with in the media. A large man with a pleasant Hampshire burr, he could restrain any intrusive photographers without appearing to be difficult and nobody bore any grudges when he had to keep them at a distance from the Queen or her family. But outward appearances can, of course, be deceptive and Ron Allison was not without personal ambition. He was quite happy to help his former colleagues whenever he could, but he never forgot that his first loyalties were to the Queen.

Nevertheless, he succeeded in an area which even in those days was full of pitfalls for the unwary. When Princess Margaret and Lord Snowdon decided to separate in 1976, prior to their divorce, which was finalized in May 1978, it was Allison who was despatched by the Queen to supervise the media arrangements. The Princess already had her own press officer, a delightful ex-Army officer named John Griffin, but the Palace felt a more experienced journalistic hand was needed and Ron Allison took personal charge of the press announcements, speaking to both Princess Margaret and her soon-to-be ex-husband.

He explained what happened next. 'I had a meeting with Princess Margaret and spoke to Lord Snowdon. What I needed to know from them was the timing of the announcement and what they wanted me to say. The timing is always of the utmost importance so that the people involved are not caught in a vulnerable position. I then drafted a short announcement which I intended to release to the Press Association at the agreed time. I sent it across for the Princess and Lord Snowdon to see, and make any changes they felt were necessary. As it happened they were happy with what was written and, of course, the Queen also needed to approve the statement.'

Allison's relationship with the Queen was remarkably close. She took an interest in his family, which in itself was unusual. She rarely involves herself in any of her household's private affairs. On one occasion when Allison was on duty with the Queen in Canada, he received news from home about a family problem. Her Majesty immediately sent him back to Britain to deal with it, in spite of his willingness to stay on. She knew his mind would be elsewhere and was thoughtful enough to realize where his presence was really needed. And since his departure from the Palace in 1978 he has remained a welcome guest at Royal functions.

Allison is one of the few in a position to know who admit

that the Queen takes an interest in her media coverage: 'The Queen was very aware of what was being said about her in the press,' he remembers. 'She always took a great interest in what was happening and she would frequently ask why a certain event had been reported in a particular way – or sometimes, why something had not been covered.'

Allison could have remained at the Palace until he reached retiring age, but after five years he decided to leave. He returned to television, and immediately trebled his salary. In 1978, the top money a press secretary could command was still only £11,000 a year.

The man who replaced Ron Allison, Michael Shea, could not have been more different, in character, profile or ambition. Shea was an academic and career Foreign Office diplomat. He had a flair for self-promotion and seemed deliberately to cultivate a high profile, in marked contrast to his predecessors in the office. He was also tremendously successful at his job and, like Ron Allison, formed a close working relationship with the Queen. Her Majesty even went to the expense of buying a large house in Pimlico, close to the Palace, for Shea and his wife to live in. It was far grander than some of the other Grace and Favour residences occupied by courtiers with much longer royal service and Shea played host there to many prominent personalities from the worlds of politics and the arts. A charismatic personality, Michael Shea enjoyed the reflected glamour of being so close to the monarch and made many useful contacts in the worlds of business, public relations and journalism during his five years at the Palace. He was also the only person in the press office to answer the telephone by announcing his name. Everyone else, past and present, always said, 'Press Office' without identifying themselves. Right from the start Shea made sure that callers knew who he was and that he was the man in charge. It might not have worked for everyone, but for him it was very effective. Shea was seen alongside the Queen in the Royal Box at Ascot and, unlike everyone else in the Palace, he was willing to be quoted when asked his views on various royal topics. He did however become slightly unstuck on one famous occasion when he was asked why the Queen was looking rather glum. It's 'her Miss Piggy look', he said – a comment that for anyone else would have meant immediate removal, but Shea got away with it.

A much more serious incident occurred in July 1986, when the *Sunday Times* published a story claiming that the Queen was unhappy with the way the Prime Minister, Margaret Thatcher, was running the country. The story went into great detail about the disagreements between Mrs Thatcher and the Queen, itemizing specific areas such as how Her Majesty felt the Government lacked compassion regarding the less privileged in British society, her feelings about the long miners' strike of 1984 to 1985 and, most important of all, the Queen's misgivings about Mrs Thatcher's decision to allow American bombers to use British airbases for their raid on Libya the previous year. The story was dynamite. Never before had a British sovereign's political opinions been made known in such dramatic fashion. It could have caused a constitutional crisis. Andrew Neil, at that time editor of the *Sunday Times*, revealed in his book *Full Disclosure*, published in 1996, the behind-the-scenes story of the revelations. It emerged that the source was none other than Michael Shea himself. The Palace denied the story's authenticity, dismissing it as 'entirely without foundation'. Neil stuck by his version and he and his newspaper became lead items in practically every country in the world, such was the interest in anything to do with royalty, particularly when it involved a row between the Queen and her Prime Minister.

A week after the original article was published, Sir William Heseltine, as the Queen's private secretary, wrote to *The Times* defending Michael Shea and refuting all that had been written by the *Sunday Times*. The main points of Heseltine's letter were: 'The Sovereign is obliged to treat her communications with the Prime Minister as entirely confidential between the two of them . . . After thirty-four years of unvarying adherence to these constitutional principles, it is preposterous to suggest that Her Majesty might suddenly depart from them. No sensible person would give a moment's credence to such a proposition.

'It is equally preposterous to suggest that any member of the Queen's household, even supposing that he or she knew what Her Majesty's opinions on government policy might be (and the press secretary certainly does not), would reveal them to the press.' The letter went on to deny the fact that the article had been read over to Michael Shea in its entirety or that any remarks he might have made could possibly be interpreted in the way the article had indicated. It ended by saying, 'As with all previous prime ministers, the Queen enjoys a relationship of the closest confidentiality with Mrs Thatcher, and reports purporting to be the Queen's opinion of government policies are entirely without foundation.'

This was by far the most serious dispute with the press there had ever been and the only one in which the Buckingham Palace press secretary has been personally involved. Some time later Shea departed, and has since written a number of books about the art of communication – nobody is better qualified. But he remains on the Royal Garden Party guest list and most years can be seen talking animatedly with his former colleagues. It was never established who the culprit was. If that had become known he or she would have immediately become *persona non grata* at the Palace. When the door closes, it bangs with chilling finality.

Shea's successor, in 1987, was a former naval officer, Robin Janvrin, a man with an easy manner which disguises an inner toughness. He was destined for the top, and his tenure of the press office was brief. Promoted to the private secretary's office as number three in a comparatively short time, he is now the most important non-royal at the Palace as the

Queen's principal private secretary. He was knighted in December 1997 and also inherited the house that was bought for Michael Shea.

In 1990 Charles Anson followed Janvrin into the press office. His spell as the Queen's official spokesman was comparatively uneventful and unfortunately will be remembered mainly for the time when he was forced to apologize to the Duchess of York. 'The knives are out for Fergie,' he had said to a reporter, referring to Palace leaks of damaging information intended to discredit the Duchess after the publication of topless photographs of her having her toes sucked by a boyfriend in the South of France.

When Charles Anson departed in 1997, to take up a highly paid position in public relations, his deputy, Geoffrey Crawford, took over. An Australian with a background in government service in his home country, Geoff Crawford had a disarming way of greeting journalists who rang him. 'Hello mate, how are you?' he would say. It was some time before callers realized that this was the way he spoke to all reporters and writers; there was nothing personal about it, but it was very effective in making people feel they were on the inside. Crawford nevertheless went out of his way more than any of his predecessors to try and help journalists with genuine enquiries. And he was punctilious about returning calls. When he was assistant press secretary he was responsible for all media queries concerning Diana, Princess of Wales, and they established a warm friendship that was strained badly when she cooperated with Andrew Morton in the writing of his book and when later she appeared on *Panorama* without telling Crawford. If he felt betrayed by her actions he never spoke about it and his handling of what was undoubtedly the most delicate situation any press secretary has had to cope with, the death of the princess in 1997, showed how professional and, at the same time, compassionate, a public servant can be.

Crawford was not without personal problems. During his term of office his first marriage broke down, but after divorcing he has since remarried happily. What was unusual about the break-up is that the press made very little of it, in spite of his high-profile position. The tabloids are not known for their loyalty and it was surprising that all the lurid details – if there were any – did not appear. It was a tribute to the high esteem in which Geoff Crawford was held by his press colleagues that no salacious stories were written and everyone wished him well. Perhaps just as astonishing was the reaction of the Queen, who was totally supportive. Twenty years earlier, he would have been forced to resign and leave the Palace immediately. Today, with three of the Queen's own children, and her only sister, divorced, the incident didn't even raise a royal eyebrow and Crawford continued to live in an elegant apartment in St James's Palace where a neighbour was the Prince of Wales.

Towards the end of his time in the press office Crawford received a great compliment from the Queen when she promoted him to be her assistant private secretary and asked him to take special responsibility for making the arrangements to celebrate her Golden Jubilee. But in December 2000 he surprised – and disappointed – Her Majesty by suddenly resigning in order to return to his native Australia to take up a much more lucrative post in public relations. A further surprise was the appointment of his deputy, Penny Russell-Smith, as the new press secretary. She was the obvious candidate with impeccable qualifications; the surprise was in the fact that she is the first woman to hold this prestigious post within the royal household. Yet another sign of the modernization of the monarchy.

The tabloid newspapers in Britain – and abroad – are always on the lookout for good royal stories, the juicier the better. But every paper, including the sober broadsheets, employs a royal correspondent who specializes in articles about the family. Some are taken seriously and build up excellent contacts within the household and occasionally even with members of the royal family themselves, but the Queen has never given an interview and is unlikely to do so despite hundreds of applications from all over the world. However, she does know several of the men and women who write about her. My own first meeting with the Queen – in a strictly informal manner – was at the Palace of Holyroodhouse in Edinburgh when, one summer afternoon, I was talking to the man who was the Princess Royal's police officer at that time, James Beaton. We were standing inside a ground floor corridor, looking through an open doorway at an inner quadrangle. The sun was shining brilliantly (unusual in itself for Scotland), when a slight female figure walked out of the sunlight into the corridor. It was one of those situations where you can see only the silhouette of the person and not the details of the face. Inspector Beaton (as he then was) said: 'Look out, here comes the boss.' Indeed, it was she. Her Majesty walked past us, saying as she went, 'What are you two up to?' That was all, nothing spectacular, but the very ordinariness made it special. I have since met her on numerous occasions and seen her, both at home and abroad, performing her role with the flawless professionalism we have come to expect.

Perhaps the best known of all royal correspondents is James Whitaker of the *Mirror*, who has now retired from day-to-day reporting but still writes a weekly column which often contains a good royal story. He is refreshingly honest about why he became a specialist in royal affairs: 'I was sent by my then editor to cover a royal engagement and I found myself eating smoked salmon and drinking champagne. From that day on I decided that this was the life for me.'

Like every one of his colleagues, James Whitaker would sell his soul to get that first exclusive interview with the Queen, and while he admits they don't actually socialize, he knows that all the family recognize him when they see him. 'They may not always approve of what I write but I am quite sure there isn't a single member of the royal family who doesn't know who I am.'

Whitaker got one of the biggest scoops in Fleet Street history when on 31 August 1989 he broke the story of Princess Anne's separation and forthcoming divorce from Mark Phillips. Like many of his colleagues, he had cultivated a relationship with some of those close to the royal family and one of these happened to be Mark's father, the late Major Peter Phillips. James made a routine telephone call to Major Phillips one evening at the time there was intense speculation about the state of the marriage. He mentioned the fact to Major Phillips and was amazed to hear the reply, 'Yes, isn't it all very sad?' That was all James Whitaker needed to break the story and give his newspaper a world exclusive. He was once asked how he got his stories and who was his contact at Buckingham Palace. He replied, 'I have eleven "moles" inside the Palace who all ring me when they have something to tell.'

Interest in the royal family is worldwide and never more so than in the United States. When the Queen visited the west coast in 1984 she received more coverage than the previous presidential election campaign. The following year over a thousand reporters and cameramen applied for accreditation to cover the tour made by the Prince and Princess of Wales. Serious commentators in America were astounded by the enthusiasm of the media and asked why it should be. Was it just that everyone wanted to hear the latest tittle-tattle about the most famous couple in the world? Was there genuine interest in the serious aspects of the monarchy, or did we simply want to see and hear what went on behind the Palace's curtains? Whatever the reason, stories about royalty still sell newspapers and magazines in their millions and some of those who write about them become rich and famous as a result.

Once Lady Diana Spencer appeared on the scene press interest reached fever pitch. It was revealed in 1985 that a photograph of her on the cover of a magazine could mean an increase in sales of as much as ten per cent.

There is also a down side. Ten years earlier, a national survey disclosed that pictures of Princess Anne or Princess Margaret, the most unpopular members of the family, could result in a decrease in sales.

Andrew Morton, a former tabloid reporter, hit the jackpot when he published the international bestseller *Diana: Her True Story* in 1992. The book was written with her cooperation, much to the disgust of the Palace press office, and immediately became number one in practically every country in the world. Translated into several languages, the slim volume made Morton a millionaire and propelled him from the obscurity of hack journalism into the rarefied heights of the celebrity circuit in Britain, the United States, where he appeared on all the major talk shows, and Australia. The difference between Morton's book and the hundreds of others which appear with monotonous regularity, is that he persuaded a member of the royal family to talk. With very few exceptions, every other author has had to make do with second-hand information from 'royal sources' or 'a Palace insider'.

Again the *Sunday Times* figured in the controversy. Andrew Neil was the successful bidder in the auction for serialization rights, paying what now appears to be the ludicrously small sum of £250,000. It was the publishing bargain of the decade. Today bidding for such a book would start at over a million. He insisted that Morton should verify all the facts and the author duly produced affidavits signed by every person quoted. Princess Diana even turned up on the doorstep of one of her closest friends, Caroline Bartholomew, who had spoken to Morton, and in a well arranged – and publicized – meeting Diana was photographed hugging her old friend, thereby letting the world know she had given her approval.

Morton was attacked for his exposé but was later vindicated by Diana herself when she gave Martin Bashir of the BBC an interview in which she admitted that everything Morton had written was true. Andrew Neil was also attacked by the establishment – and by other newspapers, who then quickly proceeded to jump on the bandwagon and follow up the startling revelations. It was the period of media coverage that the Palace would most like to forget. Every day seemed to bring fresh scandal and nothing the press office could do stemmed the tide. Morton and Neil had opened the floodgates, but no one would ever match their sensational scoop.

The relationship between the press and Buckingham Palace has always been delicate, and rightly so. It would not be in the public's interest if there were too cosy an arrangement, but in recent years the relationship has become strained almost to breaking point. The Palace refuses to cooperate in anything they cannot control, while the press has long declared 'open season' on the royals. The days when Britain's newspaper editors had a 'gentlemen's agreement' not to publish details of the affair between King Edward VIII and Mrs Wallis Simpson, when foreign papers were blazoning the story on their front pages, have gone for ever. That was in 1935.

It is now commonplace for some sections of the media to invent stories involving members of the royal family, even the Queen herself, in the hope that there will be a denial, which will then add fuel to the story. But the Queen never replies to press stories either to deny or confirm their authenticity. Her press secretary will always correct factual errors, such as stories alleging that Her Majesty pays too much money out of the public purse to maintain her race horses, when in fact those activities are financed solely from her private income. But there is never an answer to personal criticism or an opinion allegedly expressed by the Queen herself. And rightly so. Whatever she said could be misconstrued. Even a simple 'no comment' on a subject as controversial as, say, fox-hunting, would be seen by one section of the public as uncaring. It is a no-win situation.

If there are two words which are complete anathema to the royal family they are 'Public Relations'. Buckingham Palace has no public relations department as such; the press office prefers to think of itself as an information service. But when the Queen appointed Simon Lewis as her first Communications Secretary in 1998 – on loan from Centrica, a subsidiary company of British Gas – there was little doubt that his main task would be to improve the public image of the royal family. In other words, it was public relations by a more acceptable name. Lewis did not work from the press office and the press secretary was at pains to point out that the new communications secretary was not his superior. Nor would Geoff Crawford give up his elegant room opposite the Privy Purse entrance, so Lewis worked from an office in the private secretaries' corridor.

It was significant that the press office were not told of the appointment until it had happened. The interviews were held by Sir Robert Fellowes, at that time private secretary to the Queen, and his assistant, Robin Janvrin. It was on their recommendation that Simon Lewis got the job and only then were other members of the household, including the Queen's press secretary, told. The Keeper of the Privy Purse, who arranges the salaries of all royal staff, was involved and eventually it was revealed that Lewis was on secondment from his post at Centrica and his Palace salary would be supplemented by his company to maintain his reported annual stipend of around £230,000, making him by far the best paid servant the Queen has ever employed. The revelation did little to ensure his popularity in his new post.

At the end of Lewis's two-year secondment, during which time few members of the Fourth Estate had worked out what he had achieved – or indeed, what he was supposed to achieve – he was not asked to remain and a successor was found from another branch of the private sector.

This time British Airways provided Buckingham Palace with

an experienced public relations executive in the person of Simon Walters. Again he was seconded – from his position as head of corporate affairs – and has his Palace salary augmented by his normal pay at B.A. It also is well into six figures.

The royal family has a genius for maintaining public interest by providing key figures who become the focus of attention. It's a way they have of controlling the flow of the product and maintaining its quality. Princess Margaret occupied the position for many years, and when interest in her waned Prince Charles was brought on with his 'action man' style and stories about who he would eventually marry. In the seventies Princess Anne was the star with her achievements in the saddle and her marriage to Mark Phillips. Then when Diana burst on to the royal scene in 1981, she eclipsed all the others and became the centre of everyone's attention. The divorce, followed by her death, was a blow to the royal family. It disturbed the plan to have key members of the family move almost imperceptibly into the spotlight. Happily, Prince William was reaching an age when he could become a superstar, and in the final years of the millennium he emerged as the newest of the royal celebrities, and the one on whom their hopes – and those of the media – are pinned for the next decade.

William's attitude to the media had been coloured by the attention focused on his mother in the last years of her life. She led him to believe that she hated the constant presence of reporters and photographers, when in reality she displayed acute withdrawal symptoms if she was unnoticed for a few days. Diana was the great manipulator, who managed to persuade a willing public – and her own sons – that she was the reluctant victim. So, in the days following her death, and perhaps encouraged by his uncle Charles Spencer, William made no secret of the fact that he blamed the media for most of her troubles, and this attitude hasn't softened since then.

Even at the tender age of eighteen, William seems determined not to be manoeuvred into any situations where he is not in control. He does not have his own staff as yet, relying on his father's team at St James's Palace when necessary. Prince Charles's press secretary is there to help if required but does not speak on William's behalf without first getting clearance from him. Any opinions attributed to him must come from him alone.

When Prince William first went to Eton the Queen and Prince Charles asked the media to respect William's need for a little privacy to enjoy as normal a life as was possible for someone in his unique position, and generally speaking the arrangement has worked. Compared to the press treatment meted out to Prince Charles when he was at Gordonstoun, William had a fairly easy ride. He reluctantly agreed to photocalls when he started and at occasional events afterwards, such as the day when his brother, Harry, started at the school. But in general he was left alone. An exception was his eighteenth birthday, when official photographs and a scripted interview were released. Otherwise, he does not have too much to complain about, but the pressure is bound to increase in the coming years.

In September 2000 William was speaking to the press about his plans for a 'gap' year before going to university in Scotland in the autumn of 2001. With his father alongside him at Highgrove, he mentioned his 'deep regret' at the book written by Patrick Jephson, his mother's former private secretary. 'She continues to be exploited, and Harry and I regret that this is happening,' William said.

Prince William has that 'star' quality that singled out his mother, and he is exactly the right age to appeal to a new generation, a generation whose support the royal family needs if they are to prosper in the twenty-first century.

The media are also looking for a new royal 'megastar' to replace Diana. Things have never been quite the same since she died. Royals rarely appear on the front pages these days

– unless it is Prince Charles and Camilla out together or William in the company of an attractive young woman. So if William were to accommodate the press even half as much as his mother did – which, realistically, is unlikely – both the Palace and those who rely on royal stories to sell their newspapers would be well satisfied.

CHAPTER TWENTY-ONE

World Traveller

*'I am going back to Rome to have dinner with
my Pope and your Queen.'*
AN ITALIAN DELEGATE TO THE EUROPEAN
PARLIAMENT, SPEAKING AT STRASBOURG
IN OCTOBER 1980

The phrase with which this Italian Member of the European
Parliament declined an invitation to dine with some of his
British colleagues in Strasbourg, must rank as an all-time best
as a conversation stopper. It also shows how important this
titled Eurocrat felt it was to meet not only the Vatican Head
of State but also Her Majesty.

The Queen does not own a passport, never has and never
will. She crosses all borders without hindrance and is arguably
the most widely travelled head of state in the world. During
her half century on the throne she has visited practically every
country on earth, criss-crossed the oceans and continents
scores of times and met every sovereign, president and prime
minister. In the past fifty years she has been invited to every
significant country in the world, including many to whom the
very idea of an hereditary monarchy is anathema.

In 1986 the Queen visited China, where two million people waited to greet her in Shanghai and where she dazzled her hosts at the official welcoming banquet in Beijing with her dexterity with chopsticks. It was on this visit that she walked along the Great Wall of China and the tourist in her took over from the sovereign. In spite of hundreds of press photographers all snapping away, she insisted on taking out her gold Leica, handing it to her private secretary and asking him to take one of her. 'Otherwise no one will know I've been here,' she joked.

Naturally, many of her overseas visits have been to Commonwealth countries, but she has travelled also to nations outside the British family. One of her favourite places – which she openly admits and for which the Duke of Edinburgh also has a passion – is the United States.

The royal family has long had a love affair with America. The Queen's parents enjoyed a State Visit in 1937. They were fêted and welcomed wherever they went, and the trip, the Queen Mother has said, left a lasting impression on her. The Queen's Uncle David, the Duke of Windsor, made no secret of his feelings for the USA, where he was treated as a monarch long after he had abdicated. The fact that he had married an American, Wallis Simpson, helped.

Prince Philip has always enjoyed the informality of the American way of life; the lack of what he has described as 'the straitjacket regime of Court protocol'.

In 1951, when she was Princess Elizabeth, the Queen and Prince Philip made a two-day visit to Washington, where they stayed as guests of President Truman. Eight hundred reporters turned up to meet her, expecting the access they had become used to getting with their own head of state. It didn't happen. This was her first journey to the USA. Since then, as Queen, she has made several official visits, starting in 1957 as a guest of President Eisenhower, whom she had met in London when he commanded the Allied Forces during the Second World

War, and continuing during the presidencies of Gerald Ford, George Bush and Ronald Reagan.

It was in 1957, during her first visit to the United States as Queen, that an amusing but potentially embarrassing incident occurred. As part of the entertainment at a state banquet, two of America's foremost dancers were performing. The husband and wife team of Marge and Gower Champion were at the peak of their fame, starring in many of Metro-Goldwyn-Mayer's most successful musicals. Appropriately, it was on board the *QE2* that Marge Champion told me of the incident that still causes her to blush today.

'Gower and I were dancing one of our most popular routines and I was wearing a sparkling dress held up by two slim straps. Suddenly I felt one of them snap, but I knew the other would hold so I wasn't too worried. Then, a few minutes later, the remaining one parted company with the dress and the entire front collapsed, displaying rather more of me than I would have wished. Gower immediately whisked me around so that he was in front and we quickly made our exit. I was mortified, but the following morning I received a beautiful spray of orchids and a handwritten note from Prince Philip, written on White House stationery, saying, "Thank you for making last evening such a memorable one." It's an occasion I will always remember and I'm eternally grateful to His Royal Highness for his consideration and good humour. I certainly did not want to be remembered as the first dancer to perform a striptease in front of the Queen of England.'

In 1976 Her Majesty visited the United States to help mark the bicentennial celebrations. As a direct descendant of George III, the king who was the last ruler of America as a British colony, her welcome might have appeared to be surprising. But the American people are nothing if not generous and she was received as warmly as any other guest. President Gerald Ford was host and he told the present author that he was immediately struck by the friendliness of the

Queen. 'She liked to get away from the strict formalities that normally exist between heads of state. She preferred talking on a more personal level. When she arrived in Washington for the first formal occasion, my wife and I met her and Prince Philip at the front door of the White House and led her to the elevator that leads up to the private quarters. As the door of the elevator opened on the second floor, one of our sons was standing there without a shirt on – bare-chested. He said, "I'm trying to find some things for my dress clothes." Well, here were the four of us, all in white tie and full evening dress, and there was our son standing there without a shirt on. I apologized and my wife said, "I'm sorry, this is so embarrassing." Her Majesty smiled and replied, "Don't worry, we have one just like him at home." She was brilliant. There was no stiffness and she set the tone for the rest of the visit. I felt she was someone I could have got to know well in any circumstances.'

Later that evening, President Ford arranged a banquet followed by a cabaret and dancing. Two hundred and twenty-four guests were invited, including many of the Queen's favourite entertainers. Gerald Ford had gone to a lot of trouble to find the right people and he was particularly pleased with his compère for the evening. 'I chose Bob Hope to MC the event partly because of his British connections [Hope was born in London] and obviously because of his professionalism. He was magnificent and later the Queen told me she had enjoyed him very much, adding, "He is a fine entertainer." It was a fun evening altogether.'

President Ford and his royal guest opened the dancing with a slow fox-trot, 'Getting to Know You' from the musical *The King and I*. He said afterwards, 'It was a truly delightful experience to have the opportunity of dancing with the Queen of England. It sure was a long way from my origins in Omaha, Nebraska.'

The Queen returned the President's hospitality with a

dinner at the British Embassy which was another tremendous success. He recalled the event for me: 'It was a truly delightful evening with lots of easy conversation. That's the thing about the Queen, there's nothing strained or forced about her. She makes everything look so pleasant. She really is a warm, genuine woman.'

In May 1991, it was President George Bush and his wife, Barbara, who were hosts to the Queen and Prince Philip when they arrived in the United States on board Concorde. The weather was hot, humid and muggy with the Queen appearing to be the only person not affected by the heat.

To many people who watched the welcoming ceremonies on the lawn of the White House the abiding memory will be the sight of the top of the Queen's head, the only part of her still visible when she ascended the lectern to reply to President Bush's speech of welcome. The press later described it as a 'talking hat', and in one famous headline she was identified as the 'Hat of State'. The President is six feet, two inches tall, the Queen a foot shorter, and the podium had not been altered to accommodate her. She found it fairly amusing and referred to the incident two days later when she addressed the Houses of Congress, saying, 'I hope you can all see me now.' This was not an off-the-cuff remark, however. Robert Fellowes, Her Majesty's private secretary, wrote it, and in doing so adroitly turned the mishap to her own advantage.

But the President was highly embarrassed by the apparent humiliation to his guest. As he told me, 'I was troubled by the fact that we did not pull out the steps built into the podium. That failure resulted in the fact that all that was seen was her violet-coloured hat – humiliating for us. When we left the podium I bawled out our protocol chief, but he took the offensive, saying, "You were supposed to do that, Sir, after your remarks." I said, "Hell with that, I am the President. You should have had it done." I think I may have been partially guilty, but what is the protocol staff there for if not to correct glitches? Anyway, the Queen was most gracious and her remarks before Congress brought down the house and showed her grand sense of humour. She won many friends on that day with her self-deprecating humour.'

Most people have preconceptions about the Queen, and many find they are completely wrong when they eventually meet her for the first time. President Bush was not in the least surprised. 'She lived up to what I had expected – dignity, grace, willingness to do different things. I'm thinking of her trip to the [Baltimore] Orioles baseball game with us. She was a very good sport, stepping out of the Orioles dugout onto the field. The fans gave her a huge ovation.' Both the American Secret Service agents and the Royal Protection officers guarding the Queen were apprehensive about her going out onto the exposed field, but as the President had suggested it Her Majesty immediately agreed.

The President and Mrs Bush both found the Queen to be a warm and friendly guest who was not above teasing members of their family. 'On one occasion our oldest son, George W. [later Governor of Texas and now forty-third President of the United States] and his mother were having a joke. It was just before the State Dinner for the Queen and he was wearing his Texas cowboy boots. In a wonderfully warm way Her Majesty asked him "Are you the black sheep in this family?" We all loved it. He then told her that in her honour he was going to wear a special pair of boots that evening bearing the legend "God Save The Queen". At the State Dinner, as he passed by the Queen in the receiving line she glanced down. Without a word George W. pulled up his trouser leg and displayed his boots – with an American flag on them. The Queen gave a smile.'

During this visit, as with all others, the usual duties had to be carried out. Several of these were a personal pleasure for the Queen. On an earlier visit, her father, King George VI, had planted a tree which had fallen over in a violent storm.

Her Majesty replaced it. She also presented President Bush with the Winston Churchill Award, on a day that was burning hot. The President, realizing the discomfort the heat was causing, restricted his remarks to a minimum. Another duty was to place a wreath on the tomb of the Unknown Soldier when, according to the White House Chief of Protocol, Joseph Reed, the Queen saved herself a soaking and everyone else a lot of embarrassment. During the ceremony the heavens opened and a sudden downpour drenched them all. The Queen, prepared as ever, whipped a tiny umbrella out of her handbag, which was just as well as nobody else had thought to provide one.

It was during this visit that all formality was thrust aside by one woman who was so excited at meeting the Queen that she threw her arms around her and gave her a great big hug. The Queen's smile was a joy, and the happy picture was seen around the world the next day. This was in one of the poorest areas of Washington DC where drugs and guns are an everyday occurrence – and where the Queen received the warmest welcome.

Britain has long believed it has a special relationship with the United States, and the present author asked former President Bush if the Queen had contributed to the warm friendship. 'The Queen's position may be "non-Executive",' he said, 'but I don't think any President has ever questioned her genuine sense of friendship for the USA. I believe her feelings do enhance and strengthen the "special relationship" that meant so much to me and our country when I was President.'

When George and Barbara Bush attended the annual G-7 Economic Conference in London in July 1991, they were both invited to Buckingham Palace for a State Banquet. Barbara Bush recalled the evening. 'It was every little girl's dream ... We were met in the Blue [Drawing] Room by HM the Queen. She looked lovely in a yellow silk gown. No tiara! There were sixty-four participants, all the regulars and the Prince and Princess of Wales, the latter looking so beautiful in a one-shoulder, many-coloured chiffon dress. The young prince seemed sad. I felt sorry for them as they should have been the happiest people in the world [this was at the time when the Waleses' marriage was breaking down] ... There were three former Prime Ministers there, Heath, Callaghan and Margaret Thatcher ... I sat next to HRH Prince Philip ... The minute he was served he started in, down goes the food and then his plate was whisked away. Hard on [James] Callaghan as he was in what we called "starvation corner", last to be served, and HRH was waiting for the next course. I said: "Don't put your fork down, Sir, or your plate will be taken." He laughed, put down his fork and away went his dinner! Hardly a bite eaten ...'

After the meal the Queen told her guests she had a surprise for them, leading them onto a balcony overlooking the court-yard. Below, 250 musicians of the combined Air Force, Marine and Guards Bands plus twenty-four Scottish pipers marched and countermarched in a spectacular display that was followed by fireworks. Mrs Bush said it 'out-Disneyed Disney [and] Her Majesty gave us a storybook evening'.

In her book *Barbara Bush: A Memoir*, published in 1994, Mrs Bush recalled a visit to London she and President Bush made when they were invited to the Palace after seeing the then Prime Minister, John Major, at No. 10 Downing Street: 'But the highlight was going to Buckingham Palace for lunch with Her Majesty Queen Elizabeth II and His Royal Highness Prince Philip. They received us in their private quarters and the four of us sat to have a glass of sherry ... Then Her Majesty said something like, "Before we forget we must do what we are here to do," and handed George two leather boxes. One held an enormous heavy gold chain with a big burst on the end. This "Collar" with enamel on one side and gold on the other came literally well past George's waist. It was very impressive. The other box held another big burst on a large ribbon to be worn across the chest, I guess. So much for ceremony. The actual title of the award is Knight Grand Cross of the Most Honourable Order of the Bath. George is the eighth American to receive it, the other seven being Ronald Reagan and six World War Two generals ... When we got home from the luncheon, George's aide, Michael Dannenhauer, asked me to witness a paper that George had to sign. It said that if for any reason George withdrew from the order, or [when he] became deceased, the collar would be returned. So, as long as George lives, the stunning collar – valued at more than fifty thousand British pounds – will be on display in the George Bush Presidential Library Centre.'

George and Barbara Bush are also friends of Sarah and Will Farish, at whose farm, Lane's End in Versailles, the Queen and Prince Philip have often stayed in order to see their magnificent thoroughbred race horses. It happened that the Bushes had given Mr and Mrs Farish one of their own dog's springer puppies, named 'Pickles', and during a lunch at Buckingham Palace shortly after the Queen had returned from one of her visits to Kentucky, Barbara Bush asked if she had seen the animal. 'She said rather coolly that we'd talk about that later, and I thought, "Oh my, you are not supposed to ask the Queen a direct question or something."' But all was well. 'After lunch Her Majesty led us over to a table with her picture and his in lovely, silver frames. She presented them and then turned over a leather frame and gave it to me with the biggest smile. There was a signed picture of Her Majesty with "Pickles". I was so thrilled I almost cried ... Nothing could have made me happier.'

President Bush also recalled that particular incident, 'We will always treasure this very special, very thoughtful present ... Without reservation I can say that Barbara and I have great respect for the Queen. We admire her and have great affection for her too. I do not try to pretend that we are her intimate friends, but we do feel that when we are with her we are with a friend.'

Of course royal travel, like almost everything else, has changed considerably in recent years. There is no longer a Royal Yacht for Her Majesty's exclusive use, manned by 21 officers, 256 yachtsmen and its own 26-strong Royal Marines Band. That all disappeared on 11 December 1997 when *Britannia* was decommissioned in her home port of Portsmouth and towed to Edinburgh to become a major tourist attraction.

The Queen has also been deprived of the Royal Flight, at one time based at RAF Benson in Oxfordshire under the command of an Air Commodore whose sole task was to provide air transport for the royal family – and, when available, certain senior members of the Government. That too became a victim of the cost-cutting measures introduced to try and make the monarchy more economically viable. Nowadays 32 Squadron, stationed at RAF Northolt, has several aircraft which are made available to the royal family, but no longer exclusively. And some £3 million was saved in 1999 when it was decided to do away with two ancient RAF Wessex helicopters and adopt the more modern technique of leasing. The royal family now have a single Sikorsky which is financed and operated directly by the royal household and not by the Ministry of Defence. But whenever the Queen travels by air in the United Kingdom, there is still a 'Purple Airway' in force. This is the invisible carpet that unrolls as the royal aircraft proceeds and which means that for 1,000 feet (305m) above and below and ten miles (16km) on either side, no other flight is permitted. The exclusion lasts from fifteen minutes before the royal flight takes off until fifteen minutes after it has landed.

By far the most expensive form of royal travel is the Royal Train. Based at Wolferton in Norfolk, the average cost for each use in 1999 was £15,000. There is actually no such thing as a royal train; whenever a member of the royal family travels by rail, that is described as the Royal Train, but it may be a different set of coaches. So there could be two Royal Trains in different parts of the country on the same day, and the cost varies greatly according to the number of coaches used. For example, until recently when the Queen and Prince Philip travelled together, they used the maximum number of coaches, ten. This was called a 'Long Train'. But if the Princess Royal, for example, was travelling alone in what was known as a Short Train, there would be just eight. If a Short Train had been used for all royal travel in 1999, it would have resulted in a saving of £350,000, and there are now plans to reduce all future royal trains to this length.

The coaches of the Royal Train are owned by Railtrack and operated on the royal family's behalf by EW&S (English, Welsh & Scottish), a private company which is American-owned. They charge the Ministry of Transport for all royal journeys, who in turn pass on the charges to the Palace. There are some eighteen coaches in all, to enable more than one royal train to be made up on the same day, but only one each of the three personal saloons used by the Queen, Prince Philip and the Prince of Wales. The rest are special carriages that can be adapted as required. A typical royal train would consist of the Queen's personal saloon, which also contains a bedroom and bathroom for her dresser, and Prince Philip's saloon with similar accommodation for his valet. Then there is Prince Philip's dining room which can seat ten and is often used for business meetings; the household sitting room, also used as a travelling office; a household sleeping car; a household dining saloon; a kitchen and a coach for the railway staff who accompany every royal train.

In a further effort to make the royal train more cost-effective, the Queen approved plans for some of the special coaches to be hired out to government departments, a number of charities and specially vetted businesses. But there is no chance of a shrewd operator hiring the train for a mobile fashion show or to hold a firm's Christmas party, even though plenty of offers have been received. Her Majesty has the right to approve or reject each applicant.

For a State Visit overseas preparations begin at least two years in advance. Every visit is a response to an invitation from the host country – even in the Commonwealth – and the Foreign and Commonwealth Office has to approve them all. Some months before she leaves, a small group of the Queen's most senior aides departs on the 'recce' trip. The party consists of an assistant private secretary, the press secretary, the Queen's police bodyguard and the travelling yeoman, who is responsible for all the royal luggage. They meet up with their opposite numbers in the host country and go through every detail of the proposed programme: where the Queen is going to stay – if it's a Commonwealth country, it is usually at the British High Commissioner's residence, if it is outside the Commonwealth, it could be at the home of the Head of State or even a hotel, where a complete floor will be taken. Then they will need to know who is proposed to be presented to the Queen on every occasion and a briefing on each one is given. How many formal dinners are expected? Who are the other guests? The menu is subject to the most detailed scrutiny; not because the Queen is fussy about her food, she isn't, but because it is essential that she is not offered anything that might later upset her and cause the programme to be disrupted. Hosts are told that while the Queen quite likes shellfish, it should not be included on any menu because of the possible after-effects. Similarly, she does not care for desserts that are too sweet or exotic. She is quite prepared to try local dishes and in China she ate courses that included sea-slugs and shark's fins without any discomfort. Is it in order to offer the Queen an aperitif? Certainly, as long as it is fairly weak. A martini or gin and tonic can last a long time in her hand. Will there be dancing and if so who is expected to partner Her Majesty? Is it correct for a male guest to approach her and ask for a dance? No. Unless he has been commanded to do so beforehand. On royal walkabouts, will the Queen accept bouquets of flowers? Yes, provided they are unwired. Members of the royal family have been known to catch their fingers on wired bunches of flowers, and with handshaking an integral part of any royal tour their fingers need to be free of injury. If she is to attend a church service, is it permitted to offer her the collection plate? Yes, and if Prince Philip is with her, he is sometimes prepared to read one of the lessons. Clerics are also advised that sermons should not be too lengthy; twelve minutes is considered long enough.

Buckingham Palace has its own special code for the dress to be worn throughout the visit: U1 means ceremonial day uniform with decorations and medals; U2: non-ceremonial day uniform; T1: tropical day dress, slacks, shirt and tie for the men; T2: the same, but with an open-necked shirt. T on its own means the Queen will wear a tiara. One of the most important – and delicate – items to be discussed is the number and position of the 'comfort' stops. The lady-in-waiting will need to have this vital piece of information at her fingertips so that if the Queen wants to 'powder her nose' she can be guided there without having to ask the way. It is also stressed that all 'retirement rooms' must be reserved for Her Majesty's exclusive use.

Then the exchange of gifts is discussed. The Queen has been given the most extraordinary presents during her travels. In 1961 the village of Berending in the Gambia gave her a two-year-old crocodile as a present for Prince Andrew. Martin Charteris, the Queen's private secretary, kept it in his bath until they returned to Britain. Normally, the gifts are small and personal, but in some Middle Eastern countries the rulers' generosity has to be seen to be believed. On one visit to the Gulf States, Her Majesty was given carpets valued at over £2 million, which later graced the Drawing and Ante Rooms on board the Royal Yacht. In return she gave silver salvers engraved with a likeness of the Royal Yacht and a signed photograph of herself.

The business of giving photographs has its own peculiar pecking order whereby your standing is revealed by the quality of the frame. The host Head of State or Prime Minister will receive one personally signed in a solid silver frame. Next in line of precedence are those who get a photograph framed in blue leather, and right at the bottom of the ladder are those who just manage to scrape into the photo-receiving category; theirs is clad in plain brown leather – and unsigned. The household have their own way of identifying the photographs. For example, a Large Blue Pair consists of pictures of the Queen and Philip on facing pages, framed in blue leather. A Small Blue Joint is a single photograph of the couple. A Large Brown Joint is the same photograph, but slightly larger and in the definitely lower grade brown frame. They also carry a selection of small presents for the Queen to give to the households of her hosts. Powder Box (A) is a square silver box with a raised royal cypher in a stamped red leather box. Powder Box (B) is a small, round silver box, again with the cypher but in an unstamped box.

For gentlemen there are cufflinks which are again separated into categories depending on the rank of those who receive them. Cufflinks (A) Gold have a cypher on both links and come in a red stamped box. (B) are the same but of an oval shape, while (C) has the cypher in blue enamel and a blue stamped box. Right at the bottom of the pile are the wallets. One is marked (A) and is in pigskin, embossed with the royal cypher but in an unmarked box, while Wallet (B) Brown is in pin seal, with gold corners, and is packaged in an unstamped box.

During the 'recce' the press secretary will establish the ground rules for media coverage. On an American tour, up to a thousand reporters and cameramen have been known to apply for accreditation, each one trying to outdo his colleagues for a scoop. They all want that exclusive interview with the Queen. It has never happened and it never will. Her Majesty relies on Prince Philip – who accompanies her every time she goes abroad – to provide soundbites for the media. The police officer checks with his opposite number to see what security is planned. The Queen insists it is low-key and unobtrusive. Many countries have different views from Britain about the best way to protect their head of state, and while the Queen's bodyguard has to be aware of the local sensitivities, his main concern is obviously to look after his royal charge and to obey her orders. In countries where the police have the responsibility, the problems are usually not too difficult to resolve. But where the secret service is in charge, it's another matter. They can take a great deal of persuasion at the highest level to allow the Queen to meet the people she has come to see and let them see her clearly.

The travelling yeoman is well used to 'recce' trips of this nature and his duties are fairly routine. He needs to know the transport arrangements from aircraft to hotel or residence and then the times and details of all onward travel. During the visit itself he will be responsible for up to three tons of baggage for not only the Queen and her husband but for members of the household too. It includes such items as crates of still Malvern water for the Queen – Prince Philip likes the sparkling variety – and Her Majesty's own hot-water bottle, and her kettle, with the royal cypher EIIR engraved on it, along with the bottles of green ink which the Queen likes to use for personal letters of thanks. During her visit the Queen may be required to shake several thousand hands, so there will be some fifty pairs of gloves, also a plentiful supply of her favourite tea – Earl Grey – along with Scottish shortbread biscuits and a couple of boxes of peppermint cream chocolates: the little things that make travelling thousands of miles away from home more bearable. And one item without which the Queen never moves abroad is her private collection of homoeopathic remedies. She has long been a believer in this form of medicine and is living proof of its effectiveness.

Concealed in one of the wardrobe trunks is a complete set of mourning clothes: dress, coat, hat, black stockings and shoes, for if there is a royal death while she is abroad she has to return home suitably clad. So far she has only had to make use of this outfit once, when she returned from Kenya as Queen in February 1952, on the death of her father.

Once the private secretary is satisfied with the arrangements and they have been agreed by the host country, a programme is worked out in minute detail before being submitted to the Queen for her approval. Then it is photographically reduced to pocket and handbag size and circulated to all those who need to know.

When the royal travelling circus starts to move, the Queen's entourage numbers around thirty and includes two of her three dressers, her personal page, maid and bodyguard. The Master of the Household supervises all the domestic staff, while the private secretary's department looks after the administration.

It was all so much easier when there was still a Royal Yacht to use as a foreign base. Now that everything has to be transported by air, space is at a premium – even on royal flights – and the amount of luggage that accompanies the royal couple has been reduced considerably. On commercial flights, the Queen and Prince Philip occupy the first-class compartment on their own, with the senior members of the household in club. The rest are in economy, and it is here that problems can arise. The Master of the Household is responsible for arranging the seating and he has to be aware of the strict pecking order among the servants. It is important to try and keep them all happy, so it is vital that he recognizes that the Page of the Presence – a very important servant of the Queen – should not be seated next to a junior footman. Similarly, the royal chef would object strenuously to the idea of having a seat lower down the order than any of his personal staff. A system has been worked out over many years, and so far it seems to work, with the Master juggling with seating plans weeks before the actual flight, and taking into consideration the wishes of young men and women who may want to sit with their friends. Royal servants can be as temperamental as any of those they serve. It was summed up for me by a former Master of the Household: 'We have the real Queen sitting on her own up at the front of the aircraft, causing no problems at all. I then have several more sitting at the back who never stop bitching throughout the entire flight.'

On one long-distance flight, Prince Philip decided to stretch his legs and walk the length of the aircraft in the early hours of the morning. As he passed the sleeping servants in economy, he came upon a couple who were obviously not asleep but enjoying an amorous interlude. They were too engrossed in each other to notice him and he didn't disturb them. Returning to the first-class compartment he was asked by the Queen if everything was all right at the back. With a smile he reassured her that everyone was quite happy.

Supersonic flights have reduced the world to a size where just about any destination can be reached in a day. Gone are the days when a cruiser or battleship from the fleet could be summoned to escort the Royal Yacht into a foreign port with all flags flying and brass bands playing. The magic of royal travel has disappeared along with much else. But there remains a frisson of excitement wherever the Queen goes; crowds still turn out in their thousands to greet her, some out of a sense of curiosity, more because of a feeling of affectionate esteem and respect.

With the Queen in her mid-seventies and the Duke of Edinburgh at eighty, both long past the normal age of retirement, the extensive overseas long-haul journeys will inevitably diminish as the years pass. Perhaps in future, the trip from Buckingham Palace to Balmoral will be the most arduous she has to undertake; it is already the most enjoyable, the one she looks forward to the most.

CHAPTER TWENTY-TWO

Royal Style

'A good suit can go on for ever.'
PRINCESS ANNE, THE PRINCESS ROYAL

It is said that when Margaret Thatcher was first invited to Balmoral, one of her private secretaries telephoned his opposite number at Buckingham Palace to ask what the Queen would be wearing at dinner on the first evening, so that their dresses would not clash. According to the story, he received the ultimate royal 'put-down' when he was told, 'Please tell Mrs Thatcher not to worry. Her Majesty never notices what other people are wearing.' Even if the story is true – and it is highly unlikely – as neither the naive enquiry nor the graceless reply sits well with the images of either Downing Street or Buckingham Palace – the allegation that the Queen does not notice clothing is not. She takes note of everything about the people she meets, and has a particularly eagle eye for uniforms: are they correctly worn with medal ribbons in their right order?

Apart from the Queen Mother and the late Diana, Princess of Wales, the women of the present royal family are not usually considered stylish. Photographs of the Princess Royal, issued on her fiftieth birthday, showed her to have developed a sudden sense of fashion, but more often the words dowdy and frumpish have been used. In private Elizabeth II's personal style has always been 'head-scarfed and sensible'.

The Queen considers clothes a necessary but troublesome aspect of being sovereign. They have to fulfil a number of criteria: they have to be comfortable, they need to be visible and lastly they must be functional, so that she can carry out her public duties in them without any hint of embarrassment.

When she first came to the throne in 1952 she was pictured alongside the wife of Sir Winston Churchill; both were in dresses made by Norman Hartnell, but in spite of a fifty-year difference in ages, it was almost impossible to distinguish one outfit from the other. Such was the accepted style of both royalty and aristocracy in the early days of Her Majesty's reign. Hartnell went on to design her wedding dress in 1947, and the one she wore for the Coronation in 1953. The House of Hartnell continued to make the bulk of the Queen's dresses for the next twenty years. He saw no reason to change his – or her – style and she evidently agreed.

But another couturier appeared on the scene as far back as 1948, and has remained ever since. In the late forties and early fifties Hardy Amies, now over ninety and knighted, was as different from Norman Hartnell as it was possible to be. His clothes resembled the latest Paris fashions, and for the first time the word 'chic' was used to describe a royal outfit. Amies was and is a congenial man who was always relaxed in the presence of the Queen. It is one of the reasons why she was so comfortable with him. She hates anyone being on edge around her, and while she would never allow any familiarity, a friendly but respectful relationship is allowed to develop once a mutual regard has been established.

But it was not until the 1970s that the royal family acknowledged the need to become really fashion-conscious. The advent of television and the proliferation of newspapers and magazines, all anxious to devote space to their comings and goings, meant they had to become more fashion wise. The only exception was Queen Elizabeth the Queen Mother, whose unique style of flamboyant hats, colourful chiffon dresses and masses of feathers has never changed. On anyone else the look would have seemed ridiculous; on her it was perfect.

Since 1981, when Lady Diana Spencer burst on the royal scene, the ladies in the royal family have been increasingly judged on their appearance, and fashion and style have assumed an importance way beyond their true value.

If royal stories still sell newspapers, then pictures of royal women and their outfits are not far behind. When a photograph of the Princess Royal appeared recently showing her wearing a print dress that seemed familiar, the picture editors quickly delved into their libraries to prove that it was a dress she had worn fourteen years earlier. If they had gone back even further, they would have discovered pictures of her wearing outfits at least twenty years old, and she is proud of the fact. As she once explained to me, 'A good suit can go on for ever.'

The Princess has never regarded herself as a trend-setter; she once told me that her priority with clothes was that they should be suitable for the job. No one would ever have described her as a clothes-horse, though at 5'7" she is the perfect height for a fashion model. For many years, her clothes were made by Maureen Baker, who also made for Margaret Thatcher. The Princess likes blues and greens and occasionally she will return from one of her trips abroad with a bolt of silk and a couple of sketches she has done herself and order something to be made up. Shoes have to be comfortable and sensible. And, as she has told me herself, 'I hate spending money on expensive shoes.' In recent years, her sense of fashion has blossomed and the pictures released to mark her fiftieth birthday – 15 August 2000 – showed what a stunning figure she has retained and how glamorous she can look.

Among the current crop of the Queen's favoured designers is Maureen Rose, who has made dozens of outfits for Her Majesty. She first worked for Norman Hartnell. Then, when Ian Thomas left Hartnell to start up on his own, he persuaded Maureen to join him and she made her first visit to Buckingham Palace. 'I was making evening separates – skirts, waistcoats and blouses, what you would call casual evening wear. When I was told I was to fit the Queen I was petrified, particularly as one of the fabrics I had been given to make up was rather special. It was a gift to Her Majesty from the King of Thailand and it was a border print which can be difficult to work with as you can't make a dress longer than the print itself. As it was my first royal fitting I was fussing a bit and the protocol was that I would be in the dressing room with the Queen while Ian Thomas waited outside. [No male dress designer or tailor has ever been allowed to see the Queen in her underwear or to measure her.] Once the Queen was dressed I would turn the door handle and he would see that it was all right to come in. The first thing he said on that occasion was, "That skirt's a little bit short." I wanted the floor to open up and swallow me. The Queen looked at him, then at me and then down at her feet. She said, "If I have flat shoes on then there would be nothing wrong with the length of the skirt, would there?" and she smiled at me. She'd obviously heard my knees knocking. Anyway, the next time I went to fit her she was wearing flat shoes.'

The Queen's dressing-room overlooks Constitution Hill and Green Park, and used to house the wardrobe of her grandmother, Queen Mary. It is a large, comfortable room with mirrors on every wall so that Her Majesty and her dress designers can see the effect from every angle. There is also a dressing table with a triple mirror – or looking glasses as she always calls them – so the Queen can see for herself how a particular outfit looks when she is sitting down. An elegant chaise longue sits in the alcove of the bow window, facing another full-length mirror for the overall effect to be gauged.

Maureen Rose has been making and designing dresses for the Queen for nearly thirty years. Since leaving Ian Thomas to set up on her own, she has enjoyed the Queen's custom in her own right. Now able to relax and concentrate on the job in hand, she actually enjoys her royal client's company. 'I don't find her intimidating at all. There's a nice, relaxed atmosphere in her dressing-room and she chats away just like anybody else. What most people don't realize about her is her wonderful sense of humour. She loves a joke and she is a superb mimic. I dread to think what she makes of me when I've left. She probably takes me off beautifully.'

There was one occasion when the fitting session had to be suspended for a few minutes – because everyone in the room, including the Queen, was laughing so much. 'Whenever I go to the Palace, the Queen always has her corgis with her. They are inseparable. One day we were in the middle of a fitting when I stepped back to look at the full-length effect. Peter [the tailor] said, "Watch out, there's someone behind you." I glanced down and one of the corgis was stretched out asleep behind my feet. I managed to step over him but slipped and landed on a very soft feathery pouffe that I use to keep my scissors and needles on. I collapsed in a heap, showing all of next week's washing in the process. I couldn't get up and everyone exploded. The Queen's face was a sight to behold – and so was mine.' As the dogs are always present, the designers have to be careful not to leave anything sharp that could damage their paws. 'There are always lots of pins and things on the floor so the Queen keeps a magnet handy and she goes over the carpet herself, making sure nothing hurts the corgis.'

When Norman Hartnell was the Queen's sole designer he liked to boast that she never rejected any of his ideas and rarely put forward any of her own. Maureen Rose has had a different experience. 'She has very definite ideas of her own, especially when it comes to the length of anything she wears and also her shoes. Her Majesty has a particular place on her leg where she likes her dresses to reach – both standing up and sitting down. That length has never changed by so much as an inch in the twenty-seven years I've been making for her. We often have discussions about the outfits we are planning, and I encourage her, in a respectful way, to make suggestions. However, if she doesn't like what I suggest, she will always say so. Hers is the last word.'

For years there has been a debate about how the Queen manages to keep her skirts from flying up in the highest winds. It has even been suggested that her dressmakers sew tiny lead weights into the hems. Maureen Rose knows differently, 'The Queen definitely does not have lead weights sewn into her dresses to stop them flying up. As many of them are ultra-lightweight anyway – georgettes and chiffons – it wouldn't work. I always put in a straight lining fitted to the body so that even if the dress blew up, the lining wouldn't.'

On the question of hems, other (economically minded) members of the royal family sometimes have extra large ones, to let down or take up in line with the fashion of the day. As the Queen has a reputation for not wasting anything, does she also follow this practice? 'The Queen is not mean about her wardrobe, so she doesn't have the extra long hems. She does, though, tend to hang on to her clothes for quite a long time and they do get worn quite a lot. I've seen her at Buckingham Palace in a dress eighteen years old. She probably wouldn't wear it outside, but around the Palace it's all right. Most of her outfits are what I call classic, working clothes: completely dateless, and she is lucky in that she can wear almost any colour. The only one I'm not happy about is a wine or mulberry colour. When I was working for Ian Thomas, I made her a dress in that colour and I was never very pleased with the result. It's not a flattering colour for anyone and it is also rather ageing.'

The biggest demand on both the Queen's and Maureen's time is when a major overseas tour is being planned. 'I have to do a lot of homework before I see the Queen, so I look at the itinerary to see where she is going, for how long and what the climate is going to be. Then the number of formal occasions and how many other engagements are included, either indoors or outside. When I have all the information I need, I choose several different fabrics and show them to Her Majesty for her to make the final decision. Of course, this can mean journeys to Windsor, Sandringham or Balmoral if the Queen is on holiday and not returning to London until immediately before setting off. Balmoral is a special treat. I fly up to Aberdeen where a royal car is waiting to drive me to the Castle. I usually have lunch before seeing the Queen and when we have finished I am driven back to the airport, so I can still do the Scottish trip all in one day.'

One of the more high-profile occasions for which Mrs Rose dressed the Queen was the State Visit to Italy in October 2000. She recalls some of the details. 'I designed and made the dress and jacket Her Majesty wore on her arrival. It was a pale apricot, trimmed with cream. Then for the State Banquet, I designed a heavy ice-blue crepe evening gown, trimmed with silver lace and embroidered with aqua-marine.' This was the gown the Italian fashion media went wild over. They used all the superlatives in the book in describing the outfit and called Elizabeth 'the Queen of Fashion'.

When the Queen visited the Pope, she wore another of Maureen Rose's dresses. 'This was in black, as a mark of respect to His Holiness, and the extraordinary thing was, I had also made the outfit Her Majesty wore twenty years ago when she last met the Pope in the Vatican.' At that time Mrs Rose was working with Ian Thomas, who died in 1993.

Fittings can be time-consuming affairs, and naturally the Queen has to be present all the time. 'It can easily last up to two or three hours with six dresses at a time plus coats and blouses. And I also take the measurements for the tailor if suits are being made. How many women would be prepared to stand around for hours being fitted, after having spent a morning working on her papers and with, perhaps, another function that evening? The Queen never shows the slightest irritation or tiredness. We usually have two fittings and a finish. At the final fitting she will stand, sit down and walk around to see how the garment feels and looks. Then she says, "This is very comfortable. I'm really going to enjoy wearing it." She also mentions where she might wear the dress. She's always thinking of her work and how the clothes fit in with her arrangements. She has exquisite manners and always thanks me for giving her my time, instead of the other way round. I would sit up every night for a month just to hear her say those words.'

The Duke of Edinburgh sometimes passes through the dressing-room when his wife is being fitted. 'He always acknowledges us but never, ever makes a comment about the Queen's dresses.'

Maureen Rose is fully aware that she is not the only designer who makes for the Queen, but with the fact for which the Palace is famous, her rivals' outfits are never to be seen when she is there. Every couturier is allocated separate wardrobe space, and when one is attending the Queen the doors to all the others are kept firmly closed. Nor do any of the designers comment on their rivals' dresses, so Mrs Rose avoided any questions about the startling, sequined harlequin top in vivid colours, with a gold skirt, which the Queen wore to the Royal Variety Performance in 1999.

Maureen Rose has her workroom in Hampshire, on the estate of the Earl of Normanton. It's not in the stately home itself but in what was once the mews, which has now been converted into a number of small business premises around a charming courtyard. The simple legend: Maureen Rose Couture disguises the wealth of talent and priceless fabrics contained inside these modest walls. And nothing on the outside gives a hint about the firm's most famous customer apart from, in pride of place, the framed Royal Warrant, which confirms that Maureen is:

By Appointment to
Her Majesty The Queen
Designer and Maker of Couture Dresses and Evening Wear

She is the first woman to receive it and is justifiably proud. 'It means everything to me. When I was a little girl, all I ever wanted to do when I grew up was to work for Norman Hartnell and make dresses for the Queen. Now my dream has come true.'

Her tiny workforce are as dedicated as Maureen is herself, but even they don't always know whom they are making for. 'Everything is made here in our own workshop. We never let anything out. We even sew on by hand thousands of tiny sequins and pearls, and insert very subtle shoulder-pads. We avoid the "Dynasty" look. But occasionally, for really important dresses, I don't even tell the girls that they are making for the Queen. Mind you, they've been at it for so long, they can usually work it out for themselves.'

An unusual order for royal dresses came not from the Palace but from the famous waxworks, Madame Tussaud's. 'They asked me to make dresses for the figures of the Queen, Queen Elizabeth the Queen Mother, Queen Beatrix of the Netherlands, Princess Anne, and – Barbara Cartland. And every one had to have exactly the same specification as if they were being made for the real thing: fabric, decoration and fitting.'

Apart from the Royal Warrant for her professional services, Maureen Rose has also received more personal thanks from the Queen. Every year she receives a present at Christmas, 'And it's always something useful like a bedspread, a clock or glassware.'

And how does the Queen rate as a client compared with

346

other moneyed ladies? 'I've had rich clients who have made my life a nightmare with their demands, but I can honestly say – not because she is who she is – that the Queen is the easiest person I've ever made for.'

Conclusion

*'I do not want the Queen to abdicate and I do
not believe that she will.'*
LORD BLAKE, CONSTITUTIONAL HISTORIAN,
ARTICLE IN THE *DAILY MAIL*, NOVEMBER 1999

There is a strange, almost irresistible compulsion that attracts
British people to Buckingham Palace on great national
occasions. They don't get inside, not even into the forecourt.
They merely congregate outside, around the memorial to
Queen Victoria, as if, just by being there, they become an
integral part of whatever is happening.

Often no public announcement is made, none is needed;
and this mass migration is not organized in any way. It's
entirely spontaneous – and it never fails. It is as if something
almost mystical draws these people down the Mall to wait in
front of the railings, for a brief written word about a birth or
death or for the benediction of a royal wave from the first-floor
balcony. They gather either to celebrate or to mourn. This is
where they come, with equal enthusiasm, for royal weddings
and funerals, joyous and sorrowful occasions, important anni-
versaries or victories: VE Day in 1945, the end of the Falklands

Campaign in 1982, the death of Diana, Princess of Wales in 1997, the 100th birthday celebrations of the Queen Mother in 2000, and a string of other royal and state occasions in between. All roads lead to the Palace – nowhere else – with a near religious intensity that almost deifies the monarchy. Or perhaps the relationship is far more primitive; an inbuilt need to have someone or something to adore and admire. It goes far beyond mere respect and affection.

The relationship between the monarchy and the people is not easily defined. But one thing is certain, this unique phenomenon, this institution that reeks of privilege and out-dated custom, has not only proved to be the great survivor of the last hundred years, it also looks set to continue well into the 21st century. When the Queen drives out of Buckingham Palace, *en route* to St Paul's Cathedral for the service to mark her Golden Jubilee, she will be cheered by tens of thousands of men, women and children every inch of the way. And watched by millions more on television. The magic of monarchy may have been damaged by the antics of Her Majesty's children and their spouses in recent years, but more than enough remains to satisfy the mysterious longings of great numbers of her people.

As a nation, we love the image of monarchy and its immaculate appearance, but we don't know why. And while we are prepared to tolerate the occasional mild attack on the family from some of our own, so long as it is not directed at the Queen herself, the gentlest word of criticism from abroad is fiercely repelled.

Elizabeth II is the very embodiment of a matriarchal monarchy. She has not only successfully steered a course through the most turbulent of waters, but has done so while retaining her apparently impregnable hold on the imagination of her people. She has now been on the throne for half a century and throughout that period has been regarded with respect and admiration. Her devotion to public duty has never faltered and, in spite of severe setbacks in her private family life – the divorces of three of her children, the tragic and violent death of a former daughter-in-law and the break-up of her only sister's marriage – she has remained outwardly serene and composed. Her Majesty has conducted herself with dignity and self-assurance, rarely allowing a flicker of doubt to appear.

For someone who has been Britain's most public figure for fifty years, she remains arguably its most private person. Few outside her own family know her well and even those closest to her say she has secret thoughts which they can never share. In the face of criticism she has simply got on with her job as a constitutional monarch.

Her image has been of a serious woman who is rarely seen laughing or enjoying herself. Some observers claim she does not know how to relax or get fun out of life. These are the people who do not know her or have never seen her in the company of friends and relations, when she does indeed let her hair down. Certainly duty comes first, and no one works more conscientiously, but she has a highly developed sense of the ridiculous, enjoys few things more than a good joke, even a slightly risqué one, and loves to prick the bubble of pomposity that so often surrounds her.

The behaviour of some of the younger members of her family has, in the past, brought great sorrow to the Queen and, perhaps more importantly, cast a shadow over the monarchy itself. In particular, the acrimonious divorce of the Prince and Princess of Wales in the early nineties, carried out in a blaze of publicity in the press and on television, its principals each revealing acts of infidelity, resulted in massive criticism of a family which had previously been held up as an example of stability and the indissolubility of Christian marriage.

It also brought to the fore those forces which had been advocating the cause of republicanism for some time. Australia and New Zealand both made serious moves towards severing all links with the Crown. Some politicians in Britain began to express doubts about a sovereign as Head of State; even members of the public, who had in the main been loyal and understanding of the Windsor family problems, started to have second thoughts. It was not a happy time for the Queen and her family, and few would have been surprised if she had retreated into herself, much as Queen Victoria did after the death of her beloved Albert.

But Elizabeth II is nothing if not a tough woman. There is not a single shred of self-pity in her make-up and not one word of complaint was heard throughout the years of trial and tribulation. In fact, by ignoring the criticism, she was able to make a virtue of it. When people realized the Queen was carrying on as if nothing had happened attitudes changed. They saluted her courage, and support for her – and for the monarchy – reached new heights towards the end of the century. For a woman in her mid-seventies to be able to carry out her public duties in the face of such severe opposition was a lesson in fortitude for all to admire.

The last decade was difficult for the Queen. The so-called modernization of the monarchy meant a public scrutiny that cannot have been easy to accept. The private unhappiness brought about by the divorces of Charles and Andrew, and the death of Diana, all contributed to the discomfort she undoubtedly felt.

For most of the last century, the royal family had been the emotional focus of the nation. We all enjoyed their celebrations as if they were ours as well. Weddings, birthdays, Trooping the Colour, even the State Opening of Parliament, gave a vicarious thrill. But with the marriage break-ups, starting with Princess Margaret in 1978 and Princess Anne's divorce from Mark Phillips in 1992, the affection for the Windsors started to slip away.

The British relationship with the monarchy has always been ambivalent. In the past two centuries, depending on the era

– and the sovereign of the day – attitudes have changed from unqualified love and adulation, as during much of Queen Victoria's reign, to derisory contempt in the early days following the death of Diana. In between have come respect, admiration and amused tolerance towards an institution we have occasionally loved to poke fun at, but which we liked to think was always there.

By the beginning of 1999 many young people felt the royal family was an irrelevance. It was a sombre moment in the Queen's reign. So the marriage of Prince Edward and Sophie Rhys-Jones in June of that year was seen by many as the last chance for the Windsors to regain the popularity and respect they once enjoyed – and took for granted. Deliberately low-key, to avoid charges of extravagance after the ostentatious displays of Charles and Andrew at St Paul's Cathedral and Westminster Abbey, the success of the wedding came as a welcome surprise. Although it was described at Court as 'a somewhat restrained celebration', on the day itself there was an outpouring of goodwill towards both the couple and the rest of the royal family (particularly those who arrived at St George's Chapel by bus – a first for many of them).

For the Queen it was as if the wedding had been a milestone, an omen of happier days to come. The end of a disastrous period and the beginning of a new age. If appearances were anything to go by, Her Majesty seemed overjoyed – and greatly relieved – that things had gone so well. Not only that the child she and Prince Philip had thought might never marry had finally settled down, but that the day marked an end to the difficulties and problems she had endured for over ten miserable years.

The millions who watched on television witnessed a Queen looking more relaxed than they had ever seen her and saw a side of her nature that had previously been hidden behind the public face of monarchy. It was a revelation – and perhaps a turning point.

Throughout the entire period of the late eighties and early nineties, when the outlook for the monarchy could not have seemed much blacker, the Queen conducted herself with her usual dignity and confidence. Her Majesty is not plagued by self-doubt (neither are other members of the family, with the possible exception of the Prince of Wales). No one, not even her closest friends and advisers, heard a single word of complaint. A meaningful silence was the nearest she ever came to expressing her disapproval of the behaviour of her children and their spouses. In all this time the one person whose support never flagged was her husband of over fifty years. The Queen herself described Philip as 'my rock' during the celebration to mark their Golden Wedding anniversary. It was the first time she had ever acknowledged in public the debt she owed him.

The age in which the Queen was brought up could hardly be more different from the one in which we find ourselves today. Less deferential, which is all to the good, but also an age when there is less respect: for good manners, for one another and perhaps even for ourselves. For the Queen to adapt to the modern world must have taken a much greater effort than for almost any other woman of her age. It she had remained the isolated sovereign of Victorian or Edwardian times, the monarchy would probably have disappeared. That it has not only survived but prospered is due almost entirely to her pragmatic approach to her role.

In 1999 Prince Philip hinted, in a magazine interview conducted by the respected royal biographer Douglas Keay, that the Queen might consider abdicating at some time in the future, a hint that was immediately rejected by the Palace, who claimed he had been misquoted or misunderstood. It is more likely that he was having a little fun, knowing the media would leap onto his words and magnify them out of all proportion – which, of course, is exactly what happened. The year before, a much more serious view was taken after a 1998 television programme suggested that Prince Charles was becoming impatient for the throne and actively wanted his mother to abdicate. What was so unusual about this particular incident was that the Queen and the Prince of Wales took the dramatic step of issuing a joint statement denying the suggestion, saying it was 'not only offensive but also completely wrong'. The Queen was known to be extremely angry and Prince Charles shared her fury as it had been made to appear that the original suggestion had come from him.

Abdication has never been an alternative for the Queen. When she took her oath at the Coronation in June 1953, it was a sacred pledge for life, not just until she feels she has had enough. As a regular churchgoer for whom Christianity is also a lifetime commitment, so is the trust she accepted when she became Queen.

There could be an acceptable compromise, however. Prince Charles could take on more of his mother's public duties, acting as Regent but without the title, performing some of the more tiring roles. He already helps her by standing in at official functions such as investitures, which have suffered no loss of prestige or dignity as a result. This could easily be extended to such tiring ceremonial occasions as the State Opening of Parliament and receiving important visitors. He is a Counsellor of State and has acted in that capacity for years. But like the other royal Counsellors of State, he is restricted in the actions he can take in Her Majesty's name. For instance, he cannot award honours, decorations or medals. Neither can he order the disbandment of regiments in the Army or changes in military dress, or deal with any matters in connection with the General Assembly of the Church of Scotland. Perhaps most important of all, he is not allowed any jurisdiction regarding Commonwealth affairs. They are always dealt with directly by the Queen, wherever she is in the world. But Prince Charles's knowledge of constitutional affairs is deep; the Queen has allowed him access to certain state papers in order to prepare him for kinghood. So there is no reason why – as his mother gets older – he should not shoulder even more responsibility, such as travelling to distant parts of the world, which for a woman in her mid-seventies, and a man nearer eighty, must be wearisome.

Many of Prince Charles's so-called eccentricities are being adopted by those who now realize that he was far in advance of the times when he spoke out in favour of organic farming, inner city urban redevelopment and the need to care for the environment. The ridicule he suffered has turned to admiration and grudging respect. Another bonus for Charles is the way in which he has adapted to the role of being a single parent. Although he is over fifty and can have little in common with the average single father, there appears to be a feeling among many younger single parents that he is making a pretty good job of bringing up his two sons. The affection between them is obviously genuine, and while Charles can hardly be considered an ideal role model for the thousands of others in his situation, at least they can believe that he knows a little of what it's like for them.

In a modern world, it is difficult to defend a system that accords privilege simply through an accident of birth and there is a general antipathy towards the hereditary principle. But serious market research shows a consistent support for the Queen and for the monarchy in Britain to be retained. And this is reflected in the instant surveys carried out by the tabloid newspapers, whose readers might not be expected to favour the old regime.

British people do not as a rule welcome change. We like the continuity that the monarchy provides and the stability that goes with it. So, if there have been a few moments of near-panic in the last ten years or so, there has been no serious threat to the Crown. No political party has ever come out publicly in favour of abolition and it is unlikely in the foreseeable future. There may be individual parliamentarians – in all parties – who would prefer a republican constitution, but each one knows that to raise the topic in the House of Commons would alienate not only the leaders on the front benches, but also many constituents, even in the most disadvantaged areas of the country.

As we enter the 21st century the royal family know there is a feeling of indifference – if not hostility – towards them among many of the young. Gone are the days when the vast majority of the British people accepted the idea of monarchy without question. It was a benign institution, as traditional a fixture as Christmas and the Cup Final, and if people mocked the goings-on of royalty it was with kindly affection. In the fifties no one minded the flirtatious behaviour of Princess Margaret, because she was beautiful, a younger daughter and not all that important in the scheme of things. As a result when she gave up the chance of happiness with the man she loved, Group Captain Peter Townsend, out of a sense of duty to the country and the Church, she was not given the thanks she thought she deserved. But she was mercilessly attacked in the seventies, when, as a married woman, she began seeing other men.

As the Queen's children grew up and made Margaret's previous escapades seem mere peccadilloes, attitudes changed. No longer were we prepared to fund a lifestyle that was as outdated as it was unnecessary. The royals wanted their cake and also to eat it – and come back for seconds. Anne was described as the hardest working member of the family, but in reality none of those honoured by one of her visits saw any warmth or sign that she was willing to forego any of the advantages of her royal birth. When she disingenuously claimed, 'My children are not royal; their grandmother just happens to be Queen,' it was seen by some as a wonderful example of democratic ordinariness. Others, more realistically, knew that she was merely displaying a nice line in royal irony.

The other children have tried to establish themselves in

what they believe to be the real world while at the same time clinging to their royal privileges. Edward and Sophie, with their film and public relations businesses, which might never have got off the ground without their unique connections, continue to prosper and exploit their position. Theirs is also the largest house of any of the royal children. Only the Prince of Wales has stuck steadfastly to his role, not venturing into profitable commercial sidelines – apart from the products from his farms. But he does not need to justify his existence. He knows his destiny – to be a future sovereign. Everything he does is in preparation for that day. The others, however, have no future, apart from what they are doing at the present time. And what difference would it make if they were not around?

The British people have shown that they want a monarchy, and they respect the Queen as sovereign and her husband as consort. But they are concerned about the extended royal family, including the two younger children and their partners, never mind those further distanced from the throne such as the Kents and Gloucesters.

The monarchy will survive, but if it is to prosper, perhaps a close look at the Queen's family is necessary, and the questions, 'Are they indispensable and do we really need them?' should be asked. The answers to both might be 'No.' If so, perhaps, for the benefit of both the country and the monarchy itself, these 'extras' should be quietly but firmly pushed aside – allowed to become private citizens, as they often claim they would like. Their incomes are secure, so they would suffer no material loss. And if it is true – as these lesser royals sometimes claim – that they only carry out their tasks because they are so public spirited, they might welcome the relief of having no longer to undertake such boring chores.

King George VI jealously guarded the reputation of 'the Firm', and felt that its strength came partly from its size – or lack of it. When there were only four members of the immediate royal family, their rarity value added enormous prestige to the occasions they attended. It might well be to the advantage of a future royal family to follow His Majesty's example.

The Queen performs her role brilliantly and hers is a real job of work. No one challenges the need for the Prince of Wales to support an elderly mother and even older father, and to ensure that the transition will be seamless when the time comes. Prince William is also essential to the continuity of the line, so his presence in a new 'Firm' is also imperative.

The Queen has served this nation and the Commonwealth selflessly for half a century and she fully deserves the credit she receives. If the monarchy is being taken into the next century healthier than it has been for many years, it is entirely due to her. She has never sought the celebrity status that has been thrust upon her or exploited it. Her children may not have sought it either, but neither have they attempted to avoid it when it might have been not only possible but advisable for them to do so.

Many people believe that the best hope for the monarchy is that the Queen has inherited her mother's longevity, and reign for at least another 20 years. By that time Britain will, of course, be a very different nation from the one we know today. No doubt the world will have changed and maybe – just maybe – we will be ready for a new type of sovereign. An ageing Charles or a still youthful William? It will be fascinating to find out.

Bibliography

Among the books consulted are the following:

Bradford, Sarah – *King George VI* (1989)
Bradford, Sarah – *Elizabeth* (1996)
Bush, Barbara – *A Memoir* (1994)
Crawford, Marion – *Queen Elizabeth II* (1952)
Crawford, Marion – *The Little Princesses* (new edition) 1993
Davies, Nicholas – *Queen Elizabeth II* (1994)
Dean, John – *Prince Philip* (1955)
Flynn, Paul – *Commons Knowledge: How to be a Backbencher* (1997)
Goring, O. G. – *From Goring House to Buckingham Palace* (1937)
Hamilton, Archie – *My Queen and I* (1975)
Heald, Tim – *The Duke: A Portrait of Prince Philip* (1991)
Hoey, Brian – *Monarchy* (1987)
Hoey, Brian – *All the Queen's Men* (1992)
Junor, Penny – *Charles – Victim or Villain?* (1998)
Lacey, Robert – *Majesty* (1977)
Laird, Dorothy – *How the Queen Reigns* (1959)
Longford, Elizabeth – *Elizabeth R* (1983)
Morrow, Ann – *The Queen* (1983)

Morton, Andrew – *Diana, Her True Story* (1992)

Neil, Andrew – *Full Disclosure* (1996)

Pearson, John – *The Ultimate Family* (1986)

Peacock, Marguerite – *Clarence House* (1949)

Pimlott, Ben – *The Queen* (1996)

Ring, Anne – *The Story of Princess Elizabeth* (1930)

Trevelyan, Raleigh – *Grand Dukes and Diamonds* (1991)

Wilson, A. N. – *The Rise and Fall of the House of Windsor*
(1993)

Index